PRACTICAL GUIDE TO
LEADERSHIP AND MANAGEMENT
IN ACADEMIC RADIOLOGY

ABOUT THE AUTHORS

Ronald Arenson, M.D. holds degrees from Duke University (BA in Mathematics) and New York Medical College (MD). He performed his internship at Beth Israel in New York and his Diagnostic Radiology Residency at MGH in Boston. After serving in the Navy at the National Naval Medical Center in Bethesda, he joined the faculty at the University of Pennsylvania. At Penn, he served as Associate Chairman of Clinical Services, Department of Radiology, and was the interim Vice-Provost for Computing for the university. Dr. Arenson came to the Department of Radiology and Biomedical Imaging at UCSF as Chairman in 1992.

Dr. Arenson has conducted research and written extensively on informatics, workload and finances in radiology, the future of academic radiology and research training. He is a fellow in the American College of Medical Informatics, in the American College of Radiology, and in the Society for Imaging Informatics in Medicine.

Dr. Arenson is currently serving on the RSNA Board of Directors with oversight for the annual meeting and technology. He has recently served as a member of the Advisory Council of the National Institute of Biomedical Imaging and Bioengineering and the Council of Councils of the NIH. He is also the President of the Board of GE-Radiology Research Academic Fellowship (GERRAF).

Cathy Garzio is the Administrative Director of the UCSF Department of Radiology and Biomedical Imaging. She has responsibility for the financial and operational activities of Radiology, including administration of a $70 million annual budget. Prior to joining Radiology, Cathy was Administrative Director of the Clinical Cancer Center at UCSF, and practice manager in UCSF's Medical Specialties Clinics. Cathy's management skills were recognized with the Holly Smith Award for Exceptional Service to the UCSF School of Medicine in 2007. She holds a BA in Human Biology from Stanford University, and an MBA from the University Of Chicago.

A PRACTICAL GUIDE TO LEADERSHIP AND MANAGEMENT IN ACADEMIC RADIOLOGY

By

RONALD L. ARENSON, M.D.

Alexander R. Margulis Distinguished Professor of Radiology
Chairman, Department of Radiology and Biomedical Imaging
University of California
San Francisco

and

CATHY GARZIO, MBA

Director of Administration
Department of Radiology and Biomedical Imaging
University of California
San Francisco

CHARLES C THOMAS • PUBLISHER, LTD.
Springfield • Illinois • U.S.A.

Published and Distributed Throughout the World by

CHARLES C THOMAS • PUBLISHER, LTD.
2600 South First Street
Springfield, Illinois 62704

© 2012 by CHARLES C THOMAS • PUBLISHER, LTD.

ISBN 978 0 398-08702-9 (hard)
ISBN 978-0-398-08703-6 (paper)
ISBN 978-0-398-08704-3 (ebook)

Library of Congress Catalog Card Number: 2011029867

With THOMAS BOOKS *careful attention is given to all details of manufacturing and design. It is the Publisher's desire to present books that are satisfactory as to their physical qualities and artistic possibilities and appropriate for their particular use.* THOMAS BOOKS *will be true to those laws of quality that assure a good name and good will.*

Printed in the United States of America
SM-R-3

Library of Congress Cataloging-in-Publication Data

Arenson, Ronald L.
A practical guide to leadership and management in academic radiology / by Ronald L. Arenson and Cathy Garzio.
p. ; cm.
Includes bibliographical references and index.
ISBN 978-0-398-08702-9 (hard) -- ISBN 978-0-398-08703-6 (pbk.) -- ISBN 978-0-398-08704-3 (ebook)
I. Garzio, Cathy. II. Title.
[DNLM: 1. Radiology--education--United States. 2. Education, Professional--organization & administration--United States. 3. Faculty--organization & administration--United States. 4. Leadership--United States. 5. Schools, Health Occupations--organization & administration--United States. WN 18]

LC classification not assigned
616.07'57071173--dc23
                                                        2011029867

CONTENTS

Chapter   *Page*

  1. Introduction 3
  2. The Search Process and Negotiating for the Chair 5
  3. Compensation Plan and Incentives 26
  4. Financial Management 40
  5. Billing Organization 58
  6. Joint Ventures and Strategic Support 74
  7. Capital Budgets 85
  8. Clinical Services 93
  9. Turf Issues 107
10. Faculty Workload 112
11. Building Research 119
12. Building a Strong Residency Program 138
13. Fellowship Program 152
14. Faculty Recruitment and Retention 156
15. Faculty Relations and Morale 170
16. Departmental Organization 176
17. Information Systems 185
18. Leadership Development and Succession Planning 220
19. Strategic Planning and Scenario Planning 226
20. Marketing and Outreach 229
21. Fundraising and Alumni Relations 239
22. Post-graduate Education 244
23. Quality and Safety 247
24. Culture 256
25. Conclusions and Summary 260

Index 263

PRACTICAL GUIDE TO
LEADERSHIP AND MANAGEMENT
IN ACADEMIC RADIOLOGY

Chapter 1

INTRODUCTION

In this textbook we intend to provide useful information, especially for the new chair of an academic Radiology department. The topics we have selected were chosen carefully and are based on our collective years of experience attempting to manage our own department but also consult for many others. These topics are often the subjects that we are asked to comment on or present at various management and leadership conferences.

The first topic is the balance among the three primary missions of an academic department, namely, clinical care, teaching, and research. Many departments with residency programs concentrate on clinical care and resident education. These departments may not have much basic research underway but should have clinical trials and produce manuscripts that describe imaging techniques, case series, or outcome studies. As will be described further in the research discussions, only a relatively few academic Radiology departments actually have the infrastructure and faculty to conduct significant basic research.

These three major missions will be described in some depth, with an effort to provide reference materials that, hopefully, will stand the test of time and remain useful over the years to come. In addition, this text will provide guidance about faculty development, departmental organization, marketing and fundraising, and strategic perspectives.

In this book, we will be using our experiences at the University of California, San Francisco (UCSF) since that is the system that we know best. We also incorporate knowledge gained from consulting at other institutions as well as from national and international meetings where many of these topics are discussed.

Before we dive into details, there is one more generalization worth expressing, namely that it almost all boils down to people, money and space! If you have good people, most of the issues that we face can be solved with space and/or sufficient revenue. This assumes the stewards of space and funds, the leaders of the department in this case, are wise in their use of those precious resources. While we have found that enough space and money can usually overcome moderately poor management, we continue to firmly believe that the key ingredient of a great department is people: faculty, staff, and trainees. And, the leadership qualities of the chair and the few senior leaders surrounding the chair can make all of the difference in the world.

Chapter 2

THE SEARCH PROCESS AND
NEGOTIATING FOR THE CHAIR

A potential candidate for a chair position needs to understand the search process itself, including the critical political situation that might exist within an institution. Although when you have seen one institution you know about one institution, there are commonalities in the search process of importance. First of all, there is a search committee, comprised of respected members of the academic community. Usually there is at least one faculty member from the home department, but not always. For a chair of Radiology search, often an administrator from the medical center is included on the committee. The chair of the search committee will often be another chair, usually from a large department that interacts with Radiology significantly, such as Medicine or Surgery. The Dean appoints the committee and its chair, often with some input from the medical center CEO.

The committee will then begin to generate a list of potential candidates from various sources, including responses to advertisements primarily in related medical journals. Although these ads rarely generate strong candidates, they can help flush out minority candidates worthy of consideration that might otherwise not surface. For that reason alone, responses to ads must be seriously considered. The list of potential candidates is mostly generated from referrals from existing Radiology chairs or section chiefs from across the country. Sometimes a search firm is used to help with these crucial searches but usually the references are generated from solicited letters or phone calls from members of the committee.

Once this list is developed, the committee decides on which potential candidates to consider first. Often the top candidate list is determined by the frequency of recommendations for particular individuals or the apparent strength of the candidates based on the reference source. The stronger candidates are invited to submit their curriculum vitae. Those candidates that surface as the top candidates by the committee are considered on the "short list." Some or all of these are then invited to interview.

So the natural question is how do you get yourself on the "short list?" The obvious answers are strong academic credentials, leadership experience, and a good reputation. The academic credentials necessary depend on the institution under consideration. A strong research department will most likely seek an individual with significant extramural grant history as well as many first-authored, peer-reviewed manuscripts. A strong record of teaching is needed for top-notched research institutions as well as those with little basic research. Although a strong record in leadership and management would seem a major prerequisite, these critically important factors are often given little emphasis by such a committee. These committees are often dominated by individuals with strong academic records, possibly with little leadership experience or knowledge about what it takes to run a large complex department.

It is imperative that you let influential individuals know of your interest in pursuing a chair position. Obviously, the best advocate for you would be your own chair. Hopefully, your chairperson is supportive of your aspirations. But don't rely on that individual alone and let other chairs and individuals active on the national scene know of your intentions. Of course, being involved in these national organizations, especially in leadership positions, helps considerably in developing a strong reputation. In Chapter 15, we discuss some of the approaches for faculty to get involved with various national and international organizations. This involvement on the national scene will certainly help establish your reputation and keep you in the minds of those leaders who recommend names for consideration of chair recruitments.

You do not want to be pushy about these opportunities, but certainly let influential leaders know of your willingness to serve on various committees and lead some of these activities. You want a reputation for not only being a great academician but also for being a leader, a thoughtful participant who is willing to roll up his sleeves and work. And you want to demonstrate your initiative and wisdom. You want these leaders to say "wow, that person is really terrific and would make a great chair."

Certainly becoming a section chief or a vice chair is a big step in the right direction. Having recognition as a leader at your home institution and getting experience leading a group are very important for gaining leadership credentials. Taking courses in leadership offered by the Radiological Society of North America (RSNA) and the Association of University Radiologists (AUR) is another step toward recognition for consideration for chair positions. Sometimes these efforts will lead one to the conclusion that becoming the chair of the department is not all that it is cracked up to be! But that is a very useful lesson as well, especially if your personality or disposition does not fit such a role very well.

One other consideration, whether we like it or not, is age. A candidate who is youthful but has already excelled academically and has leadership experience would be a strong candidate. Most successful chairs are in their positions for ten to twenty years and older candidates would find it difficult to accomplish very much in their tenure. Ideally age is not a major consideration but investments in these leadership positions by the institution demand a good return on that investment and a longer term is desirable.

Let's assume you have secured an invitation to interview. How do you prepare for that event? First, one must consider the expected audience for the visit. In addition to the search committee members, the candidates are likely to see the Dean even on the first visit. Other chairs may be asked to meet with the candidates, either alone or in small groups. Sometimes multiple candidates will be seen on the same day or consecutive days. You may be asked to meet with key members of the department, but often those meetings are held until at least the second visit or until there is some other indication that you are a serious "final" candidate. It is sometimes a deliberate choice to have candidates avoid meeting leaders or others in the department; keep in mind that this could tell you something important about the reputation of the department, and you should consider this as you formulate questions for those in the institution.

Candidates for chair of an academic Radiology department really have two key institutional stakeholders: the Dean of the School of

Medicine and the CEO of the medical center. We will explore the negotiations with these stakeholders later in this chapter, but you need to recognize the special relationship between Radiology and the medical center. Unlike other clinical departments, there is a partnership, or should be, between the department and the medical center. Not only does the department generate a large portion of the profit for the medical center but is critical to the operational efficiency and care processes for the entire clinical enterprise.

A candidate has to be fairly clever when it comes to early discussions. He/she has to be careful not to make demands early on, while also assessing the likelihood that the needed resources are or will be available to be successful. It is critical to articulate a vision and direction for the department in order to make it to the next round of negotiations. You must present a coherent vision with enough understanding of the department and institution to make a case. Advance preparation through external and internal sources, and your own Radiology network is absolutely crucial.

Websites are a good place to start and much about a department's organization, people, and emphasis can be gleaned from such a search. Personal contacts with individuals at that institution with whom one can confide can ascertain a lot of useful information, especially about attitudes and philosophy. The more one knows about the skeletons in the closet before a search visit, the better. For example, if there are internal candidates that are convinced they should be the next chair, that information would be very useful for an outside candidate expecting a warm reception from the department's leadership. Likewise, if the prior chair was removed because of an argument with the Dean, one would like to know more about that dispute going into consideration for that position.

After the first visit, some candidates will be invited to return for a second round. Such a return visit is a strong indication of interest on the part of the institution and the candidates need to be as prepared as possible. This preparation includes learning as much about the department and institution as possible and thinking about the points covered in the next section. The candidate should have received a fairly detailed set of documents about the department including the following:

1. Clinical procedure volume broken out by sections
2. Number of faculty in each clinical section including any cur-

rent openings

3. Number of research faculty in each area of research
4. Relative Value Unit (RVU) and Fulltime-Equivalent (FTE) data or if not available, some proxy for that workload data
5. Numbers and size of extramural grants and standing in National Institutes of Health (NIH) rankings by the Academy of Radiology Research and similar data for the school of medicine
6. Numbers of residents and fellows and some information about match history
7. Medical student teaching opportunities and expectations
8. Some information on leadership roles of the faculty in school and in the medical center
9. CVs or biosketches of the faculty
10. Organizational chart for the department including information about department administrative staff
11. Information about the hospital staff and the medical center organization as it relates to the department
12. Any department brochures or other documents showing the breadth and depth of the department
13. Information about the capital equipment in the department including the age of installed base and the replacement process
14. Information systems in the department and the relationship of department IT to the school and medical center
15. Space inventory for clinical and academic needs (this subject is covered more later)
16. Financial overview of department and information on faculty and staff salaries/retention
17. Information about the school such as the organizational chart and school data on NIH rankings and research space

Perhaps not every piece of information on the list above will be distributed to the candidates but whatever is missing will be worthy of investigation. If this type of information is not provided, then a wise candidate would ask for it, at least in advance of the second visit. Obviously, armed with information such as that above, you would be informed and able to better articulate your own vision and your view of the needs for the department.

The interview schedule for your visit is also very important. You want to be sure that you have the opportunity to meet with the key decision makers in the institution, not only the search committee. Key members of the department should also be on your schedule unless they are hiding them from view! Don't be bashful about asking to meet with individuals not already on the schedule if you feel they are critical at this juncture. You probably want to meet with the department's administrator as well as other department chairs. This may be the last visit before an offer is made to the top candidate.

When a tentative offer is made or the search committee or Dean indicates that they are ready to negotiate for the chair's potential package, the candidate must be prepared to cover a number of important areas. Let's start with the Dean's package and then move on to the medical center CEO.

NEGOTIATING WITH THE DEAN OF THE SCHOOL OF MEDICINE (SOM)

As was mentioned in the introduction, space and money are among the top three requirements for success as chair. A candidate must be assured that sufficient research and education spaces are either in place or available for a new chair. Space is often the rarest commodity and without adequate space, a new chair is not likely to be successful. How much space do you need for academic success? Unfortunately, there is no hard and fast formula, but this is where your preparation and careful questions for the institutional and departmental leadership can help. Many think the answer to "how much space is enough?" is "more is always better!" It is important to remember that space comes with a cost too. Yet lack of research space, for example, can prevent faculty from obtaining grants or keeping graduate students, and lack of space overall for offices and classrooms can discourage the most devoted faculty member and resident. Here are some questions we would ask, as a candidate, to begin to assess space needs, and we will go into more depth below.

Assessing Space Needs – Key Questions:

1. How much square footage by category (wet lab, clinical research, desk-based research, clinical, educational, administrative, etc.) exists in the department?
2. When was the last space allocation made to the department?

3. What measures does the institution use to evaluate the use of space, if any? (e.g., RVUs per square foot of clinical space, or indirect or total costs per square foot of research space).
4. How many times were space needs mentioned by members of the department as you interviewed?
5. What did you actually see on your tour – crowded, empty, somewhere in the middle?
6. Does the department have faculty spread across multiple campuses or sites? If so – why?
7. How is space assigned to other departments on campus and in the medical center?
8. Is there an institutional space committee and if so, how do they view Radiology?
9. Are there differences in costs between on-campus and off-campus space?
10. Are departments allowed autonomy in finding, modifying, and occupying space?

This is not meant to be an exhaustive list but gives you an idea of the kinds of issues to think about as you negotiate for space.

Research Space

Since many Deans measure a department's space allotment in terms of indirect cost recovery dollars per square foot, we should start our discussion looking at that metric. Depending on how research core space is allocated (to responsible departments, to the schools, or to a central pot for the campus), the price per square foot (sq. ft.) can vary greatly. Figures around $150-$200/sq. ft. are reasonable but the data for the specific campus must be examined carefully. The point is that Radiology should not be an outlier; it's important to be close to the mean for the particular campus or school.

If a department has less than the average or threshold values for the school's particular metric, then it may be difficult to argue for substantially more space unless that space is part of a start-up package with expectations for significantly more research dollars coming from entities that provide indirect (or overhead) cost recovery. Keep in mind that not all sources of research funding will support indirect costs and that might be a problem for departments with significant foundation or non-federal funding. Many foundations limit overhead or indirects and sometimes the campus will then expect rent or some other payment for use of research space for those programs.

It is very important to understand the campus or school policy and practice regarding space costs. If you are to receive space as part of the recruitment, pay very close attention to the agreement for building research programs to support the costs – how long will it last? What are the expectations, if any, for paying back the campus or Dean? Again, this is where preparation and asking questions of your future chair colleagues at that institution is critical. They can tell you what the institutional practice has been, and when or if exceptions are made. As a new chair with many issues to tackle, you need breathing room to build a research program without worry about throwing the department into deficit because of space costs that are not covered.

What is clear is that a department cannot build a successful research program without adequate research space. Do not accept the challenge of increasing research funding without the Dean's commitment for space to support it, unless the department is far below the established metric. You should be very clear about the type of research the department does. Basic science wet labs and instrumentation space is clearly more expensive than desk-based research space. You must ask the department to provide you with accurate information about the existing researchers, their existing programs and grants, and their plans for the future. In this way, you can begin to identify gaps that will assist your negotiation. (See the list for information above).

At UCSF, research success is defined by the number and size of federally funded grants and by NIH rankings. When we arrived at UCSF, we found that Radiology was outside the top ten departments in NIH funding in the country, and at UCSF, this lower ranking made the department an outlier. The major departments at our institution are all in the top ten. By analyzing the top departments in the country and talking to peers and colleagues, we could understand the gaps that existed at UCSF. There was very little basic science and instrumentation space, and at that time – the early 1990s – this was holding the department back. We use this as an example of the type of gap analysis that is essential to complete as you begin to speak about space with your future Dean. Where does the department fit among research programs at the school? Again – understand the expectations as you craft your research and space strategy.

Education Space

The space required for educational needs is relatively modest but critical for success. A department needs a library, conference room or rooms, space for medical student small group education (if not available elsewhere), and office space for the residency coordinator and other administrative personnel. The space needed for medical student education could be more expansive if that activity needs administrative help and if the department has computers for individualized instruction. Most departments have moved in that direction and planning a large workroom with multiple workstations is probably a good idea.

The residents need a space to study or relax and that space is often the department's library. Almost every department at UCSF has a library or gathering space for residents, and it is surprising how important this availability is to resident candidates. It is worth asking the department residency coordinator for a tour of space designated for residents and other students. If you want to grow a research program, or are taking on an existing program, you should also ask about space for graduate students and post-doctoral scholars. They are often ignored in favor of the residents; Radiology is a clinical specialty after all. We have found, however, that strong principal investigators depend on post-docs and graduate students in a significant way, and having work rooms and cubicles in and around labs and research spaces definitely leads to funding. Again, it depends on the individual department and your goals as chair. At UCSF, we use a ratio of four cubicles per funded principle investigator (PI), or roughly 200 square feet for post-doctoral scholars and students. In addition, ACGME requires designated space for fellows. We have found that shared cubicle space in larger rooms is the only way to accommodate this requirement. It is very important as you interview to really observe space in the department and how it is used, and to ask a lot of questions about utilization.

Recruitment Start-Up Packages

Whether you are an internal or external candidate for the chair position, it is extremely important to negotiate a solid start-up package. This may be the only chance you will get to secure space and funds for developing academic programs, which most likely you are being courted to achieve. It is in these negotiations that you lay out what you need to be successful. Yet you must not start making demands until you know you are the front-runner for the job. Pushing for space or other resources too early in the process will backfire and turn the recruiting Dean to look to others instead. Once you are informed that you are indeed the leading candidate, it is critical to remember that the job is clearly not worth having if they have tied your hands behind your back by not providing resources necessary for success.

If you are asked to present what you need while still on a short list and not the finalist, be careful not to ask for too much yet, but be sure to specify what you believe you need based on the knowledge you have acquired so far. Remember that at this point in the process you have only had a superficial peak into the department and have not had a chance for an in-depth review. Make it clear that your thoughts are preliminary and will be refined after you have more time for talking with others and gathering data. Present a general outline and be sure to comment, perhaps more than once, that you are providing information based on a limited understanding about the department so far. You would be pleased to provide more detail when and if you have the opportunity to explore these issues with key individuals in the department and outside.

Once you are the front-runner, you need to map out a plan for getting as much information as possible to develop your needs assessment. At this point you definitely need to visit the department and talk with key individuals about their perceptions of the department's needs. If the department has had an external or even an internal review in the recent past, you definitely want a copy of the report. Don't simply let the Dean's office or someone in the department set up the interviews for you. You want to let them know the individuals you wish to see and places you want to visit. And you need to keep the three main missions in mind: clinical, teaching, and research.

Financial assessment is critical at some point in this process. You need to understand the financial capacity of the clinical engine and you need to assess the current financial commitments for salaries and academic expenses. Chapter 4 will deal in more details concerning the financial picture but the importance of a 50,000-foot view of the financial health of the department is vital for these negotiations. Again, I would not simply accept financial documents or assurances provided by the Dean's office, but would highly recommend talking to competent financial staff in the department and make sure there is agreement between the department's view of its finances and the Dean's office view.

Billing Arrangements and Taxes

As part of the financial assessment, it is important to understand the compensation plan, the taxes assessed by the Dean or others, and to understand the billing arrangements. This information will help you understand the income side of the balance sheet.

Designing a compensation plan is described in Chapter 3. You need to determine how the plan rewards performance and if the faculty are generally happy with it. You should quickly analyze the salaries and bonuses for the faculty to see if they are adequately compensated compared to benchmarks such as the Association of American Medical Colleges (AAMC) and the Medical Group Management Association (MGMA). And you need to assess the faculty workloads as will be discussed in Chapter 10. Basically you need to find out if the faculty are working reasonably hard (balance of work and manpower), whether they are adequately paid, if the proper incentives are in place, and if you have enough income from clinical operations to support them. Remember that faculty salaries will be the largest part of the department expenses, probably over 75 percent.

You should determine if taxes and billing costs leave you with sufficient net income to support the department. Chapter 4 will detail some of the financial issues and Chapter 10 will discuss faculty workload and the financial implications of that effort. The bottom line is that it is difficult, even in an efficient department, to live on professional fees alone. You will most likely need access to technical fees, in one form or another.

Funds for Laboratory Renovations and Expansion

As with so many other items, the ability for the department to get funding from the school or from other sources is never as great as it is at the time the new chair is negotiating. Once you have determined the amount and kind of space needed, then it is essential to identify the source of funds for both the facilities and equipment. Equipment for animal studies will be discussed later, but keep in mind that clinical research can be performed on equipment owned by the medical center. The charges for such use have to be at least equal to Medicare rates and, therefore, is often not very attractive to cost-conscious investigators. Usually, if volume of cases justifies the expense, it is better to have dedicated research equipment for humans as well as for animals.

Another concern is where will research space be located? Remember, "location, location, location!" Try as best you can to secure space that is convenient to the investigators who will be using that space and try to keep research space aggregated in the same location. Doing so will keep overhead costs down and encourage interaction of the investigators working there. Whether you build a stand-alone facility, renovate existing space, or develop an off-campus facility, will depend on what is available and where. If on-campus space is available and well located, that would be best. If no on-campus space is available, then you should be able to negotiate for off-campus space. The indirects will obviously be less and sometimes the rent and tenant improvements are paid out of indirect cost recovery. Individual campuses handle these differently based on the negotiated arrangement with the NIH. But as stated in the beginning, location and proximity to investigators, including those outside the department is critical. If you locate the research imaging facilities across town from the basic scientists who have knock-out mice behind the barrier, forget getting them to use your facilities.

Animal and Human Imaging as Campus Cores

Although you need research imaging for the faculty in Radiology, supporting and maintaining such facilities and equipment will be a real challenge even for the largest basic research departments of Radiology. Outside users are important and making the facilities easy to use, cost-effective, and convenient is difficult at best. The ideal arrangement is to have these facilities declared as campus cores, which should mean that funds are available to construct and equip these laboratories. Hopefully, in addition, funds will be available to provide ongoing support for operations, including supplies and personnel for operating the equipment. You should expect some operating costs will be covered by recharges. Chapter 11 will cover this subject in more detail.

As you negotiate with the Dean, it is very important to have a good understanding of his or her viewpoint about this type of facility. Radiology equipment, as we all know, is incredibly expensive. If future "customers" of imaging research facilities such as investigators in other departments expect low costs to write the use into grants, then you will fail unless there is campus or school support. I would ask how other large research investments have been handled at this institution. Does the campus or school invest capital or philanthropic funds in research facilities? Does the Dean loan money for investment in research facilities and if so, what are the payback expectations? If you were to incur a deficit from the investment, what would happen? The answers to these questions will guide you as you negotiate a package and will either encourage or temper your research space and equipment requests.

Turf

If the department appears to be having major turf issues (see Chapter 9), then we advise you to discuss this issue with the Dean. You should negotiate with both the Dean and the medical center director so you can come to an understanding that the department of Radiology is the primary imaging entity and that either clinical care or research involving imaging should be in the domain of Radiology. Of course, there are exceptions and probably there is already established encroachment on various fronts that you have to accept. But you want to protect the core of the department in CT and MR and you want to convince yourself that too much has not been given away already. You want at least to be able to comment before any new imaging is handed over to others, if not real veto power accordingly. But keep in mind that you also don't want to be viewed as unreasonable or unwilling to share. More on this subject can be found in Chapter 9.

Role of Chairs in the Organization

Although this may not be the first topic of discussion in chair negotiations, the role of chairs should not be dismissed. The organization of the school, practice plan, and medical center are very important, especially with a department that is viewed as a service entity for the other departments and is often considered a "hospital-based" specialty. Is the medical center organized by service lines? Who controls those and what is the role of the Radiology chair or section chief in management and strategic direction? Are the technical fees shared with other departments through this mechanism or others? All of these questions are very important in determining the relative strength of the Radiology chair in the big picture.

Similarly, who runs the practice plan? What role does the Radiology chair play in that arena? Perhaps you want to negotiate a seat at the table for some of these activities. And is there a Council of Chairs? What role do they have and how often do they meet with the Dean or CEO of the medical center?

Start-Up Personnel

In the negotiations for the chair position, you need to plan on recruiting the needed personnel. Certainly research faculty need to be brought in if the Dean has desires, as is often the case, to move up the ladder of NIH-funded schools. If the Dean makes a strong pitch for improving the department's grant status (more in Chapter 11), then you need to determine how you will be able to attract faculty who will be able to bring in grant funding. Of course, these can be radiologists who are good at both clinical work and research, but you need to consider the opportunities to recruit pure researchers, most likely PhDs.

Don't forget to consider the needs for other personnel besides the faculty such as grant administrators or financial personnel who will be able to manage a growing portfolio of grant funding. These positions can rarely be funded directly from grants, so it will be important to ask for start-up funds for the necessary administrative help.

MEDICAL CENTER NEGOTIATIONS

Capital Budget

Perhaps the most important aspect of the relationship between the chair/department and the medical center is the support for capital equipment for the department. The department's lifeblood is the availability of state-of-the-art imaging equipment. During negotiations for the chair position, in addition to securing the equipment needed right away, it is imperative to establish a firm commitment that the medical center will keep the department well equipped and to replace the aging equipment on a reasonable time schedule. This commitment should be in writing.

The medical center is likely to focus on a capital budget committee and process that makes all of the decisions. In reality, these committees are always advisory to the leadership of the medical center and they expect that new chairs will demand items outside of the usual processes. You will probably have to compete for new types of equipment beyond the start-up negotiations but you want to at least establish a depreciation fund for replacement equipment. You should not have to compete through a capital budget process for replacement equipment. Please see Chapter 7 for more details on capital budgets.

As for the immediate needs, most medical centers delay major equipment replacements and expansion once it is announced that the current chair is stepping down. So the department may have substantial needs at the time the new chair is negotiating. During this process you must establish your role in equipment selection for the future. Will the medical center allow you to make such decisions? Is there a required request for proposal process and what freedom of choice do you have? How binding is the low bid?

The best argument for expansion of certain services such as MR or CT is a long waiting list in spite of adequate hours of efficient operation. Or new services that would be available and marketable based on new equipment. Some of these might fall under the category of good prospects for joint ventures (see below).

Don't forget to make sure Radiology is well represented on the Capital Budget Committee if one exists. Remember that your negotiating power is the strongest before you say "yes" to accepting the chair position. And capital commitments are absolutely key to your future. This area is one of the "show stoppers" for accepting the job.

Strategic Support and Joint Ventures

Similar to capital budgets, this subject is critical to your success. As part of the negotiation process, it is imperative that early on you establish the "50,000 foot" view of the department's finances. The ability for the department to support all of its missions depends heavily on the financial strength of the clinical enterprise, mainly the professional fees from clinical work. Most Radiology departments no longer can compete and thrive on professional fees alone. Access to technical fees in one fashion or another is essential. If a department is part of a state university and receives substantial state funding, this may not be necessary. But such state schools often carry a heavy load of underinsured and uninsured patients and, therefore, have relatively low reimbursement. The other factor in this equation is the faculty workload. If the faculty are not carrying a reasonable workload yet have competitive salaries, the system is going to be strained. (See Chapter 10 for faculty workload calculations.)

Chapter 4 discusses more details about finances and Chapter 6 delves into strategic support and joint ventures in much more detail. We cannot emphasize enough, however, that your best chance for success at some type of medical center financial support is during the negotiation period. You may need to share more about the finances of the department than you would otherwise like, but if you are making the argument that you will need financial help, you will probably have to open the department's books, at least partially. Of course, this step assumes you have been given access to these financial records either by the Dean or the department's administrator. Once you have established that you have insufficient funds to be competitive, you should be able to argue for help. Keep in mind that the medical center is unlikely to want to hear about the research and educational needs. They will only be interested in the clinical enterprise and being able to recruit and retain top-notched clinical faculty.

They will also care deeply about the service the Radiology department provides to physicians and patients. If you have discovered, through your due diligence, that this is an area that is lacking, then you might weave improvements to service (with concrete metrics) into your argument for support. In the reverse situation, if you are lucky enough to inherit a department with excellent, documented service standards, then make the argument that you need financial support to maintain excellence. The point is, there has to be something in the investment for the medical center, and a smart chair will use this to his or her advantage.

So do you ask for strategic support or joint ventures? The answer is probably both. As you will see in Chapter 6, strategic support is the best way to go for recruitments, especially where you expect to build clinical business. And that kind of support is ideal for demands for service that cannot be adequately reimbursed, such as off-hours coverage and services with low reimbursement such as Mammography or Pediatric Radiology. Strategic support should be just that, strategic. If possible, try to learn what other departments are getting, not so much in dollars, but in kinds of services that the medical center is paying for. Keep in mind that the medical center will most likely want to see strategic support be time-limited, often going down over several years. Sometimes they will want to establish not-to-exceed limits such as for start-up salary support for new faculty recruitments. They will expect you to reduce the subsidy based on the actual earnings for that individual and, of course, will not start the payments until the recruit has actually started working.

Joint ventures are quite different and should be expected to last for many years. Unless precedents have already been set with other arrangements, the medical center is likely to want the department to provide the proportional share of the startup costs. If the joint venture (JV) is 50-50, which is highly recommended to keep the balance of power, then the department would have to pay 50 percent of the equipment and construction costs (if necessary) as well as 50 percent of the operating costs. Unless federal legislation cuts the legs out of outpatient imaging entirely, these joint ventures for CT, MR, PET, etc., can be very lucrative if operated at a reasonable cost and patient volume is moderate to high. Because these imaging centers are so successful, the medical center may be reluctant to enter the JV. In addition, the department may not have sufficient funds to put in a proportional or reasonable capital share. Perhaps you can ask the Dean for the school to provide the funds to the new chair or perhaps, although less attractive financially, for the school to participate in the joint venture. Please see Chapter 6 for much more in-depth discussion and analysis.

Access to Technical Revenues

Although strategic support or joint ventures are the two most common means of getting medical center financial support, one other approach that has great merit is a straight RVU-based payment. Such a methodology provides a strong incentive to keep the interests of the department and the medical center aligned. Because the outpatient technical revenues from imaging often represent such a large portion of the medical center's profits, they should be more than willing to provide incentives for Radiology to be successful. These payments can also be strictly incentive-based and can depend on the department reaching specific goals established each year. Obviously, if the goals are set higher each year, the probability of sustaining adequate payments over time is in jeopardy. The straight payments per RVU are much more dependable, but many departments across the country that have had such arrangements have experienced reductions in payments over the years. The medical centers have argued that they can no longer afford these payments or that the department is doing too well even without such support.

The best approach for your future department will be based on your analysis of its strengths and weaknesses as part of the medical center's strategic direction. If this type of review cannot be accomplished before your negotiations are concluded, then it would be important to insist that the discussion be held within three months of your arrival, after you have had a chance to look at data and analyze your situation, and you should make sure your offer letter includes a to-be-determined, mutually agreeable level of support.

Managing Radiology Clinical Service

One more approach to securing a revenue stream from the medical center that potentially has other substantial benefits is a management contract with the medical center. Under such a contract, you are the administrative head of the technical side of the business as well as the professional side. You can more easily maintain control of the hospital operations in Radiology and the medical center is more able to hold you responsible for the clinical service in its entirety.

To be successful with this model, you need to be the responsible leader for both the operating budget and for the staffing authority/control. Ideally you would report directly to the COO and be included in the administrative decision making for the medical center. However, you can avoid spending too much time by delegating much of this activity to a clinical administrator who clearly reports to you. Be careful with this one – you can't blame the hospital for problems if you are the chief!

If you convince the medical center to go down this route, try upfront to negotiate some freedom to act without several layers of approval above you (or your designee). If the medical center leadership tends to micro-manage operations, this arrangement could be difficult. At UCSF, the Chair of Radiology is responsible for the clinical operations and our Clinical Operations Director reports jointly to the chair and to a medical center executive for ancillary services. It has been very important to the relationship to communicate regularly, to be honest and open and share information, and to engage the hospital administration in the department's planning and thinking for the future. (See Chapter 8 and 16 for more information about these relationships.)

Strategic support or funds from the medical center can be based on RVUs, or various performance measures, such as excess revenue over costs, exceeded budgets, etc. Obviously, the more stable arrangements are less risky and the RVU methodology allows for increases with an increased volume of work. However, there may be a tendency for the medical center to want to reduce these subsidies over time, especially if finances are not as good or if the department appears to be performing too well financially. And if the payments are linked to improvement in performance, it may be difficult to show marked improvement year after year.

Space for Clinical Operations and Offices

If the department is expected to grow clinical volume or if current space for clinical operations is insufficient for an adequate modern facility, then the new chair should secure more clinical space during negotiations. Obviously, the medical center should be supportive of a reasonably well-articulated plan since their revenue stream, in large part, depends on your clinical success. If the medical center is not very responsive to the needs for more clinical space for Radiology, you might want to consider having the medical center bring in a consultant. Such consultants usually recommend more space than you would imagine yourself. However, that might delay the negotiation process and be unacceptable. Again, although not desirable, you could ask for a commitment to hire the consultant and follow his recommendations after your arrival as chair.

If the current space for clinical operations is run-down and unattractive or simply no longer efficiently organized, now is the time to ask for funds for renovations. Once you accept the job, the likelihood of ever getting funds for such renovations is low, simply because there will be so many other competing priorities. In a perfect world, you should get space for future expansion of services. One way of reserving space for the next MR scanner is to design the space and place offices or other easily movable purposes in that space. Of course, you will need to find alternate space for those functions later on. Renovating old or unattractive space often falls to the bottom of the priority list. It is useful if you can point to experiences where renovation or remodeling projects have resulted in improved service, better care, more efficient throughput, and so on. It is essential to know what the medical center wants to achieve and explain how Radiology can assist this mission. Take the focus off your individual needs as a chair candidate and put it on jointly building a great department.

We want to say a word about faculty office space because it is remarkable to us how much time and energy is spent discussing this topic inside academic departments (all specialties – not just Radiology!) You must assess the number and adequacy of existing faculty offices. At some institutions, office space is the responsibility of the school of medicine, even for clinical offices. In Radiology, the clinical office space is often a medical center responsibility. If you are planning on a major expansion of the clinical operations, you will also need to consider future office needs. At UCSF, we assign office space based on certain principles. The first is only one office per faculty member, and then size/amenities of the office depend on rank and position. Junior faculty often have the smaller or less-conveniently located offices, but we have found it relatively easy to make changes over time. We also use hotel offices effectively at our various campuses to provide convenience despite our one-person, one-office rule. We are also extremely careful to keep research activities out of medical center space, and respect the medical center's clinical boundaries.

You know you have successfully concluded your negotiations when both the Dean and medical center CEO have agreed with most of your requests but begin to push back a bit, hopefully on less important items. You should look over the package and convince yourself that the ingredients are there for success. You should not wait until every aspect you can imagine is nailed down. There will always be issues later on that you will need to get resolved and you should feel comfortable that your relationship with the Dean and CEO is such that they will support reasonable requests in the future.

We have seen more than one "finalist" go down in flames because they were not acting reasonably and continued to add demands on top of demands with little explanation why they were important to the school or the medical center. And it is important to assess the ability of the school or medical center to fulfill your request, whether it is money or space. You can't expect them to give you what they do not have to give.

Chapter 3

COMPENSATION PLAN AND INCENTIVES

As in most fields, although often considered of lesser importance in academia, adequate financial compensation is critical to success whether dealing with faculty or staff. Designing the ideal compensation plan is a challenge and above all else must convey a sense of fairness to all involved. A new chair has an opportunity during the brief honeymoon period to implement a new compensation plan. Once in place, making changes will be very difficult, if not impossible.

What are the components of a good plan? First of all, a decision concerning whether or not to include financial incentives or bonuses needs to be made. Although such incentives are often considered of great value, they may have unintended consequences and are difficult to remove or significantly change once in place. And usually you can change behavior by incentives so make sure you encourage behavior that you want and recognize that other behaviors will likely decline. How much do you need to provide in incentives? That question is difficult to answer but most experts talk about needing incentives to be large enough to have an effect, usually in the range of 15–20 percent of the base salary. At UCSF, clinical incentives have ranged widely, depending on Radiology subspecialty, but have hovered around 20 percent with a few notable exceptions. One question we have asked over time is whether a clinical incentive bonus should be capped at a certain percentage of base salary. The market drove Radiology salaries quite high between 2000 and 2008, but has begun to normalize more recently. A cap on clinical incentives in the early part of the decade, when our compensation plan was redesigned, might have caused us to lose key faculty to peer institutions or to private practice. Interestingly, we have also found that some behaviors can be encouraged by simple peer-pressure, such as report signature and report turnaround.

Besides identifying and designing strong incentives, a good faculty compensation plan does the following:

- Guarantees faculty reasonably competitive compensation
- Provides incentives for clinical and academic productivity
- Provides incentives to achieve desired outcomes
- Gives subspecialty sections incentive to control costs (adding faculty, fellows, and staff)
- Promotes entrepreneurial spirit/section chief authority/decentralized responsibility

Yet the plan must accommodate the overall department's need to:

- Support research infrastructure/education/administrative costs
- Set aside funds for program development/recruitment/start-up costs

And as stated earlier, the plan must provide a sense of fairness to all faculty. Rewards for clinical and academic achievement should be balanced so that neither area is disadvantaged by incentives for the other. The compensation plan cannot have such a large component in incentives for either clinical work or academic achievements that the base guaranteed pay is insufficient for faculty recruitment. The compensation plan has to provide enough funds outside of salaries and bonuses so that the department can adequately support education and research initiatives. We will discuss those areas later in Chapters 11 and 12. The other area that needs adequate funding is administrative costs but it is important to manage these carefully so that they do not drag revenue away from the faculty salaries and academic support. Administrative costs usually run between 5 and 10 percent of the direct costs for the department. When designing a compensation plan, many questions come to mind that require decisions before completing the plan. We will discuss each of these in the following paragraphs, but it might be useful to consider them all now in order to understand the issues involved. These questions include:

- Should salaries be tied to academic rank, productivity or years of service?
- Should incentives be used at all? Are incentives the right size (large enough to have the desired effect)?

- Should sections be rewarded based on profitability or clinical productivity (RVUs/adjusted RVUs)?
- Should individual radiologists get clinical incentives or should the sections? What about unprofitable sections?
- Are grant incentives competitive with clinical incentives? Should they be?
- Should off-hours clinical work be compensated more?
- How much should go to reserves?
- How much discretion should the chair exercise?

For the rest of this chapter, the UCSF Radiology compensation plan will be used as a model for what is believed to be a reasonably fair and effective plan. We will point out some of the difficulties with this plan as we go along.

BASIC COMPENSATION PLAN

In the University of California system, similar to many others, the X component is the base salary on which the retirement allocation is calculated. The Y is the so-called negotiated salary and can be used for determining mortgages or setting an expense budget since it is "guaranteed" at least for the year. These amounts could conceivably get reduced if funding were an issue. The Z component is the truly optional payments for bonuses of all varieties. In our compensation plan, they consist of the clinical bonus, the end-of-the-year bonus, and the quarterly report turnaround bonus. Grant bonuses are given for those clinical faculty who obtain extramural grant support and save the department partial costs for their salaries. The faculty member gets a bonus of 25 percent of the salary savings if they do not require more academic time to fulfill the time required by the grant. If they do require more time, the bonus is adjusted including such factors as whether or not they take full off-hours call.

At the present time, all such clinical faculty with research support carry the full off-hours call and collect the grant bonuses. If we offered additional compensation for call, this policy might not be as important.

The compensation plan consists of the following basic parts:

- Salary (X + Y) based on AAMC averages scaled for steps within

rank
- Bonus (Z) based on section clinical revenues less expenses (section Profit and Loss, P&L)
- End of year bonus for individual academic productivity and good citizenship
- Grant bonus and report turnaround bonus

Section Profit and Loss Statement

The clinical Z is determined by the section profitability and all faculty in that section share in the bonuses based on their clinical percentage of a FTE. All calculations are based upon a clinical FTE effort of four or four and a half days per week clinical service, and one-half or one day per week academic time, exclusive of meeting and vacation time. The department is divided into section subspecialties and the section profit and loss statement is used for these calculations. The section P&L statement consists of the following parts:

- Gross revenue (after billing) less Dean's Tax (6%) and medical group tax (2%)
- Net revenue less 10 percent for departmental overhead (academic expenses)
- Direct section expenses
- Faculty salaries and benefits
- Fellows salaries and benefits
- Administrative and office expenses
- Profit (excess revenue less expenses) split 75 percent to department, 25 percent to faculty

The Dean's tax and the medical group tax as well as the billing charges are taken off the top along with the 10 percent departmental academic expense tax that covers the following items:

- Administrative costs/business office
- Residency programs
- Medical student education
- Computer/network infrastructure
- Individual faculty support
- Minimal travel (rest out of section accounts – see description below)

- Computers, society dues/reprints
- Malpractice expenses
- Investment in retirement funds
- Departmental events and publications
- Library and facilities
- Compliance/shared expenses

We will explore a few of these in more detail in later chapters. After subtracting these "off-the-top" expenses, the section expenses are subtracted to determine the profitability of the section. Items included in these section expenses include the salaries and benefits for the faculty and fellows in that section along with staff assigned to that section. General office expenses are also included. If there are any revenues left after these expenses are deducted, then those revenues are profit for the section. Twenty-five percent of these profits are divided up according to the percent clinical FTE for each faculty member in the section and this calculation is done twice a year. The department's 75 percent share of the profit is put toward the chair's discretionary funds for other academic support. Of course, those sections that are not profitable do not generate any discretionary funds for the department.

Incentives

What is the right size for bonuses to have the impact desired? When are clinical bonuses too small or too large to have the desired effect? Perhaps the primary considerations are that we wish to provide encouragement for doing clinical work, up to a point, and to encourage cost-effective management on the part of the section chiefs. The ideal sized bonuses would balance the actual clinical needs of the section against the desire to have additional faculty to share in the work. If a section adds a faculty member, the bonuses would decline. We believe we have chosen the right percentage, 25 percent, since overall sections are fairly conservative in requesting additional clinical faculty or adding more fellows. Remember that any such recruit would cost the department 75 percent and the section faculty 25 percent.

What about sections that are not profitable? That problem is very real and several of our sections do not generate sufficient funds to be in the black after expenses. Those sections include Pediatric Radiology, our General Radiology Section, and Nuclear Medicine. All three are special cases. Pediatric Radiology and the General Radiology Section do primarily plain x-ray imaging. Nuclear Medicine is occasionally profitable due to PET/CT studies which are reasonably reimbursed. Nuclear Medicine suffers from high faculty salary expense, because we pay them all as if they were radiologists although a number of them are internists who became board certified in Nuclear Medicine.

The clinical bonuses range from zero to $150,000 annually. With these bonuses, total annual compensation is quite competitive (between the 50th and the 75th percentiles of the AAMC total compensation figures). Obviously, the differences among the sections are fairly large and probably not completely fair. In hindsight, we would consider capping bonuses at a percent of total base salary, while also keeping a close eye on the subspecialty market rate. Yet those sections with very high annual bonuses are also among our most productive when work RVUs are measured against national benchmarks. This demonstrates that setting up incentive formulas is as much an art as science, and a department chair and team needs to consider multiple factors in the design.

Subspecialty Section Accounts

Separate from the section on P&Ls, which focus on the clinical revenue and expenses, section accounts hold the section's discretionary funds. These funds are accumulated from continuing medical education (CME), paid visiting fellowships, and from other sources such as consulting. The primary source for these funds are the CME courses, and UCSF Radiology offers over twenty courses per year. One could argue that the success of these courses is at least in part due to the entrepreneurial approach which passes the vast majority of any profits to the sections conducting these courses. The sections, through their chiefs, can use these funds for any legitimate academic expense such as additional travel, computers, society dues, or section events.

Departments at other institutions use some of their clinical income to support section discretionary accounts. We have found this not to be necessary, and the current system is a strong incentive to support our successful CME program. Another method used elsewhere is to allow faculty members to designate a portion of bonus funds to be used for legitimate academic meeting travel and other purposes, such as textbooks and electronic aids, as a before tax benefit. Both of these methods are commonly used in private practice. We have also resisted these approaches as a disincentive to our CME program. Not all of us believe the CME program is vital to our department's success. These courses certainly pull clinical faculty away from interpreting images and generating income but they are a source of enjoyment for some faculty to spend time at nice places while educating practicing radiologists. Certainly the revenue generated is relatively small compared to the administrative effort and financial risk associated with these courses, but as long as the faculty believe these courses are of value, we will continue. Our department enhances its reputation through these CME courses (see Chapter 22).

Salary Benchmarks

There are at least three benchmarks for both productivity and salaries for Diagnostic Radiologists. They are the AAMC, the MGMA, and the Association of Administrators in Academic Radiology Departments in cooperation with the Society of Chairmen of Academic Radiology Departments (AAARAD/SCARD). Which benchmark to use depends heavily on your school's favorite approach. By far the most accurate benchmarks are those produced every year by AAARAD. They do not publish the data as SCARD used to do, but instead circulate the results to those departments that have participated in the survey. In this fashion, they have excellent results, based on a large number of departments. In fact, over eighty departments participated this year (2010). The following data is from last year's AAARAD data so it is a year behind and is presented with permission from AAARAD.

As you can see from the chart on the next page, some subspecialists such as Body and Neurointerventionalists and Neuroradiology are now enjoying higher pay than others. Certainly market demands are playing a big role in these differences. As you can see from the chart, Nuclear Medicine faculty have the lowest average compensation, although this is not true in our department at UCSF. You can see from this chart, which measures total compensation, that "General" radiologists are also well compensated. At UCSF, since the General Radiologists interpret primarily plain radiographic images, not much CT or MR, and do not perform procedures, they are not compensat-

RADIOLOGY	ALL RADIOLOGY EXCLUDING FELLOWS & CHAIRS			
All Radiology	25th	298	COUNT	3,191
	50th	343		
	75th	400	MEAN	352
Abd/Body Imaging	25th	288	COUNT	581
	50th	332		
	75th	386	MEAN	344
Breast Imaging	25th	300	COUNT	257
	50th	351		
	75th	399	MEAN	350
Chest/Thoracic	25th	282	COUNT	258
	50th	327		
	75th	372	MEAN	335
ED	25th	287	COUNT	125
	50th	342		
	75th	386	MEAN	341
Gen Rad	25th	310	COUNT	235
	50th	361		
	75th	414	MEAN	366
INR	25th	346	COUNT	111
	50th	388		
	75th	454	MEAN	398
MRI	25th	314	COUNT	31
	50th	384		
	75th	433	MEAN	376
MSK	25th	289	COUNT	267
	50th	328		
	75th	381	MEAN	339
Neuroradiology	25th	306	COUNT	461
	50th	347		
	75th	414	MEAN	361
Nuc Med	25th	258	COUNT	239
	50th	309		
	75th	362	MEAN	310
Peds	25th	308	COUNT	220
	50th	340		
	75th	380	MEAN	350
Ultrasound	25th	300	COUNT	63
	50th	355		
	75th	394	MEAN	352
VIR	25th	333	COUNT	343
	50th	384		
	75th	441	MEAN	389

ed more than other faculty. At some institutions General Radiologists also handle attending calls on nights and weekends, as well as teleradiology, which probably helps explain the General Radiologists' higher salaries.

One more comment about salaries is that often in private practice and in many academic departments, radiologists are paid the same amount or based on seniority or faculty rank. Paying everyone the same has a number of advantages including a real team attitude and a sense that everyone contributes to the whole. In these departments, there are no specific incentives for performance.

Before you go down the route of such incentives, make sure you are convinced that the rewards are worth the effort and negative consequences. No matter what you do, keep in mind that the overarching consideration is for a real sense of fairness in compensation. And after the first year of such incentive bonuses, will the faculty just expect them to continue and not see them as at risk? It is important to continuously stress that these payments are not guaranteed and that this income is, indeed, at risk.

Workload

This discussion leads us into another very important topic, namely, faculty workloads. We have stressed the philosophy that if faculty want to be well compensated AND maintain academic time; they need to work hard and efficiently when on service. It is no surprise to anyone that the sections which are not profitable also have very low work RVUs/FTE. Work RVUs and profits track quite well together, which is quite logical since insurers most often pay us based on total RVUs, of which a large proportion are the work RVUs. The subject of faculty workload is covered in detail in Chapter 10.

So if a section has reasonable levels of workload but still cannot generate a profit, how can they be adequately compensated? Either the X + Y salary is high enough or some other means of making bonus payments should be considered. Bonuses could be made based on RVUs rather than revenue or section profit. This approach would reduce the variation some but may not be enough and is not as obvious as money! One could use the adjusted RVUs as will be explained in Chapter 10. Adjusted RVUs allow one to compare radiologists' workloads across sections by reducing the value of MRs and CTs in comparison to simpler exams. A compensation plan could reward those with RVUs per FTE above the expected threshold. Some departments use a combined approach of RVUs and number of studies interpreted, which gives more balanced weighting to sections which read principally plain radiographs. Keep in mind that once you have a compensation plan in effect, any changes will be negatively received by those faculty who see diminished income.

Perhaps now is a good time to discuss the changes in the compensation plan that we introduced when the current chair started. During the hiatus between the former chair and the current chair, the interim chair agreed to a compensation arrangement that provided strong incentives to just a few sections. This approach was considered unfair but the new administration did not want to penalize the advantaged faculty. Therefore, their salaries (X + Y) were adjusted upward to make up for the expected decline in Z bonus. Over the next few years, their increases in salary were less than others in order to bring their total compensation into line. Of course, as their salaries went up, the Z bonus declined further. In that fashion, we were able to reach fairness in the X + Y salary so that every member of the clinical faculty was treated the same for that portion of their compensation. Such fairness is the cornerstone to success and a department chair will not be viewed favorably by many of the faculty without it.

In retrospect, the only aspect we would have done differently is some kind of cap on the magnitude of the Z clinical bonus related to the revenue generated by the section. A few sections have Z bonuses in excess of reasonable levels at the current time and it would be very difficult to reduce those at this time. Of course, they may be reduced by the anticipated changes in the healthcare system over the next few years.

Off-Hours Compensation

Some practices and academic departments provide incentive pay for those individuals working off-hours, nights, and weekends. The UCSF Compensation Plan does not provide for such payments, on the basis that the evening and weekend work is simply part of the job and that the billing for these off-hours procedures are reimbursed and calculated in the section P&Ls. All faculty are assumed to provide their fair share of off-hours coverage. One of the biggest issues associated with such extra compensation is how to make it fair. Should an Interventional Radiologist who comes in on an urgent basis occasionally at all hours of the night get paid the same as someone who has to come in early in the morning on a frequent basis to check the residents' work from the night before? No two radiologists have the same weighting factor for intensity versus frequency.

Different schemes have been devised to make the payments fair based on frequency and duration of call but we do not know of any that have been considered fair by most of the radiologists involved. And a complicated system is hard to administer. One other comment on this topic is that once such an off-hours call payment is instituted, the faculty may well want to get paid for everything they view as "extra" causing dissent among the ranks.

Academic Productivity

We have now provided for financial incentives and rewards for clinical productivity. How do you recognize and reward academic productivity? In the UCSF compensation plan, we provide end-of-the-year bonuses for individual academic successes as well as for good citizenship. Faculty are also rewarded for their academic achievements by getting step increases and promotions in the academic series. In the UC system, faculty are "promoted" by steps within each rank: assistant, associate, and full-professor. The typical time between each step is two or three years. And finally we provide for the grant bonuses described earlier.

At the University of Maryland, Reubin Mezrich, MD, PhD, and colleagues have developed the concept of an academic RVU that is a measure of many attributes of a faculty member's academic achievements (Mezrich & Nagy, 2007). It is calculated from the electronic curriculum vitae. At UCSF we manually create a score for each faculty once a year based on their achievements and consider the following:

- Teaching evaluations
- Publications
- Research and grants – submitted and awarded
- Community and university service
- Awards

In addition to these measurements, we also consider good citizenship as defined as:

- Leadership qualities
- Professionalism
- Service excellence
- Attendance at grand rounds and/or faculty meetings
- Willingness to work at other sites

These components are obviously more subjective and the leadership of the department helps measure these attributes along with the section leaders. The size of the annual bonuses are based on the overall financial performance of the department but typically range from $5,000 to $10,000 for those faculty doing reasonably well.

Because these bonuses are relatively small and because we have so many possible contributing factors, none of the individual items are strong enough incentives to really change behavior. It does give the faculty a clear idea of what the departmental leadership is striving for. Each year we probably should stress some more than others early in the year to encourage compliance.

Other institutions have a combined "pie" bonus for clinical, academic, and institutional citizenship activity with defined published percentages of the pie. This actually works well for departments trying to move up the scale of academic activity, because low overall department activity makes the dollar amount of the academic bonus larger for those who are successful at publishing papers and receiving grants. If the department is progressively successful however, the individual magnitude of this incentive begins to diminish and can then be counter-productive, for example, relative to clinical productivity.

How do we determine the size of the end-of-the-year bonus pool? The source of these funds is from the 75 percent department tax on section profits. This pot of funds is determined by how well the department has performed overall for the year. The first consideration is to make sure enough funds are set aside to keep reserves at a reasonable level and to provide enough funding for departmental investments, such as recruitments or research funding. These issues will be discussed in more detail in Chapter 4, Financial Management.

The chair, getting input from the subspecialty section chiefs and from the Vice Chairs of the department as well as using the scoring for the academic measures described above, decides the end-of-the-year bonuses. However, this is one important example of the chair maintaining discretion and being viewed as having direct influence over the faculty's lives. In this fashion, the faculty are more likely to listen when the chair asks for their cooperation.

Grant Bonuses

The last item in the compensation plan is the payments for radiologists who have obtained extramural grant support for their salaries. It does not matter if they are the Principal Investigator (PI) or not, as long as they are saving the department part of their salary cost. If a faculty member has 20 percent of salary covered by a grant, then they will receive a bonus of 25 percent of that savings or 5 percent of their salary. The percentage salary covered is not the percentage officially on the grant since radiologists' salaries are generally over the cap on NIH funding. So if the funding is from the NIH, the actual percentage of the salary savings will be less than the NIH FTE percentage.

These grant bonuses are reduced if the faculty member needs extra academic time to fulfill the obligations of the grant. But the section chiefs have some discretion to provide the faculty with a larger portion of their savings payback if they take full call, for example. As mentioned earlier, the overall policy of the department is to have these faculty take full call and receive the grant bonus.

This investment of departmental financial resources is part of the formula of encouraging and rewarding academic activity. Being academically productive is the principle challenge that all academic departments strive for, but relatively few achieve.

Motivation

The incentive discussions above assume a basic premise that money is a good motivator. We have already explored the size of monetary rewards that might influence behavior. But there is a more fundamental question and that is, does money motivate everyone and under all circumstances? There is a video about motivation that we recommend viewing, which is available from YouTube or from its source, the Royal Society for the Encouragement of the Arts (RSA) located in England. The website for the RSA is http://www.thersa.org/ and the particular video we are referring to is an animated video from Daniel Pink created on April 1, 2010, and can be viewed at: http://www.youtube.com/watch?v=u6XAPnuFjJc&feature=player_embedded.

This presentation describes how well money motivates for low-level cerebral activities, such as mechanical tasks. But for creativity and innovative thinking, cash rewards seem to have a negative effect. He goes on to argue that the best motivators for high-level thinking are autonomy, mastery (against challenges), and purpose. Although not mainstream thought perhaps, these three concepts are certainly the major drivers for very talented individuals who volunteer their precious time to further various causes.

Compensation for PhD Scientists

Up to now, we have concentrated these discussions to the clinical faculty. But what about the PhDs in the department? We use a similar methodology for calculating target X + Y based on the AAMC data and scaled to rank and step. At UCSF, we have little flexibility regarding bonuses for these scientists but we do pay up to 25 percent extra for a small group of faculty with a sustained track record of substantial grant funding for a number of years. A large factor in determining increases for the next year is the ability of the faculty to fund any such increases. Of course, our research faculty are encouraged to build in inflation into their personnel portion of their research grant budgets.

The department has had a long tradition of bridging these productive faculty so that we do not cut salaries if they have temporary lapses in their funding, assuming that they are continuing to submit quality grant applications and are otherwise good citizens in the department.

Those research faculty that are Research Interest Group (RIG) leaders (which will be described in Chapter 11), get some administrative support and a few leaders are augmented more based on their service to the department. A few research faculty are more heavily supported by the department due to heavy service demands on their time.

REFERENCES

Mezrich R., & Nagy, P. G. (2007). The academic RVU: A system for measuring academic productivity. *Journal of the American College of Radiology, 7*: 471–478.

Chapter 4

FINANCIAL MANAGEMENT

In this chapter, we will discuss some of the key management tools needed to direct and operate a financially solvent department of Radiology. More than solvency, strong financial management should lead you to develop a pool of reserves to further the department's academic mission. Clearly, finance and financial management is a very broad topic with entire books devoted to the subject and many available resources at your disposal. This chapter is intended to provide you highlights of what we have found useful in managing money in Radiology at UCSF, and to suggest to the chair candidate or novice chair what questions he or she might ask in approaching a new department and its finances. At the outset, we suggest that as chair, you carefully hire a strong financial team including an excellent Chief Financial Officer. This might be the one single decision that could have the most impact on your situation and tenure as chair. It is probably more important than any vice chair or other administrative position you hire. We will provide some suggestions for building a strong team and the key positions you should consider filling as you develop your department.

BUDGETING AND FORECASTING

How much money do you have at your discretion as chair? How much money do you expect to generate in terms of professional fees, indirect cost recovery, gifts, or other sources of revenue? These are the key questions at the heart of the department's finances. Nearly every financially strong department, in our experience, spends considerable effort developing a budget, following it, and understanding variances from it. It is important to remember that a budget is really a plan – it pulls together your assumptions about the future, based on information you have in the present, and some variance from the budget is to be expected over the course of a fiscal year or years. We want to start this discussion by talking about assumptions. The quality of your financial assumptions will drive the level and amount of variances, and will impact your ability to control your other activities that are driven by the money you generate.

At UCSF, our department chair and leadership devote 90 percent of our budgeting time and effort into creating the chair's discretionary budget. We are required by our School of Medicine to create a three year consolidated budget that encompasses all funds, including contract and grant revenue. However, philosophically, we disagree that "budgeting" for contracts and grants and creating projections of extramural fund sources is a useful exercise. For our purposes, we definitely look at our past history of grant success and we review those grants that are in process for the budget period. We expect contract and grant revenue and expense to balance each year, and we will discuss later in this chapter some of the steps we take in managing extramural funds. Because no discretionary funds accrue back to our chair from research (we allow clinical trial residuals to remain with the individual PI), these dollars are not really relevant from our budgeting and forecasting perspective. In our world, we focus our efforts on carefully budgeting, forecasting, and managing professional fee revenue. We strive to create a surplus each year in order to generate the critical cash we need to further our research and educational mission. We admit up front that it is increasingly difficult to manage the department with only professional fees, and the technical revenue we receive from a joint venture with our hospital (discussed in Chapter 6) has been essential to our financial success in the last three years.

At UCSF, we have created a framework for budgeting that divides the budget into two primary parts: (1) an operating budget that reflects revenue and current expenses for activities that are considered "operational" in nature, and (2) an investment budget (Reserves and Commitments) that includes as income the operating budget net revenue and, as expenditures, major facilities and equipment, recruitments, and other strategic investments. We make an attempt to reflect our expenses by mission: clinical, research, education, and public service, though many expenses (such as faculty recruitment) do not fall neatly into a single mission-based category.

Flexible Operating Budget: Revenue

At UCSF professional fee income represents over 90 percent of flexible operating budget revenue. We spend a considerable amount of time up front in the budgeting cycle talking about our professional fee revenue assumptions. We start from prior year actuals and estimates for each year, adjusting for a variety of factors to develop our professional fee and other revenue stream projections. We definitely use the past as our guide, but particularly for professional fee revenue projections, we do not simply assume a percent increase year to year. Rather, we analyze our professional fee stream by payer mix and by cost center (modality) adjusting for volume and contracting/payment changes. We seek information and data that will allow us to develop a strong budget number. Because professional fee revenue is most often the single largest source of discretionary funds for a chair, we suggest that you invest time and tools in creating valid pro fee projections for your budget each year. We have been very pleased over the last several years that this approach has created variances for us that have been less than one percent in either direction in our pro fee budget. This has allowed us great flexibility in our decision making, because we have confidence that we will bring in the amount of money we project.

Some steps we take each year to develop a strong professional fee revenue forecast includes:

1. Reviewing the past three years of volume, charge, and payment data.
2. Analyzing payer trends – particularly for government payers and contracts. We pay particularly close attention to any notices of change in Medicare payments and applicability to private payers. We often analyze this at a modality level.
3. Reviewing trends in payer behavior – e.g., the move to radiology benefit managers, increased requests for prior authorization, or any significant change in payer practice that might impact collections.

4. Considering/analyzing any new equipment planned to be brought on line during the fiscal year; we are extremely conservative in estimating the impact of new equipment whether from a timing perspective or an increased volume perspective.
5. Reviewing other significant changes in the professional operating environment – e.g., addition of faculty or retirement/departure of productive faculty; changes to the hospital operating environment or billing structure; changes to the medical group or Dean's office tax structure.

We engage a number of individuals in formulating the pro fee assumptions for our budget each year. These include our Chair, Executive Vice Chair, Clinical Vice Chair, Hospital Operations Director, Revenue Director, CFO, and medical group leadership. We are often provided assumptions by our medical group and medical center, but we tend to use these in the context of our own analysis, and do not simply apply them at face value to our projections. Our department leadership has preferred to take a very conservative approach, preferring to act carefully and prudently until sure that money is actually coming in to the department in a way that matches our projections.

In addition to professional fee and joint venture revenue, we also factor in other revenue sources, to the extent that they are largely discretionary to the chair. Specifically, we include state support, unrestricted gifts, department share of CME net revenues, medical center strategic support, and interest income on discretionary fund sources. medical center strategic support revenue tends to be offset by associated expenses, but to the extent that resources are generally available for medical direction or other open-ended purposes, they are discretionary revenue to the department chair.

Once we have created a reasonable, flexible operating budget revenue projection that we have confidence in – including timing of revenue over the course of the year – we can then proceed to create the other key pieces of our budget.

Flexible Operating Budget: Expenditures

In our department, we create a program expense budget covering all the major areas that must be paid from the chair's discretionary funds. The largest item – about 75 percent in our case – is faculty, staff, and fellow salaries and benefits associated with professional fee activities. The lion's share of these costs are faculty salaries and benefits. We have discussed salary setting in other chapters, but because this is the largest expense item, and because it has such an impact on the bottom line, it is worthwhile to give a few suggestions that have worked for us as we budget and forecast.

While our fiscal year always begins on July 1, we actually begin our faculty salary planning the previous December. We start by reviewing the list of "annual appointments" which in our environment are faculty in the purely clinical series, adjunct PhD faculty, and retired faculty who have been recalled part-time for clinical or other duties in the department. Our chair indicates if anyone on the MD side will not be eligible for reappointment. This occurs if, for example, a section has hired new junior faculty and so retired recall faculty might be thanked and excused.

On the PhD side, we engage in an entire evaluation process that involves review of existing and pipeline grant funding for each individual with the RIG (see Chapter 11) leader, and projections from our extramural funds manager on the PhD's grant portfolio.

By January, we also have projections of the faculty eligible for merit or promotional raises from our Academic Personnel Director and can include these projections in our expense budget. In this timeframe, as well, we are usually given our campus' assumptions of benefit rates and will know about any extreme changes to the faculty compensation plan that might impact our budgeting. Because UCSF is a public institution, we have been particularly hard hit in recent years by the state of California's economic difficulties. This has resulted, for example, in a sudden, significant and mandated department contribution to the retirement plan that has added about $1 million in projected benefit expense in each of the next three fiscal years – another argument for having a well-developed budget, strong planning assumptions, and some reserves.

In February, we begin a series of meetings between our Executive Vice Chair and Vice Chair Research, with the leaders of our Research Interest Groups and Specialized Resource Groups (SRGs). These RIGs and SRGs include 100 percent of the PhD faculty and non-faculty academics in our department. We inform these meetings with a list of each PI's existing and projected research portfolio, his/her use of our recharge resources, and a financial projection of the PI's grant resources and expenditures covering eighteen months beginning with the upcoming fiscal year. We have a team of post-award financial analysts (more on this later) who follow a set of standardized procedures in putting together the projections. We do this to avoid differences in projections among PIs – e.g., some are overly conservative, and others tend toward pre-spending, neither of which lends itself to accurate budgeting. When faced with a PI's potential funding shortfall, our leadership can then make a reasonable judgment about whether we need to plan for bridge funds, whether the PI will be asked to leave or reduce his/her appointment percentage, or whether other actions should be considered. By completing this process by March, we are better able to inform our budget and also act in a fair and reasonable manner with the PIs before the close of the academic year in June.

During this same timeframe, February and March prior to the new fiscal year, we also review market rate salaries for the radiologists. We use two major sources of data – the AAMC salary survey which provides us median salaries for Diagnostic and Interventional Radiology and Nuclear Medicine; and, the AAARAD Faculty Salary and Productivity survey. AAARAD's data is more detailed, providing percentile salary data at the level of rank and subspecialty. Using these sources, we set a target salary for the Assistant Professor level one, and we scale up from there, establishing a target salary for each of our MD faculty based on rank and step. Depending on distance from the target, we will then establish an overall percent increase which we use in our budget planning. In recent years, we have assumed a three percent salary increase for our budget, but some faculty receives more and some less depending on distance from the target. Unlike many institutions and other departments within UCSF, we do not vary salary by subspecialty and feel this equitable method has brought us the best results.

Once we have projected faculty salary and benefits, the rest of our expense budget is determined by making reasonable assumptions based on history and planned changes in programs or activities. We look at expenses for operations by activity: residency program, medical center support expenses, research administration, departmental administration (computer support, finance, human resources), and faculty support (e.g., academic affairs office and section and travel subsidies). We look carefully at our staff budgets and discuss needed additions to the senior staff with the Chair and Vice Chairs, if necessary, in a given year. We are provided detailed assumptions by our campus and medical center on staff salary increases based on bargaining unit contracts, merit adjustments if applicable, staff bonus programs if applicable, and so on. Our Chair and senior administrators discuss other line item additions to the budget that might be relevant in a given year, but these items tend to be minor in the scheme of a $75 million overall budget.

Our budgeting and forecasting advice then really boils down to two key pieces: first, careful professional fee revenue projections; and, second, detailed faculty salary setting, completed well in advance of the budget deadline.

DEPARTMENT INVESTMENT BUDGET: RESERVES AND COMMITMENTS

Once we have developed an acceptable operating budget, with a four-year projection going forward, we have an idea of our cash flow and what money might be available to place in reserves. At UCSF, we have also been careful to keep at least three months of operating expenses available as a reserve for contingencies in case something goes terribly wrong and our bottom line falls apart – this is about $5 million in our department. We believe we could take appropriate action to handle a financial crisis with three months of "savings" available. Beyond this, any remaining surplus is directed into the Chair's reserves account, and we develop a separate budget and forecast for the department's commitments against those reserves. The UCSF Radiology reserves and commitments forecast is our strategic budget: it is what we use to plan ahead for our research and educational missions. We update it quarterly and analyze variances aggressively. While contributions to reserves from the operating budget net have been less guaranteed in recent years, it was a large amount of reserves built over a decade that allowed us the flexibility to open offsite research space and invest in a full 50-50 joint venture with our medical center, so the importance of managing to create reserves cannot be overemphasized. What types of commitments utilize department reserves? Large categories tend to be:

1. Research support – including bridge funds for key PhD faculty who might run into trouble with funding, as well as subsidy of core facilities as required and rent subsidy for research enterprise activities in off-campus facilities which cannot legitimately be charged to grants.
2. Faculty support – in addition to bridging salaries occasionally, on a case-by-case basis, we also fund extra research time for some MD faculty, fund the NIH "cap-gap" for MD researchers, and occasionally fund staff support positions for key faculty.
3. Capital commitments – we have leased significant core equipment such as 3T MRIs, a cyclotron, 7T animal MRI – sometimes this is done as part of a match within a grant, or as a subsidy if research recharge revenue is not adequate.
4. Faculty recruitments – in our case, most of the dollars invested in Molecular Imaging at UCSF have come from Radiology reserves.

COST MANAGEMENT

While it is definitely more interesting to talk about revenue generation, marketing, and science, it is often old-fashioned, disciplined cost management that has made the difference on our bottom line. We strongly urge new chairs to understand their department's cost structure, and to benchmark as much as possible both within their own school and outside among peer institutions. Here are a few key issues to consider.

What is Your True Overhead Expense?

At UCSF, the department tax is 10 percent of net professional fee revenue, and we consider this as what is required to cover administrative overhead. If you have a similar structure, when did you last reconcile this number? That is, look at administrative expenses line by line and determine whether the amount brought in by the department tax covers the actual overhead expenses. We participate in benchmarking surveys through AAARAD and AAMC to help determine whether this 10–12 percent overhead cost is acceptable or too high or too low. Other departments at UCSF often change the tax year to year to cover overhead, but we have noticed that this is extremely unpopular among the rank and file faculty. On the other hand, Radiology has probably kept the tax rate steady for too long. We know, for example, with the mandated contribution to the retirement plan, our department will probably need to review the tax rate to come up with the contribution. Our communication around this will be crucial and we will discuss this a little later in the chapter.

Can Every Salary be Justified?

Because faculty and staff salary and benefits are the overwhelming expense in Radiology, we like to feel confident that we are getting the most benefit from every position. On the MD side, this means that we monitor our faculty RVU productivity against benchmarks, and on the PhD side, we expect grants to pay for salaries and benefits. We are not uncomfortable asking difficult questions of our faculty (at least most of the time) and we have made tough decisions about ending appointments, reducing appointments, changing series to clinical, and so on in order to create more of a balance between income and expense.

On the staff side, our administrators try to be equally disciplined. When positions open on the staff side, each one – from an administrative assistant to an IT professional – is reviewed and discussed. We often move staff around, share positions, and we promote from within. We have five bargaining units (unions) operating within Radiology, which might be different than other parts of the country, so in many cases, employee salaries are determined by contract. For those managers who are exempt and outside of a contract, we have more flexibility to adjust hours, pay, and so on, depending on the situation. Recently, our department participated in a mandated furlough/pay cut program for non-represented staff, and it did result in substantial cost savings. However, the morale impact was significant, and it is not something our campus hopes to repeat. The learning experience we took from it, however, is that we probably do have the capacity to reduce our staff salary base by about five percent without significantly reducing the amount of work we can do. We plan to implement this lesson in the coming year's budget.

What Programs Do You Support With Reserves and When Were They Last Reviewed?

For example, about two years ago, we took a careful look at our medical student education program and found that despite a very large department subsidy (more than $400,000 per year), satisfaction from students and the medical school was quite low. We slashed expenses through some painful personnel decisions and took a year to entirely restructure the program. While we still have some level of department expense, it is smaller, and more importantly, we are creating a better product. It is critically important to avoid a "sacred cow" mentality in the department and stay focused on what is working and what could work better. IT is another arena where the potential for tremendous cost is high, and it is absolutely essential to ask – must we do this ourselves? Does the IT service add value? Could it be handled by the hospital or school without a decrease in service or satisfaction?

Have You Reviewed Small but Truly Discretionary Expenditures?

Sometimes these expenses – such as travel to meetings, or events such as parties, graduations, resident celebrations, and so on – are so small as to be insignificant in a department as large as Radiology. However, when staff are taking pay cuts, and faculty are being asked to work to a higher RVU standard, eliminating these small expenses become symbolic of an attitude of "everything counts," and can help morale. For example, we chose to become tougher on reimbursed expenses, yet continued to fund a training and development budget for our staff. We eliminated operating a booth at the RSNA, but kept the annual holiday party. Each department needs to find its own balance and fund the initiatives that matter to its mission and culture – it's important to understand what your faculty and employees value most.

EXTRAMURAL FUNDS MANAGEMENT

We have discussed the critical importance of professional fee revenues in creating discretionary funds for the department's initiatives. This section is less about discretion and more about control, yet it is essential as a chair strives to build a research enterprise within Radiology. As a department begins to build a research infrastructure, the fun and excitement is clearly in the science and in the translational research that often comes from imaging investigation. The less glamorous side of research is managing the money, particularly if it comes from the NIH or other government sources. The compliance requirements can be staggering, and universities differ in the amount of centralized control and support they provide. Our campus is evolving from one of decentralization to one of greater centralization and standardization, and in many ways this is probably better for funds management. Why should you as a chair care about this topic? The reasons are mainly negative – penalties for compliance violations are severe and expensive, and discovering that a strong investigator, perhaps a major recruitment, is in financial distress, is difficult and politically sensitive. Chairs don't like financial surprises, and we have learned through trial and error that this arena of post-award grants management can often offer the most unpleasant surprises in a Radiology department. We have struggled with very poor financial reporting systems at UCSF, although new investment in systems hopes to change this. Internally, however, we have structured personnel and reports to create an "early-warning system" for our Chair and leadership that will signal whether a PI is heading into difficult waters.

At UCSF our research administrative staff is divided into those who handle pre-award activities and those who focus on post-award management. A departmental research administrator who oversees both areas manages them. This division of responsibility has allowed staff to become "experts" in each area and allows the all-important post-award administration to be managed in a timely and accurate way. Where pre- and post-award activities are managed by the same staff, we find that post-award activities (reporting, ledger reconciliation) tends to fall to the bottom of the "to do" list when the excitement of deadlines for grant applications push other priorities aside. It is precisely these post-award activities when neglected that can cause audit and compliance problems and penalties.

We cannot emphasize enough the importance of having highly qualified and well trained staff to manage grant portfolios post award. Departments that leave post-award funds management in the hands of PIs directly are asking for trouble; we have seen it over and over. Even if you have a small grant portfolio, take the time to assign a competent financial staff member to structure reports or analyze reports provided and actively manage these funds. It has taken several years for us to create the mentality that the post-award financial analysts represent the department and its interests – namely the Chair's desire to avoid having to support a PIs financial liability if he/she overspends on a grant – rather than the individual PI. We do not allow post-award fund managers to change faculty funding without review by someone more senior, and we do not allow customized reporting templates. We expect the PIs to review and sign off on their financial projections regularly, but based on a template and standards that are set by the department. We try our best to give an eighteen to twenty-four month view to the Chair so that he knows in advance if a PI is running into financial trouble. He expects our staff to make cost-cutting suggestions, even when difficult, to a PI to avoid this situation. Our department is not averse to bridging a PI with a proven track record, but we do not want it to be because an investigator refuses to reduce or rearrange staffing on a project, or re-budget expenses to avoid the problem. Through aggressive funds management, we have created a culture where our faculty knows they will be supported if they have a successful track record, but where we expect them to make hard decisions before coming to the department for help.

We also ask our financial analysts to be on alert for pre-spending on grants, e.g., a grant "will probably" be awarded, but the funds have not arrived, and yet people are being hired or money is being spent on the expectation of the award. This is a recipe for financial disaster. If you are going to get into the business of imaging research, please focus on the post-award backend as much as the pre-award frontend. And we highly recommend that these functions, if assigned to staff, reside in separate people rather than in a combined "research services analyst." In our opinion, the skillset required is very different and the training needs and compliance requirements are also different. Then, as chair, set the tone for your researchers. Back up the financial staff, and communicate your expectations of the researchers about how much of their time you will support, when you will provide bridge funding, and so on. Let the PIs know they are ultimately responsible, but give them the people and tools to make sure they are successful. We have found that a strong Vice Chair Research makes a great partner with the financial team in managing awards and setting expectations. In our case, the Vice Chair Research, has had, and continues to have, an outstanding track record in obtaining and managing her own grants, and is a mentor and example to more junior researchers around how to develop good financial processes within a research group.

COMMUNICATING FINANCIAL INFORMATION

We value and protect our department reserves. In our School of Medicine, the Dean (so far) has taken a hands-off approach to department reserves, but at the same time, those departments with money like Radiology, rarely gain school support for research or academic initiatives. Reserves are so important to us, that after our budget is prepared, if we do not believe we will be contributing to reserves in the fiscal year, we go back and develop either revenue strategies or cost reduction strategies to assure some contribution to reserves is achievable. We try to be conservative and disciplined when it comes to this topic, but have struggled with how best to communicate this to the faculty. Our leadership has taken the position of communicating some basic financial principles, rather than providing extraordinary detail to the faculty, and we do not believe there is one right approach. Every department is different and a chair needs to gauge his/her faculty level of interest in financial matters. Here are some of the key financial reports we share regularly with our faculty leadership and with the rank and file:

1. Pro fee revenue collections by section and section profit and loss – shared semi-annually with section leadership and used as the base for calculating clinical bonuses if earned.
2. Revenue and payer trends by section as well as audit results – we self-audit regularly and by section and routinely share results with the section members to allow them to understand what is billed, how payers communicate about what is billed, and the impact on patients themselves.
3. RVU statistics – by faculty member compared to a subspecialty benchmark and tracked quarterly and annually.
4. Department budget with year-to-year comparisons of major categories, e.g., salaries, research support, and education. We also share actual to budget performance quarterly and at the close of the fiscal year.

5. Use of reserves by major categories – shared annually.
6. Performance of the Joint Venture – quarterly review of volume, cash, and distributions.

It is important to note that we have enough breadth in our financial staff that almost any financial question posed can be answered. However, we try to be judicious in understanding why someone is asking a question and what they really want to know. We prefer to keep the details of our reserves and planned commitments within a smaller circle of the department leadership; however, we are most willing to talk about the larger categories of commitments, particularly funding competitive faculty salaries and recruitments. In recent years, our faculty leadership has become more educated on the professional fee revenue cycle, and our department Revenue Director devotes a large percentage of her time to section education. This can take the form of audits of billing practices and presenting the results to a section; or in some cases, she has educated faculty on terminology, documentation requests, coding and other topics that they have questions about. We have made it a point to have a standing item around billing and compliance at all of our MD faculty meetings, and we create an annual financial report as part of our Chair's "state of the department" talk.

INTEGRITY, ACCOUNTABILITY, AND CONTROLS

It seems that it should go without saying that having proper controls and accountability in place in the department is essential. Most universities certainly have policies and procedures in place to assure financial control and accountability. We think it is important for the chair, again, to set the tone in the department. It is very easy for busy faculty to view these policies and procedures as irritants and annoyances – at least until there is a problem. Whether the rules are around Medicare fraud and abuse, or around extramural funds management, lack of compliance carries serious penalty, usually financial and sometimes more. A chair's credibility can be seriously damaged with the Dean or university leadership if it appears that compliance is taken lightly or not considered at all in the department. What financial policies should you be most familiar with as chair?

1. Conflict of Interest and Conflict of Commitment – critical in a public university but essential in any department setting.
2. Compensation plan rules for the faculty – are you following and applying the same rules for everyone on the faculty? Is salary setting applied fairly and can you demonstrate this with data?
3. Vendor relationships – most universities have very strict policies around vendor relationships and chairs need to comply themselves as well as advise faculty appropriately.
4. Purchasing decisions – because Radiology departments routinely purchase large and costly equipment, it is very important to have a purchasing process and decision-making process that is criteria and benefit based, rather than based on a chair's relationship with a sales team or vendor.

The next section will talk about developing a financial team within your department, but a word needs to be said here around accountability as well. The most important advice we can give you when discussing financial accountability and integrity is to hire great people and then allow them and trust them to give you straightforward advice. It will not help you to hire a strong financial manager, but then discount her advice or apply it only in certain situations. The Radiology administrators at UCSF feel fortunate that our chair listens carefully to what they say, and backs them up without question in situations that involve the faculty either receiving or spending funds. It is part of our system of controls, checks, and balances, and works very well for us. We have also found at UCSF that allowing some of the senior staff to have the final word on financial policy creates a buffer around the chair and allows him to avoid some negativity with faculty. He can then focus on the larger financial issues that really require his input – budgeting, planning, new revenue streams, new research venues, and so on. He can avoid becoming a referee over small financial decisions – for example, is this expense appropriate on a grant? Can I be reimbursed if I buy an iPod for teaching? Can I have a section meeting at an expensive restaurant? Our senior staff take this responsibility seriously (some of our faculty think too seriously) but it works for us. Again, assess your faculty and your culture and make your own decision about what level of financial accountability should reside with you alone.

THE RADIOLOGY FINANCE TEAM

This is where UCSF Radiology is spoiled – we have outstanding financial administrators and great depth and breadth. We share our structure here as an example, but clearly the size and scope of your staff will entirely depend on the number, size, and type of funds that you manage. By way of perspective, UCSF Radiology is a $75+ million department, with about 55 percent of funds coming from clinical activity, and 45 percent from research activity. We have approximately 130 academic employees, about evenly divided between MDs and PhDs, and our clinical practice covers five sites. We have 200+ employees on the school side, and another 250 on the hospital side. Our clinical technical activity at our primary hospital generates more than $200 million in charge and generates about 30 percent of the hospital's bottom line. We are responsible for clinical compliance on both the hospital, technical, and professional side. This is a large operation, with thousands of transactions, both clinical and research, every day, at a university that has invested very little in financial systems – clearly, we have invested in a large and competent staff. Here are the key positions:

1. Chief Financial Officer – reports to the Department Administrative Director and has complete responsibility for the financial management of the department. (See organization chart, Chapter 16). Reports directly to the Chair for purposes of compliance, compensation plan issues, and works directly with the Executive Vice Chair and Vice Chair Research on funds management and faculty salary setting. In our department, the CFO is a highly experienced, respected individual with broad experience at the school and campus levels, and with strong skills in budgeting, planning, EMF management, research administration, NIH requirements, and campus financial policy. Every chair needs someone like this in his/her department.

2. Director of Revenue and Reporting – this individual is responsible for the professional and technical billing functions within Radiology (jointly reports to the hospital) and also directs the scheduling call center. She is an expert on coding, compliance, revenue cycle management as well as call center operations. She supervises a team of nearly ten people on the revenue

cycle side. She is increasingly drawn to IT, EMR, and business intelligence reporting which are areas we find more and more important as we manage these critical fund sources.

3. Director of Research Administration – reporting to the CFO, this is again a high-level and experienced research administrator who supervises a team of about eight pre- and post-award research analysts. She is responsible for grant budget preparation, extramural funds management and reporting, and of course, compliance. Less than a decade ago, this position and her team did not exist in Radiology, but as research grew, the need for administrative control over the process and the funds grew as well. This investment, we believe, has demonstrated success in terms of our corresponding rise in the NIH research rankings.

4. Senior Financial Analysts – reporting to the CFO, these individuals prepare the section profit and loss statements, interact with the medical group and Dean's office for purposes of reporting; prepare the three year consolidated budget required by the School of Medicine; create custom reports for the Chair; and, create, monitor, update, and analyze the department's reserves and commitments report, which is the primary report used by the chair to assess the department's financial health.

5. Recharge Services Manager – reporting to the CFO, this individual manages the financial activity and reporting for our imaging cores, including our cyclotron, research MRIs, preclinical imaging core, research computing, and quantitative image processing. He is responsible for compliance with our campus budget office procedures. He routinely produces analyses for the chair, Vice Chair Research, administrative director, and for the RIG/SRG leadership.

These are the core positions, and obviously, a department chair can start with a strong CFO or CFO-type role, and scale up as activities change and the department grows. In many small departments, the administrator acts as the CFO, and the pro fee revenue director or billing director – as it is sometimes called – is critically important. Some universities and schools centralize the research administration and only a reporting function resides in the department. Your circumstances will dictate what you need, but we strongly advise you to hire at least one person you trust in a critical financial role and then listen to the person and follow his or her advice. Nothing can pull down a chair like poor financial control, inadequate respect for compliance procedures, or consistently poor financial performance, so this is not an area where you should avoid spending money on either people or systems.

Chapter 5

BILLING ORGANIZATION

Radiology charges are composed of technical and professional components. The technical component covers the expenses associated with the process of obtaining the images including the technologist's time, the cost of the supplies and the depreciation for the equipment used as well as utilities and charges for the space used. In the hospital, the technical fees are usually billed by the medical center although they may be billed by the radiologist in free-standing imaging centers owned and operated by the radiologist. On the other hand, the professional charges are associated with the direct expenses of the radiologist including his time, individuals directly employed by him/her, and malpractice insurance. The technical and professional billing can be combined into global charges, which will be discussed more fully later.

The professional billing in Radiology can be done by the medical center, as a stand-alone operation in the department, or as part of the medical group or Practice Plan of the school. Billing can also be a combination of the above. Interventional Radiology (IR) is often handled separately from the rest of the department, sometimes combined with Surgery. We will explore these approaches as well as describe the advantages and disadvantages of each organization.

The Medical Group Practice approach brings the advantages and the scale of a larger entity. Expenses including personnel and information technology (IT) are shared. Also the personnel in a larger organization can develop specialized skills so that one individual may be primarily dealing with Medicare while another can handle managed care. Some can specialize in getting the bills out while others deal with denials.

In a larger entity such as a medical group, the department may lose control and influence. Negotiations for reimbursement rates with payers are always a compromise and Radiology may not fare well in comparison to others such as primary care or even other specialties such as Surgery. Often primary care needs special rates in order to make up for such low reimbursement for Evaluation and Management (E & M) codes. Primary care usually needs some subsidy, either through the medical center or the school. As long as all of the specialties share in the "cost" of helping primary care, Radiology has little to complain about.

Another model is in partnership with the medical center. Hospital-based practices may contract with the medical center for the billing of professional fees. The medical center is often better able to negotiate with payers for reimbursement rates. But it is important to link the professional billing in these arrangements to the technical fees so that the hospital is not tempted to get higher reimbursement on the technical side at the expense of the professional contracts. One way to keep the payments in synchronization is to use the ratio of charges as the determinant. If the professional fees are 20 percent of the total charges, then the professional practice should get 20 percent of what is collected. If the hospital raises the technical charges, then the radiologists need to raise the professional charges or else the ratio will change and the percentage of the collections for the radiologists will diminish. And if the medical group is billing as a separate Medicare provider from the medical center, the physicians will lose out on the higher reimbursement rates generally given to hospital outpatient facilities.

However, medical center billing systems are usually designed to send to their insurers combined electronic bills (UB92) and do not itemize or provide line-item details. If there are multiple charges such as lab or outpatient visits in addition to the Radiology charges, dividing up payments equitably can be a challenge. That problem is especially true if some of the charges are denied. A system designed for outpatient practice billing usually provides for such line-item details that makes follow-up for each charge easier to handle with multiple departments involved using form HCFA1500 (Redmond, 2011).

Some institutions have gone to a contractual model with the medical center that is a strong departure from the independent approaches described so far. The medical center, in this approach, does all of the billing for the various practices and then passes payments based strictly on RVUs to the clinical departments. The departments are freed from responsibility of clinic expenses and do not have to worry directly about the billing process. The downside is that the departments lose complete control over the clinic operations and over the billing process. The medical center, in this scenario, has to carefully design incentives to keep physicians engaged in the practice in other ways and to monitor payer mix. Radiology can be disadvantaged under a pure RVU payment model. Remember that Radiology generally does not have a very large practice expense as part of the RVU and often needs technical fee support in order to compete with salaries with those radiologists who own imaging centers or have joint ventures with their medical centers.

One variation on this theme that is the practice at a few multidisciplinary centers provides salaries for physicians that are not directly linked to income or RVUs generated. These institutions usually have incentives for performance and enjoy relatively few turf battles. But the physicians at these institutions do not have strong incentives to worry about billing, collecting, or even marketing.

IR is often misunderstood by commercial carriers. Often these payers do not realize that IR is just like Surgery from a billing perspective and not like the rest of Diagnostic Radiology. Managed care contracts can be a problem for IR and the IR billing may be better suited as part of the medical center charges. Each Radiology department needs to analyze their particular circumstances before deciding the best approach. As mentioned earlier, sometimes it is attractive to bill for IR along with Surgery and, similarly, it might be advantageous to bill with Neurosurgery for Neurointerventional Radiology. No matter what billing arrangement works best, make sure that the billing fees are a lower percentage of the charges for these high-end procedures as compared to the rest of Diagnostic Radiology. The billing fees are the costs for billing each procedure done and most often are charged as a percentage of the professional fee that is billed to the insurance company or individual. The billing and collections for a neurointerventional procedure is not much more complicated than for a chest x-ray, yet the fees are substantially greater. Billing fees are often in the range of 7–12 percent for simple imaging but should not be more than 6–8 percent for the high-end procedures.

PATIENT MIX IMPLICATION

In order to effectively manage contracts, you must fully understand your reimbursement not in percent of charges, but in relationship to some standard. Most managers use Medicare payments as the single best benchmark, although Medicare reimbursement changes somewhat year to year. At least it is a relatively fixed and well understood entity that we can use. You need to calculate your reimbursement in terms of Medicare, such as 130 percent of Medicare reimbursement overall. Of course, you need to perform this calculation for each payer to understand the particular issues with each one. And these calculations should be done at the procedure level to see what outliers exist for each payer. Some will reimburse reasonably well for CT but not MR, etc. The more you know about these variations going into contract negotiations, the better.

Keep in mind that Medicare reimbursement itself will never exactly equal Medicare rates because of denials for one reason or another. The best you can hope for with Medicare is actually slightly less than Medicare rates. Medicaid will be substantially less than Medicare and does not reimburse at all for a number of procedures now in routine clinical use. This has significant relevance as the Obama administration rolls out healthcare reform, where many who are currently uninsured are expected to enroll in a Medicaid type payment system. It is difficult to recommend an overall percent of Medicare target for reimbursement or contract negotiation. Each department needs to examine its own professional cost profile and determine what is acceptable.

At UCSF, we have found that maintaining a strong presence and position in medical group governance and on the contracting committee have helped us to achieve a reasonable target rate of reimbursement. Early on, we recommend developing a deep knowledge of reimbursement yourself, or cultivating this skill in a key faculty member, perhaps a Vice Chair for Finance. In either case, you and your faculty experts should be backed up by strong and effective staff support in clinical finance. This staff member can function as your early warning system and should be expected to monitor the entire revenue cycle, start to finish, in detail. We have found at UCSF and in reviewing other departments, that this detailed focus separates successful departments from those on the margin.

SELF-PAY

There are two distinct groups within so-called self-pay. They are the indigent and the wealthy who choose not to have health insurance. One experienced healthcare CFO referred to this group as "full pay/no pay" (personal communication). But as you well know, there is a growing group of individuals who do not have insurance either because they are young and healthy and are willing to risk not having insurance or they have recently lost their jobs and are now unemployed and struggling to meet house payments or pay for food. In fact, studies show this group to be approximately 16–19 percent of the population, an estimated fifty million people in 2010 (The Huffington Post, 2010).

Medical centers have recently been criticized for charging self-pay patients full charges or offering only small discounts. Public institutions and non-profit hospitals are particularly scrutinized for this practice. The problem is that "scheduled" or "retail" published charges are often excessive because they are driven up by institutions' desire to stay ahead of discount rates negotiated with fee-for-service payers, which will be discussed more in the next section. Because of this concern, institutions – both medical groups and hospitals – are often offering larger discounts to self-pay patients, usually tied to their ability to pay. In this fashion, those wealthy patients who simply have chosen to self-insure can be charged more while those who simply cannot afford even lower charges are given a break. Determining one's ability to pay is not so easy and can be a humiliating process for the patient if not handled quite delicately.

COMMERCIAL PAYERS

Most payers today are discounted fee-for-service contractors who typically negotiate the contracts with the physician groups and hospitals every two to three years. The game is to raise prices in between negotiations and take advantage of the fact that most contracts are a discount off of the published charges so that more revenue can be brought in at least until the next round of negotiations.

Many such payers will try to impose their own proprietary fee schedule, often not even published or fully available. You have to specifically ask them for representative payments to get an idea of how good of a contract it might be. They often insist on the right to change the payment amount in between contract negotiations, sometimes without notification. Obviously, these arrangements should be avoided and, in fact, you need to carefully consider termination of contracts that include these proprietary fee schedules. More and more contractors are going to fee schedules that are a percentage of Medicare which both sides understand and can relate to easily as well as monitor compliance.

Radiology tends to be reimbursed more poorly than other specialties in proprietary fee schedules. In fact, you must be careful in any negotiations with commercial payers that Radiology is not singled out for special consideration, which usually means a larger discount off charges. Sometimes payers will agree to the across the board discount rate but will specifically target Radiology by identifying non-covered services such as Computerized Tomography Angiography (CTA) or Magnetic Resonance Angiography (MRA).

Recently a chair from another institution circulated an email message seeking help from other chairs of Radiology departments because their medical group was asking Radiology to take a lower percentage of Medicare so the rest of the group could get a higher rate. This type of "divide and conquer" strategy usually works against Radiology.

Preferred Provider Networks (PPNs) are now quite popular and insurance companies are using these large networks of providers in a region to cut costs. They can do so by first negotiating a special set of rates for providers to be in the network, but then to select from among the network providers those where the best rates are contracted. In this fashion, they offer a wide selection to their clients but steer them to lower priced providers. They will often give the patients an incentive to use these lower cost providers by charging them smaller co-pays, for example. At UCSF, we have experienced payers "steering" patients away from imaging at our academic medical center and toward lower cost community-based providers. It is discouraging to us, and extremely inconvenient for patients and their doctors. We have not found an ideal solution, except to offer as much help as possible to our internal practices in terms of obtaining authorizations to allow imaging to occur in the same place as the specialty visit or consult.

This needs to be handled carefully, as there are compliance issues and we recommend clear communication with your local compliance officer if you are considering a similar strategy.

Often the referring physicians will ask the faculty in our department to render a "second opinion" for their patients who were steered to other imaging centers for their scans. Of course, it is often difficult or impossible to get paid for such second opinions. Another point is that this steering to other centers is often mostly caused by high technical fees at our medical center which are usually about 80 percent of the total charge. The competing imaging centers are owned by the radiologists who can afford to charge lower technical fees and still see large profits.

MANAGED CARE

In addition to government payers, self-pay, and commercial insurance, we still have managed care, especially in Northern California. In many parts of the country, managed care has disappeared, mainly due to client discomfort with their loss of control over whom they may see. Even where managed care persists in some form, typically it applies mostly to primary care and specialty care is offered as a discounted fee-for-service.

Managed care, which is also called prepaid care, is based on capitation whereby a primary care provider is paid a fixed amount per person that is signed up in his panel. These payments are typically a fee per person per month (PPM) and do not vary depending on how often the individual sees the physician or otherwise requires his attention. Obviously a physician can have severe adverse selection in which a large number of patients who have chronic illnesses sign up either because of his/her reputation or special areas of expertise.

These primary care physicians under capitation are usually offered bonuses if they can keep their referrals in control and especially if they can keep medical imaging and laboratory tests in check. They are viewed as the gatekeepers to specialty care of other referrals and their permission is often needed to proceed to see a specialist or get MRs or CTs. Now even their authorization is insufficient and they must get authorization from the insurance company or a third-party clearinghouse. We will deal more with authorizations later.

The only control on patients seeking to visit their primary care physician is usually a co-pay. These co-pays are often around $20 per visit and most capitated plans do not have deductible amounts that must be met before the insurance covers anything. On the contrary, these deductibles are common in straight fee-for-service insurance plans and can be hundreds to thousands of dollars per year.

A new variant on straight managed care plans is the so-called tiered approach. In such a plan, which is usually more expensive than traditional managed care, the individual has a choice of seeking the usual primary care physician (tier one) or going directly to a specialist in the network (tier two). If the patient goes out of network, they fall into tier three. Needless to say, the co-pays and deductibles go up with the higher tiers.

PREFERRED PROVIDER NETWORKS

As mentioned earlier, PPNs are now quite common. Insurance companies claim they choose these providers based on "quality" indicators. However, some companies refuse to publish the criteria for such selection and often the physicians left out are those with high referral rates or high utilization of imaging or lab work. In other words, they select the most cost effective providers under the guise of quality.

As we described earlier, the insurance companies provide incentives to their clients to choose physicians in the PPN by offering reduced co-pays or deductibles if you use these preferred providers. And the preferred providers are given a bonus to be in the PPN and usually understand clearly that to stay in the preferred group, they must continue to be less expensive to the insurance company than other physicians around.

FOUNDATION MODEL

Another approach to prepaid or capitated care is the foundation model, such as offered by the Kaiser Permanente system. In these arrangements, patients are often in what looks like managed care with a first-line primary care physician with specialist referrals. There are co-pays and perhaps deductibles, but the cost overall tends to be less. Why? These foundations, by virtue of their organizational structure, can control the entire spectrum. They can carefully choose members to begin with, with marketing campaigns often designed to attract the young and healthy. Some facilities do not have emergency rooms or have limited emergency services available, so that higher-risk, less affluent populations must access other alternatives in their communities. Probably most important, they manage very large populations and can carefully control risk. In California, we have also seen heavy investment in information technology by these foundations to allow rapid sharing of patient information, but also self-care, which again is attractive to a young and tech-savvy population. The Kaiser system has also used very strategic contracting with other hospitals for specialties such as radiation therapy or cardiovascular surgery. The contracts offer large volume for low rates, but they have been outstanding at dropping the contract and adding a regional facility as soon as the financials justify it.

The advantage to the physician (as we have seen by the numbers of UCSF residents taking positions with Kaiser in every medical specialty) is a guaranteed salary and benefits, reasonable working hours, and bonuses based on both financial performance and outcomes or quality measures. Removing the uncertainty of reimbursement from government programs, medical group choices and selectivity, and the need to pay so much attention to the practice expense side, pushes physicians to choose foundation models even if they lose direct control of their professional lives.

PAY FOR PERFORMANCE (P4P)

Another wrinkle in healthcare reimbursement is the so-called P4P program which Medicare is trying to embrace. The concept is that Medicare will pay physicians more if they reach certain thresholds for quality indicators. The American College of Radiology (ACR) tried to define these indicators at its summer intersociety conference a few years ago. Please keep in mind that Medicare does not intend to provide higher payments but instead to lower payments for those physicians not in compliance. The latest approach is the push toward using information systems, specifically the Electronic Medical Record (EMR). The "meaningful use" criteria have recently been described and radiologists do fall under the umbrella of eligible physicians if they do a substantial amount of outpatient work. The radiologists were originally excluded but the ACR worked hard to be sure they were included. In the long run, we are not sure that was a wise decision since there will be more penalties for non-compliance than rewards for compliance down the road. But for now, physicians can expect $40,000 more income from Medicare patients over the next five years. That is, unless the institution, the medical center, has provided the EMR. In that case, they can claim the payments since they incurred the expense.

CONTRACTING STRATEGY

As I mentioned earlier, think Medicare as a metric when you are negotiating reimbursement contracts. You need to pick a base year for Medicare since it does change slightly year to year. If you want to use current year Medicare each year, run the numbers to see the difference in what you collect based on Medicare rates one year to the next. To do so, you need to multiply the quantity of each procedure code times the new rate from Medicare for that code as compared to the last rate. The overall sum of these differences would represent your change from one year to the next, assuming the only payer you experience is Medicare. In this manner, you can determine your overall reimbursement as a percentage of Medicare. Let's say you collect $1,300,000 overall and you would collect $1,000,000 if every patient had Medicare. Then your reimbursement is 130 percent of Medicare overall.

You can calculate the percentage of Medicare for each payer in this fashion and figure out which insurance carriers are adequately reimbursing you and which are not. Of course, these calculations can be done on an individual procedure code basis or on the entire book of business for that carrier.

Before you enter into negotiations with a carrier, you need to have a clearly articulated plan that sets a target and a floor for the negotiations. Of course, these two levels need to be in terms of a multiplier times Medicare. Let's say for the particular insurer in question you are currently at 130 percent of Medicare and you would like to increase that to 140 percent of Medicare. You should determine the floor and if you have history with the insurance company, then your floor will likely be the current rate, in this case, 130 percent. If it is a new company and you do not have any prior history, you will have to pick a target and floor based on the expected volume of work. Most insurance companies want a steeper discount if they are offering a larger volume of work. And, conversely, if a company promised a certain level and failed to reach it since the last contract was negotiated, you should be able to argue for higher rates this time.

Keep in mind that although you might be able to get higher rates, you may be pushing the carrier to shift patients to other providers if they can. Obviously, for more specialized services for which there may not be any competition in the area, you will be able to negotiate higher compensation. If after successfully negotiating a higher rate, you notice a decline in patient referrals, you might want to analyze where those patients are going to see if you have priced yourself out of a market. Such information is invaluable in planning for negotiations when the contract is up for renewal.

I have been using the term, "you" in this context although the actual negotiations for a medical group are likely to be done by a small group experienced in that task. The medical group governing board, often a subset or all of the clinical chairs, needs to decide on the floor which they would allow the negotiators to go down to without coming back to the board for approval. If they fail to get agreement at or over the floor figure, then the board needs to be involved again and either decide to walk away from the contract or lower the floor.

A few words of caution might be appropriate here. Medical group negotiations with insurance plans can be tricky. These expert negotiators from these companies often try to trade off some practitioners for deals with others. As an example, all too often, the negotiators will offer better rates for most practitioners at the expense of Radiology. If Radiology is not at the table, these special deals could be agreed to.

Also look out for deals that establish the need for prior authorizations for Radiology procedures such as CT/MR or PET, in exchange for better deals for others. Or sometimes the offer would simply acknowledge that certain procedures are not covered under the plan such as CTA or MRA. Another trick is to deny payment for procedures that are changed from one Current Procedural Terminology

(CPT) to another from what is authorized, such as CT head without contrast to one with contrast. For these procedures that require prior authorizations, try to perform the process to protocol the examination before getting authorization. In that fashion, changes from the procedure ordered can be managed. For outpatients, any changes need to be confirmed with the referring physician. Reaching such a busy person can be a difficult challenge. If you can get your referring physicians to order generic procedures, such as simple CTs of the head, with no reference to the exact CPT code or contrast use, then you can establish the best exam based on the history and other patient information and have the authorization obtained for that precise procedure.

NEGOTIATING TACTICS

As stated before, the most important strategy is to know the target and floor in relation to Medicare rates and push hard to use Medicare as the basis of the fee schedule. It is critical that you know the competition. You are not supposed to know their rates but at least understand the physician groups and hospitals around you and figure out if you offer unique services, are more comprehensive, have a better reputation, or are more conveniently located as compared to them. Only then will you be in a strong position at the negotiating table. Are you the only show in town? If so, you will be in a very strong negotiating position with practically any carrier.

Next it is important to know what the insurance company wants. Do they emphasize convenience for their clients such as geographic location, one-stop service, or easy access to specialists (short wait times for appointments)? Do they pride themselves in covering many of the larger medical groups and hospitals in the area? Are they primarily looking for a good deal and do you expect them to play hardball? Were they difficult in the last negotiation?

The last point is that you must be prepared to walk from the table if they are unwilling to reach the floor of your negotiations. If they represent a large portion of your business currently, walking away, not accepting their best offer, could be very difficult. If they are more than 10 percent of your activities, you will definitely need the buy-in of the executive board of the medical group and/or the medical center before you give up with a particular insurance company. Obviously, if your beds are full, you have patients waiting to see physicians in the outpatient arena, and you are confident that other patients will come to you, then walking away from a poor deal makes sense. On the other hand, if your hospital has a low occupancy, your physicians are eager to take on more patients, and you have a dominant insurance carrier in your area, turning down a deal with that carrier would be foolhardy.

Let us examine the UCSF situation regarding competition. We are a large academic institution in a medium sized city that is reasonably well off financially. We have for competition California Pacific Medical Center (CPMC), San Francisco General Hospital (SFGH) and its network of clinics, Kaiser Permanente, and Stanford University to the south. CPMC is a large multiple hospital institution in the Sutter system which is now pushing the foundation model very tenaciously. Kaiser is the definition of the foundation model and owns their physicians completely. SFGH is the county hospital dealing mostly with indigent and Medicaid patients but is also the only Level 1 Trauma Center in the city. SFGH is staffed by UCSF faculty. Kaiser has 50 percent of the population in their network.

Stanford is similar to UCSF in that they offer the full spectrum of specialties and unique services including transplants. So we are certainly not the only show in town. Both Stanford and UCSF enjoy some special treatments because of our reputations and because we offer package deals for transplants and other high-end services. And we have a very strong neuroscience program (Neurosurgery, Neurology, and Neuroradiology) whereas Stanford has great strength in Cardiothoracic services. Both institutions have children's care but the major pediatric population is in the East Bay area and is served by Oakland Children's Hospital.

It is fair to say we have ample competition and are really not that unique. Our reputation serves us well as we have a small but real advantage at the negotiating table. Also, although we are not that dominant, practically all insurance plans include us in one way or another. Yet because we do demand higher rates, some plans actively steer patients away from us for services like high-end imaging.

What you need to keep in mind is that as a large university system, we take indigent patients along with Medicaid. In fact, our underinsured financial burden is over $90 million per year and we must earn that before we can even break even. And, as you know, health systems must earn profits in order to reinvest in capital budgets and facilities improvements. On the other hand, CPMC actively discourages indigent patients and we have already commented on Kaiser's ability to cherry-pick young, well patients. In addition, patients with significant chronic problems are attracted to institutions like ours. We have suffered with adverse selection by costlier patients who require much more expensive care. The trick to keeping costs down is to have a large diverse pool of patients which include as many generally healthy patients as possible.

PITFALLS FOR RADIOLOGY

Let's get back to Radiology specific issues. As stated before, be wary of a negotiating team that might accept lower reimbursement rates for Radiology in return for higher rates for others. All specialists might have to accept slightly lower rates in order to get reimbursement to reasonable levels for primary care, but make sure Radiology is not singled out.

Make sure that special authorizations for Radiology are not part of the deal. More and more, health plans are demanding prior authorizations for MRs and PET/CTs and some are going after other CTs and even other Nuclear Medicine procedures. You will most likely have to live with some of these but be sure that mechanisms are in place to get after the fact authorizations without too much difficulty. You will certainly need those processes for urgent or emergent scans and you want some way to appeal denials when the exact procedure ordered and authorized is changed to another procedure such as adding contrast to a CT or MR scan.

If the medical center technical fees are too high, then even with very competitive professional fees, outpatients may be steered to lower cost imaging centers by the insurance plans or even by physician groups. Your own referring physicians, under pressure from their patients, may send patients to outside imaging centers, if the co-pays and deductibles are too high for imaging studies.

And if you global bill with the medical center, make sure your pro fees (charges) are kept in synchronization with the medical center tech fees, that is, if you get paid a ratio of the collected amount of the global bill. This issue was discussed earlier in this chapter.

Capitation is always bad for Radiology. The medical group should avoid capitation in any form but may be forced to accept it for primary care services. The group should strenuously avoid capitation for specialists and you need to avoid it for Radiology at all costs. If you are forced to accept it, be careful to include risk corridors so that unnecessary procedures or adverse patient selection does not overwhelm you. Try to insist that all Radiology contracts in the geographic area are treated the same – all in capitation or all out.

PACKAGE PRICING

For specialized services such as transplants, the institution will often negotiate carve-outs, or fixed prices for particular patients. Let's take a liver transplant that has a fixed payment of around $50,000. The "retail" charges for these services for an average patient may be around $150,000, which translates into a discount of around 66 percent off of charges. But if the patient is complicated and has a prolonged hospital stay and extra services by interventional radiology (IR) are required, for example, then the charges may be $300,000, which translates into a discount of 75 percent. All services who have charges submitted for the particular patient then collect their proportion, each getting 25 percent of charges in the simpler case presented.

But in the average, less complicated case, IR may not even be involved and, therefore, does not have any charges in the mix. For the more complicated case, IR may have lots of charges but is only able to collect 25 percent of charges at best. The easiest method of distributing the revenue is as a ratio of charges, but works to the disadvantage of services like IR that only get involved in difficult cases. It would be preferable to average reimbursement over a large number of patients.

SUMMARY

Fee schedules, billing arrangements with your institution, negotiating with outside payers, and working with your clinical colleagues, are complex and challenging issues. It is difficult to predict the outcome of any single arrangement. However, if you understand the issues described in this chapter, and you understand your cost structure, you will be more likely to achieve your financial goals for the benefit of your department and faculty. At the same time, we must keep the patient in mind and be careful that we are sensitive to their costs, especially their out-of-pocket expenses.

REFERENCES

Number of uninsured Americans soars to over 50 million. *The Huffington Post*, February 18. http://www.huffingtonpost.com/2010/12/27/uninsured-americans-50-million_n_801695. html.

Redmond, M. (2011). Ub92 medical claim forms – When and how to use them. Ezine articles, February 22. http://ezinearticles.com/?Ub92-Medical-Claim-Forms---When-And-How-To-Use-Them&id=272557.

The Henry J. Kaiser Family Foundation. The uninsured, a primer, February 18. http:// www.kff.org/uninsured/upload/7451-06_Data_Tables.pdf.

Chapter 6

JOINT VENTURES AND
STRATEGIC SUPPORT

At UCSF, our mantra is "We can't live on pro fees alone" and we will refer to this theme again in the section under faculty workload in Chapter 10. In order to understand why joint ventures and strategic support are so important, it is critical to realize that most academic Radiology departments simply do not have the volume of work per faculty and reimbursement from professional fees to support the faculty salaries and other academic expenses of the department. Either the department needs to own outpatient-imaging centers and collect the technical fees or get funding from the medical center. Other than owning imaging centers, the only realistic source of more revenue is from the medical center, either in so-called strategic support or joint ventures. Keep in mind that typically outpatient Radiology represents a large portion of a medical center's profits because they are able to collect the technical fees. In the outpatient Radiology arena, there are large fixed costs and relatively small variable costs. Whoever owns the facility simply needs to make sure the volume of cases is sufficient to benefit from the profits realized. The Radiology department leadership is most capable of driving that volume through efficient workflow, in conjunction with capturing all of the imaging demand of the enterprise (no outside "leakage"). Some of that excess technical fee revenue must be returned to the department in one way or the other.

JOINT VENTURES

Joint ventures with the medical center can be a lifesaver for a department trying to build reserves for either faculty salary support over time, or to support the academic mission. However, think about the medical center perspective – they will be sharing revenue with no guarantee that there will be more to share. Medical center administration in the beginning will almost surely view a JV as a take away for them. It is so important for the Radiology department to have its own house in order before proposing a joint venture. By this we mean you have carefully reviewed your own operational expenses. You have monitored faculty productivity and set up appropriate incentives through your compensation plan so that clinical practice and revenue generation is not viewed as a sideline. The department has paid close attention to both patient and referring physician satisfaction and you have taken steps to improve access, reporting, and communication. If you have highly paid faculty, you have documentation to show you are in line with the market and not excessive. In sum, you need to show that your department has done everything it can with its own resources before asking the medical center for a share of technical fees. If your department has poor relationships with other clinical specialties, has not worried too much about productivity or otherwise has obvious improvements it needs to make in operations, do this first and talk about a joint venture second.

The ideal joint venture is an arrangement in which the department and the medical center split, say 50-50, the costs, risks, and rewards (net revenue) for a venture such as an outpatient imaging center. In this case, they would share, equally, in the management and oversight/governance of the entity. All decisions from location, selection of equipment and facility renovations, hiring personnel, marketing, and operations would be shared. Obviously, the two parties come to the table with different expertise, and the efforts should be divided accordingly. If there are disputes, then some process for arbitration needs to be in place, such as turning to the Dean and hospital CEO. In the ideal situation, even with a 50-50 arrangement, the department leadership and management are the "operating partner" and the medical center is the "silent partner," but with some veto control.

Why would the medical center want to get involved in a joint venture if they have the capital dollars and expect to capture the business anyway? Unless they believe that the department can generate more business than would come to the institution normally, they are reluctant to share in their revenue-generating business. At UCSF, the medical center leadership came up with some guiding principles regarding JVs:

- Procedure driven specialties that derive much of their volume from community referrals or patient self-selection (MD driven)
- Competition is often in free-standing facilities
- Significant cost and service benefits accrue from a focused operation
- Ancillary revenue potential is substantial
- Economies of scale create much higher profits with volume growth
- Significant capital costs create a barrier to entry
- Outpatient activity is not closely tied to inpatient activity

It is probably evident that these guidelines were not created for Radiology. While these principles were developed for a different specialty, we were in fact able to use them to our advantage in setting up an imaging center JV. We particularly focused on radiologist driven programs which were unique in the community and could drive business to both the medical center and other specialists in our clinical enterprise. In many ways, it was useful to have the other specialty and chair drive open the door; their arrangement actually broke open a discussion with our medical center that had gone on for far too long.

JVs can be established with arrangements other than 50-50 and then all of the investments and profits would be split according to that ratio. Whoever is over 50 percent would be dominant in decision making and, therefore, the minority stakeholder would have to establish minority rights to be protected from the majority owner. These JVs could be separately incorporated entities, but then favorable contracts with insurance companies would not be available to the JV. Usually it is best to fall under the hospital's license for outpatient facilities, unless the department or practice plan owns the imaging center outright. In the UCSF clinical enterprise, independent, and free-standing arrangements outside of the hospital license are prohibited for the time being, a position that the Medical School Dean supports.

Even with expected changes in reimbursement on the outpatient side under healthcare reform, these imaging centers should be profitable if enough patients are imaged daily. And existing imaging centers may well be available for purchase, at a fair price, if they do not have enough patients, especially with the changes in legislation.

Sometimes medical centers establish profit-sharing arrangements where a department enters into an agreement with the medical center in which profits over a set amount – perhaps any profits – are split in some fashion even without the department's initial investment or risk. The percentage available for the department's use is usually relatively small, approximately 10–15 percent, but is real and can amount to significant revenue. These profits are almost always calculated after the medical center takes its overhead, which can be quite high. In fact, whether a JV or profit sharing arrangement, this overhead probably needs close examination and negotiation between you and the medical center. This overhead often contains a number of items that are more appropriate for inpatient services or even specific outpatient services. You need to review what is included in hospital overhead and try to negotiate away those items that are clearly unrelated to the JV activity. At UCSF, after an initial bid to set hospital overhead at 60 percent, we eventually agreed on 20 percent for the medical center and 10 percent for the department, a much more favorable arrangement.

For JVs, the department may not have sufficient funds for its share of the initial investment. Since these JVs tend to be quite lucrative, they may provide a mechanism for the department to fund their share by either borrowing from the medical center until the net earnings are sufficient to pay back its share, or by taking responsibility for the equipment through a lease mechanism. That reduces the cash requirements up front. Of course, if the department has sufficient reserves, you might use those first. Some faculty may not be happy that you are taking their hard-earned reserves for such a purpose, but make sure to point out that this is an investment in the future. As described in Chapter 2, the other approach would be to ask the Dean for the school to provide the funds or perhaps, although less attractive financially for the department, for the school to participate in the joint venture.

One important point about JVs is that they maintain a sense of alignment between the medical center and the department, unlike when the department owns its imaging centers separately. If the medical center believes, correctly or not, that the department is in competition with it, then the whole relationship is in trouble. Capital budgets may suffer and, as stated earlier and in Chapter 7, that could be disastrous for the department. On the other hand, if the medical center is unwilling to consider JVs and the department has reserves, then owning imaging centers may be the only way to go. This approach would require support from at least the Dean.

A good JV could spin off close to one million dollars for each partner, each year, for each scanner involved, which could mean the difference between a financially borderline department and a successful one. And if set up properly, the JV management should be outside the normal operating processes and certainly needs to have more flexibility and departmental control than normal hospital operations. It is important that separate cost centers and revenue accounting be established for the JV so that the expenses and revenues are tracked separately from other activities. You should also build in the possibility of expansion if the JV is successful.

One more point about JVs is the advantage of establishing a depreciation fund within the joint venture. In this fashion, either expansion of activities or replacement/upgrades for the equipment can be accomplished without going back to the capital budget committee.

STRATEGIC SUPPORT

Strategic support is funding from the medical center to the clinical departments in the school of medicine (SOM) generally for three categories of activities: purchased services, program support, and graduate medical education. The following paragraphs will detail each of these categories. This flow of revenue from the medical center to the clinical departments in the SOM can take different forms and be called various names, but in almost all academic institutions, significant funds flow in this fashion. These revenue sources for the clinical departments exist even when the medical center is owned and operated separately from the university and SOM. The medical center often talks about the total amount transferred to the school with considerable pride. However, the graduate medical education support and the purchased services should be viewed quite differently from the program support. For determining the amount of the program support, the total amount is often calculated as a percentage of the profits from the medical center, sometimes on a sliding scale based on the average of several years to reduce the year-to-year variability.

Purchased Services

Purchased services are those activities considered essential work by the departments on behalf of the medical center, such as medical directors of various hospital services, physician or physician extender performing clinical services that are not billable, and support of technical personnel employed through the department (usually in SOM).

Medical directors should be capped at a certain percentage of effort and should be calculated as reimbursement for direct salary expense and benefits without departmental overhead, for example. Expectations need to be set, perhaps in a job description so that both sides know what the medical director is supposed to accomplish.

The physician clinical services that are supported by the medical center are usually those for which no billing is possible such as the ethics consultants, clinical laboratory supervision, and employee health services. Such support may also cover onsite hospitalist coverage or on-call duties for specialists covering the emergency room at night.

These technical services are often in information systems or perhaps laboratory technicians or even nurses for one reason or another employed by the SOM. Purchased services are strictly used to buy services from the departments for these individuals who would normally be employed by the medical center. Sometimes these purchased services cover physicist support for Radiology and Radiation Oncology where portions of faculty are paid by the medical center very much like medical directors.

In our department, computer personnel that support our Picture Archiving and Communication System (PACS) and Radiology Information System (RIS) are included in this category, mainly because of historic reasons. And we have physicists, although we would like more support for them. The Chair or the Vice Chair for Clinical Affairs is the only medical director supported in our department but a strong case can be made for clinical service chiefs.

Program Support

A variety of activities may be the beneficiary of program support, such as start-up funds for recruitment, negotiated support for new program development, and deficit support for departments not able to make it on their own in their clinical mission. This kind of support from the medical center is ideal for demands for services that cannot be adequately reimbursed, such as off-hours coverage and services with low reimbursement such as Mammography or Pediatric Radiology. Keep in mind that the medical center will most likely want to see program support be time-limited, often going down by schedule over several years. Our medical center likes to structure such subsidies to last no more than three years with interim reviews each year. Sometimes they will want to establish not-to-exceed limits such as for start-up salary support for new faculty recruitments. They will expect you to reduce the subsidy based on the actual earnings for that individual and, of course, will not start the payments until the recruit has actually started working.

In our department, the medical center supports our ultrasound faculty to cover the surgeons in the operating rooms at Mt. Zion Hospital. This is a service which was viewed as essential to get the surgeons to agree to operate at Mt. Zion, but was not a service we wanted to commit to without financial help because we needed to add a faculty member to provide this remote service and we did not receive adequate reimbursement for the time spent.

A large category for program support is for recruitment of new chairs. Every applicant for chair positions, like Radiology, wants to get promises in writing for the support they need to achieve a variety of goals. These new chair packages can easily trump other requests for strategic support.

For deficit support, the medical center needs complete transparency and the department's books must be open. The medical center is not going to be interested in subsidizing academic activities and the school should support the academic aspects of these departments truly in deficit. The basic concept behind deficit support is that the medical center recognizes that some departments will not be able to provide reasonable and necessary clinical activities and still break even financially. A decision to support a deficit department is contingent on the faculty in that department performing clinical work at benchmark levels, have compensation that is consistent with the market or other institutions, and that practice expenses are not out of line. At UCSF, practice expenses are typically benchmarked against MGMA medians; benchmarks for both private and academic practices are available. However, sometimes high practice expenses may be out of the department's control (e.g., nurse or technologist salaries set by contract with different labor unions; or requirement to participate in the medical group's billing plan) and the department should be expected to efficiently manage what they can control directly.

Another principle is that departments are expected to cross subsidize troubled divisions or sections and only turn to the medical center if their overall finances are in trouble. Some departments, however, do not agree with that principle and would rather limit or shut down services that are financially in trouble, even if those services are critical to the institution. Such an attitude requires intervention by the Dean of the SOM or by the other chairs.

A variety of methodologies have been used by academic medical centers to calculate the appropriate level of deficit support. Most of these approaches impute the necessary faculty in FTEs to do the clinical work. These calculations are usually based on the RVUs generated by the department. This workload data is generally available from the University Health Consortium (UHC), from the AAMC, or from the MGMA. These organizations take a slightly different approach that we will not spend a lot of time on, but please see Chapter 10 for more in-depth discussion of workloads, especially related to Radiology.

Then the costs for the department are calculated based on the appropriate number of practitioners needed to do the work and the practice expense as taken directly from cost reports. The appropriate level of practice expense can also be calculated from benchmark data. MGMA is one source of these benchmarks. In the ideal setting, the appropriate income that is needed is calculated and the shortfall between reality and this idealized scenario is determined. The medical center may want to reduce this subsidy over time or may be willing to continue to underwrite the department going forward. Often some reward is established for the departments who improve compared to benchmarks. The percentage time of clinical activity by faculty should be reasonable.

Another approach used by at least one leading institution on the West Coast to deal with strategic support in general and deficit support in particular is an RVU based payment system, instead of actual collections minus expenses. The income is calculated from the RVUs that are billed and all of the practice expense is covered by the medical center.

Several flaws are evident. The first is that the department no longer has control over managing expenses in the practice. Any additional nurse practitioners, for example, would require consent by the medical center. And there are no incentives for improving the collection process. In this scenario, the physicians are just employees of the medical center. And sometimes perverse incentives are established that are just rewards for more RVUs with little care for the appropriateness of such RVUs. This issue will increase the turf issues for Radiology since RVU creation is enhanced by doing procedures. This approach will undermine efforts to move toward the "Mayo" model where physicians are salaried by the institution and do not compete for various procedures. If we are forced in this direction by health reform, this approach for departments getting paid for RVUs generated will not work.

Radiology is often viewed as generating sizeable revenues and in general gets little sympathy from the Dean, medical center leadership or other department chairs when it comes to financial difficulty. Obviously, it is much more difficult now than it used to be for Radiology departments to be profitable, but, unfortunately, some institutional leaders have not yet learned that fact. Our prior comments about having the department's own house in order apply to asking for increased strategic support as well, in our experience. However, the best time to negotiate for strategic support is when someone is being recruited as a new chair. In fact, that is probably the best time to negotiate for almost everything! Another approach that has worked at UCSF is to petition the medical center together with a partner department such as Medicine or Neurosurgery; strategic support for key recruitments is an excellent example of how a cross-department partnership might improve the support for everyone.

Graduate Medical Education

The medical center receives reimbursement from Medicare for most or all of its expenses for house staff, including residents and partially for fellows who are recognized by the Accreditation Council for Graduate Medical Education (ACGME). Therefore, the medical center should pay for the residents' salaries and benefits along with at least half of the fellows' salaries and benefits. The medical center is usually quite willing to do so and, in fact, gets into trouble if they charged the federal government for their services and did not cover the expenses incurred. The problem is that Medicare placed a cap on reimbursement for residents in 1996 (Medicare Update, 2009). Since that time, the number of residents supported by Medicare has remained constant and many medical centers now exceed the limits imposed. For that reason, they are usually reluctant to add additional funded slots.

How do they choose which residents to support? A variety of approaches are utilized including just keeping the funding the same as it was back in 1996 or whenever the particular medical center reached the cap. Some hospitals have tried to rationalize the distribution of funding for residents and some have established review committees to help advise them on the proper numbers. Of course, no hospital wants to fund positions for residency programs in trouble, possibly losing their accreditation. Volume data may be used to argue for support as compared with benchmark data, some from the Residency Review Committees (RRCs) established to provide oversight for residencies by the ACGME.

Since reimbursement is limited for activities outside of the hospital functions, research rotations and clinical rotations at other sites are generally excluded from medical center support. Since departments incur costs associated with running the residency programs – such as residency directors and residency coordinators – the medical centers often support at least a portion of those costs. This support is often calculated as a percent or dollar amount per resident. These calculations favor larger departments with more residents. Small departments with just a few residents may need additional administrative support.

In addition, the SOM must have a central office for graduate education. The medical center should fund at least a portion of that expense since the hospital benefits from having house staff in the first place. Some institutions split these costs between the medical center and the Dean's office.

Oversight

At UCSF, the medical center leadership created an advisory committee for strategic support to advise them about the distribution of support year to year. After the medical center distributes the strategic support based on previous years, the committee hears arguments from the various departments seeking additions to the established support. The committee then recommends which requests should be funded based on the overall budget for strategic support established by the medical center. The committee is composed of various department chairs, elected by all the chairs, who serve three year staggered terms. Other members of the committee are financial and administrative personnel from the medical center as well as representatives from the Dean's office.

This committee not only hears requests from the various departments, but also attempts to establish principles for the program support so that the committee and the medical center leadership are not bombarded with unnecessary requests. This committee is also wrestling with alternate financial models – such as described above – that would have physicians directly employed by the medical center. Although only in operation a few years, this committee has created an atmosphere of transparency among the departments and with the medical center and has certainly leveled out what were large discrepancies in funding among the departments.

REFERENCES

Medicare Update. (2009). Legislation introduced to increase hospital FTE resident caps for residency programs. Accessed February 18. http://medicareupdate. typepad.com/ medicare_update/2009/05/medicarefteresidentlimits.html.

Chapter 7

CAPITAL BUDGETS

Capital budgets are incredibly important for Radiology. Without new equipment, the latest and greatest scanners, the faculty and staff will be unhappy. You will have difficulty recruiting and retaining faculty, fellows, residents, PhD scientists, technologists, and other personnel. Without the opportunity to select new equipment, you will not be considered for strategic alliances with industry while other academic departments are doing so. But, perhaps more importantly, you will have difficulty in competing for your patients with the surrounding imaging centers or hospitals. That fact will affect your pocketbook as well as the hospital's bottom line.

Radiology typically consumes a large portion of the hospital's capital budget dedicated to clinical equipment, often as much as 20–25 percent in any given year. Unfortunately, the clinical needs are now eclipsed by IT which has taken the honors as the biggest line item with facilities (construction) not far behind. If the construction for imaging is managed as part of the facilities budget, then it will obviously be larger and imaging somewhat less. For large pieces of equipment, the renovation costs can exceed the equipment costs. For simple radiographic or fluoroscopic equipment, the construction costs can be considerably more than the equipment in the hospital setting. Space renovations to support MR can be particularly expensive. These costs will be substantially less in an outpatient facility especially away from the hospital.

How do you approach developing your capital budget requests? The first part of your analysis must be the age and condition of your existing plant, the wait times for patients for both inpatient and outpatient procedures, and the kinds of new equipment that you would like to consider. You should use the depreciation data from the American Hospital Association (AHA) but typically most radiographic equipment lasts about seven years. Although the AHA may suggest that MR scanners only last five years, they do not have moving parts like CT and actually have lived longer than seven years in our experience. Although they may need software or hardware updates more frequently.

One of the critical elements in your capital budget strategy should be to separate requests for replacements for aging and failing equipment from new programs. You should argue that the medical center should have two capital pots, one for depreciation/replacement of older equipment and one for new equipment and new programs. This approach can be very beneficial to Radiology as a major consumer of capital. That fact is especially true if there is a capital advisory committee composed of individuals who would prefer to see their pet projects funded before yours.

If you can convince your medical center to establish a depreciation pot, then you should have enough funds in that bucket to replace almost all of your aging equipment. You should try to keep construction costs out of the equation since there are so many variables in those numbers due to local building considerations. If you need to put a couple of items from your wish list for replacement in the new equipment list, that might be fine if you can make a good argument for its replacement, competing with all other new projects. And you probably do not have to write up very much about the replacement items, other than simply needing it. Current use case volume can support that argument. Of course, showing that older equipment is breaking down frequently or that it is out-dated and difficult, if not impossible, to find replacement parts, helps make the argument for replacement.

RETURN ON INVESTMENT

For new equipment, if you can demonstrate a return-on-investment (ROI), you will be much more likely to get support, especially from the medical center leadership. But new equipment may also be justified by long waiting times for patients to get scheduled for procedures like CT/PET or MR. Or perhaps a new inpatient scanner will reduce the chance of patients getting bumped until the next day delaying the hospital discharge. There is probably no better argument than you can reduce length of stay (LOS) or hospital days. Of course, arguments for patient safety are always powerful, such as having angio rooms shut down in the middle of an endovascular procedure.

The ROI calculation will probably be led by the hospital's financial team and will most likely include their overhead calculation as we mentioned earlier. Unlike the JV discussion, it is probably of little value to argue about the overhead in these calculations unless it is in a freestanding imaging center where a number of their costs are hard to justify. You do need to include the depreciation of the equipment and renovations, personnel and maintenance, supplies, furniture, and other operating expenses, and rent if there is any. On the revenue side, you should be able to use the standard payer mix for your department, unless there are unique attributes of the patients you expect to serve by this new or expanded program. We would recommend that you be somewhat conservative in your projections for new patients and have everyone pleased when you exceed your projections. The inclusion of the cost of construction or renovation in the ROI is valid but the medical center may argue for its exclusion since that cost is in the overall facilities budget. Excluding the construction obviously will improve the ROI.

There are several standard ways of calculating ROI, with the variations discussed above included. An alternative calculation that you may be requested or desire to make is Internal Rate of Return (IRR). This can be performed with spreadsheet formulas available in Mic-.rosoft Excel or other spreadsheet software. It looks at the outflows and inflows over a series of time intervals (e.g., yearly) for the expected life of the equipment, and yields a single number indicating an equivalent interest rate return for the investment or use of capital. Some institutions rank new programs and equipment projects in the order of their expected IRR, where high rates of return are preferred and funded to those that have low IRR. Other institutions establish a "hurdle rate" annually that sets a qualifying IRR in order to be funded. You or your departmental financial team should understand this method, at least by example.

A very important part of a new project, unless you are guaranteed all the patients you can handle, is marketing. Marketing, which is mostly focused on outpatients, is often not well handled by hospitals, especially if they are generally full of inpatients without it. They often dismiss the importance of feeding their lucrative inpatient business with a steady stream of outpatients. You may have to go out and hire your own marketing specialist to lead this effort and expect to spend more money on marketing than you would likely plan. We will discuss marketing in Chapter 20, but as a rule of thumb, we assume a marketing budget equivalent to two percent of net revenue in every IRR spreadsheet we complete on the outpatient side.

Another aspect of capital budgeting is to have a multi-year plan, at least five years ahead. Figure 7–1 is the five-year plan for UCSF Radiology this year. In this fashion, you can determine in which years you need to replace which pieces of equipment. You can also titrate your requests to the availability of funding which may vary from year to year. Of course, your five year plan should include a section for replacement and one for new projects. Keep in mind that for many of your projects, more than one year will be required to complete the installation, especially for inpatient locations where state oversight of the construction project is required. These multi-year projects can be funded over at least a couple of years, with the bulk of the expense for both facilities and equipment in the second year (see discussion below). Spreading out the cash layout can be very helpful but obviously the commitment needs to be in place from the start.

In California, inpatient projects are regulated by the Office of Statewide Health Planning and Development (OSHPD.) Most states have similar organizations if not outright certificate of need (CON) requirements. All of these approaches slow down such projects considerably and usually drive up the costs. CONs were originally designed to limit the introduction of new "unproven" technologies and apply mostly to hospital facilities. Some Radiology departments have dealt with CONs by arguing for true freestanding imaging centers owned by the departments. Right now in California, OSHPD may require up to nine months to get approval for imaging equipment installation.

Because of these delays and the fact that construction, especially in an existing facility might require multiple phases, you need to split the costs of some projects over a couple of years. You need to work with your facilities planning group to figure out how long projects will take and plan your capital requests accordingly. For the equipment, you only need to spend 10–20 percent as a down payment in the beginning

Equipment	Location	Yr. installed	Current age	Action	FY12 Cost	FY13 Cost	FY14 Cost	FY15 Cost	FY16 Cost
*Toshiba biplane angio**	M/L	1998	13	Replace	2300				
DR/CR portables (2x)	M/L	Various	7+	Replace	400				
Ultrasound replacements (2x)	All	Various	7+	Replace	350				
CT low dose reconstruction hw./sw.	All	Various	N/A	Upgrade	175				
CR reader (including plates)	ACC	2002	9	Replace	175				
*XMR (magnet and angio)**	M/L	2001	10	Replace		3500			
*UCIC magnet (1.5T)**	UCIC	1996	15	Upgrade		600			
Mammo. unit w/tomo.	MZ	2005	6	Replace		550			
DR/CR portables (2x)	MZ	Various	7+	Replace		400			
Decision support sw.	All			New		300			
Mobile C-arm	M/L	2004	7	Replace		225			
*PET replacement (with PET-CT)**	M/L	1995	16	Replace			3000		
*Body IR angio room (Rm. 7)**	M/L	1998	13	Replace			1500		
Mammo. unit replacement	MZ	2005	6	Replace			450		
Ultrasound replacements	All	Various	7+	Replace			350		
Mobile C-arm	MZ	2006	5	Replace			225		
CR reader (w/plates)	MZ	2004	7	Replace			175		
*PET-MR**	CB?			New				3800	
*Nucs. camera replacement**	M/L	2000	11	Replace				500	
*Moff. rad rm.**	M/L	2004	7	Replace				500	
Mammo. unit w/tomo.	MZ	2007	4	Replace				550	
HIFU (clinical unit)	M/L			New					1250
CB 1.5T MR (2x)	CB	2006	5	Upgrade					1300
*ED rad rm.**	M/L	2005	6	Replace					500
*Moff. rad rm.**	M/L	2004	7	Replace					500
DR/CR portables (2x)	All	Various	7+	Replace					450
Ultrasound replacements	All	Various	7+	Replace					350
Mobile C-arm	M/L	2006	7+	Replace					225
CR reader (w/plates)	MZ	2004	7	Replace					175
TOTAL (Dollars in 1000s)					3,400	5,575	5,700	5,350	4,750

* significant construction projects

Figure 7–1. UCSF five-year capital budget request.

and pay around 70–80 percent on installation and the remaining 10 percent or so on successful operation of the equipment. Don't be too fast to pay the last 10 percent since that is the leverage you have for getting remaining issues resolved with the vendor. Companies don't like delays in payments and are likely to have the engineers work a little harder and to have applications specialists, so be more flexible with scheduling time with your personnel if you have not paid yet.

PENDING CHANGES IN REGULATIONS

What impact will new legislation have on your capital planning? No one knows the full answer to that question yet, but we have some clues. Certainly some reduction in payments for outpatient technical fees will occur soon. The increase in utilization factor by Medicare from its current 50 percent to either 60 percent, 75 percent or more will have a dramatic impact on our payments. This utilization factor is based on the expected number of patients that can be accommodated in a CT or MR scanner, for example. The assumption has been that the typical scanner in an outpatient environment can only handle a certain number of patients and will be used about half the time. Of course, newer scanners can handle patients much faster and the growth in such imaging has driven utilization up dramatically. So Medicare has found a very defensible position in arguing that they should not be paying so much per scan, if capital cost is the main factor for high technology imaging costs. Primarily isolated scanners in mostly rural or less populated areas drove the prior figures and those locations will likely suffer more under the new rules, unless there is a dispensation for under-served areas. There is still debate about how quickly these new rules will go into effect, but most likely in the next few years they will be phased in. These new numbers translate into as much as a 50 percent or more reduction in payment per scan. Obviously, this legislation will have a serious impact on imaging equipment purchases and the vendors are fighting this as best they can.

The fears of radiation from CT scanners and the fact that imaging costs have risen so fast in the last decade are further threats to imaging reimbursement. Legislation will likely require reporting and standardization of ionizing radiation use and that alone could drive the costs for imaging upward. The cost of developing and administering the reporting process will certainly add to the cost of imaging. And the fear of radiation has already reduced the use of CT scans at our institution and many across the country.

Additional legislation could further erode payments for imaging, probably more so on the technical side. But the biggest potential threat to reimbursement is the possible implementation of outpatient Diagnosis-Related Groups (DRGs). Medicare implemented DRGs for inpatient services in 1983 for hospitals in the United States. These 500 or so DRGs are based on ICD diagnosis codes, procedures used, complications, and co-morbidities for each patient.

For outpatients, similar groupings are being considered which would dampen the use of additional tests or new techniques unless they can clearly reduce costs. The medical centers/medical group would get paid for a diagnosis group whether or not they used advanced imaging. Outpatient imaging would become simply a cost center for the medical center rather than a revenue source. The enthusiasm for the medical center to invest in new imaging equipment would greatly diminish.

The only good news related to outpatient DRGs is that the interest in investing in imaging centers on the part of private practice radiologist competitors or other specialists will greatly diminish. The academic medical center interest in such investments will decrease as well, but there may be more opportunity to run highly efficient outpatient operations.

CAPITAL BUDGET ADVISORY COMMITTEE

We mentioned the capital budget advisory committee earlier in this chapter. Not every institution has such a group, but if it does, Radiology must be represented on such a committee and if there are other chairs on the committee, then the Radiology Chair needs to be there as well. Medical center CEOs often use these kinds of committees to give them political cover concerning decisions about capital investments. Because these deliberations must occur in advance of the capital year, which is usually the same as the fiscal year, you must be prepared with your five year plan well in advance of when you plan to start buying equipment. And you may need to get quotes and determine configurations of equipment long before the capital budgeting process is started for the year. And don't forget about the sales tax, if there is one. Although we are a state institution and a non-profit hospital, we still get sales tax – which is substantial – added on to the cost of equipment.

Therefore, if your fiscal year is July to June, then you need to have some idea of the equipment you would like to buy by the end of the Radiological Society of North America (RSNA) annual meeting, which is held in early December. The RSNA meeting is an ideal place to see equipment, "kick the tires," and get quotations or at least ballpark numbers for budgeting purposes.

In the past, academic departments used purchasing of equipment for the medical center as an entry into research collaborations with industry. These partnerships often included free imaging equipment and industry support for research fellows or other contractual arrangements. Much more scrutiny is now being devoted to these relationships. See Chapter 21 for more information about such relationships.

Don't forget that the facilities group needs plenty of time to get their estimates together for the companion construction or renovations needed to install the equipment. Such coordination with the facilities organization needs to happen whether or not the construction is included in your equipment budget.

Chapter 8

CLINICAL SERVICES

This entire book could easily be filled with discussions about clinical services, although this is only one of an academic department's primary missions. The clinical activities of the department are at the heart of the academic endeavors and are the key to the financial well-being and happiness of the faculty. We will only deal with some of the more problematic aspects of clinical services and we assume the rest is well-known to the experienced imaging practitioners who are reading this text.

CLINICAL ORGANIZATION

The first issue is the organization of the clinical department. Most large academic departments today are divided into subspecialty sections or divisions. The distinction between a section and a division may be subtle but could be significant at certain institutions. And whether it is a division with a small "d" or with a capital "D" sometimes has local significance. We are not referring here to Divisions that have almost complete autonomy but to sections or divisions that have separate P&Ls as mentioned in Chapter 4 but otherwise are not financially separate from the department or each other.

These subspecialty sections could be organized in a variety of ways but most departments attempt to have so-called organ system sections for the most part. The following is a list of clinical sections at UCSF:

1. Abdominal Imaging
2. Cardiac and Pulmonary Imaging

3. Interventional Radiology
4. Musculoskeletal Radiology
5. Neuroradiology
6. Neurointerventional Radiology
7. Nuclear Medicine
8. Pediatric Radiology
9. Ultrasound
10. Women's Imaging
11. General Radiology/Outpatient Radiology

As you can see, not all of the sections fit the mold of organ systems and at least two of them are closer to modality sections than anything else. Many departments have variations on the theme based on local history or expertise. Perhaps the most important organizational criteria relates to the referring physicians with whom they work most frequently. Examples are Neuroradiology and Neurointerventional Radiology who work with Neurology, Neurosurgery, and ENT most of the time. Abdominal Imaging usually interacts with General Surgery, Urology and Oncology, while Musculoskeletal Radiology deals mostly with Orthopedics and Rheumatology. The exceptions include Ultrasound because that particular specialty interacts with everyone, but perhaps more with Obstetrics and Gynecology, and include Nuclear Medicine working mostly with Oncology and Cardiology.

Having strong clinical relationships with their referring colleagues also enhances the research and teaching relationships and keeps turf issues in check. Many of these departments and others have close interactions in research projects that will be covered in more depth in Chapter 11. Training is more and more interdisciplinary and we have many examples of trainees working in our department, from Obstetrical fellows in Ultrasound to Vascular Surgery residents and fellows in Interventional Radiology. We have even trained a neurologist in Neurointerventional Radiology and we partially support his faculty position in both departments.

General radiologists deserve further comment. If they mostly interpret plain images and do not read CT or MR, they will not likely be able to generate revenue sufficient to cover their expenses. Often these same individuals are expected to cover injections for the CTs and MRs interpreted by subspecialists and they also frequently provide online services for outpatient practices and the emergency room. Special consideration should be made for these kinds of circumstances.

At UCSF, each section has a Chief, responsible for the schedule, call coverage, fellows, teaching, and overall leadership. We expect section leaders to be role models in terms of interaction with referring colleagues and in running reading rooms that are efficient, physician-friendly and responsive to the medical center's needs. In recent years, we have taken the time to develop formal job descriptions for section chiefs and to establish goals to be achieved. In fiscal year 11 (July, 2010, through June, 2011), we will also establish term limits so to speak. In reality, this probably should have happened years ago, to avoid the "section chief for life" phenomena which can sometimes be excellent for a department, and sometime detrimental. We strongly recommend job descriptions and goals and a formal evaluation process for the clinical section leaders. We also believe this process creates better morale for junior faculty in a section.

OFF-HOURS CLINICAL COVERAGE

How best to provide twenty-four hour, seven day clinical coverage is a challenge for every Radiology department and there is no magic bullet that fits all situations. A few guiding principles that are worthy of consideration will be presented here. First of all, it is vital that your referring physicians are comfortable that you are providing good clinical care all of the time. There is no doubt that a double standard exists in that many other specialties are only covered by junior house staff through the night and weekends yet referring clinicians expect top-notched subspecialty coverage from Radiology. But we have one major advantage called PACS, which today extends out to the web with security for teleradiology coverage. We can actually provide some coverage from home, reducing the need to actually come into the hospital, except for interventional procedures.

Many departments still have residents alone in the hospital at night to provide most clinical readings, so-called "wet reads," which is a carry-over from the days that film would be dripping wet out of the hand processor (that residents or practicing radiologists had to handle when alone) and would be literally read on a view-box in the dark-room in that state. Attending radiologists in the morning provide the final reading as well as bill for the procedure.

More and more referring physicians want an attending reading during the night. Those readings are especially desired for patients on whom they may make a major therapeutic decision or disposition, such as patients who they may take to the operating room or even those patients in the emergency room who may be discharged home or admitted. The biggest concerns are for those imaging studies that are read by the residents as negative for acute findings where the referring physicians suspect a problem. Cases with obvious findings are less often a problem.

How well do our residents perform? The answer has been documented a number of times and is almost always the same: those residents who have completed even just one year but with significant exposure to the types of cases they are likely to encounter in the emergent setting do remarkably well (*American Journal of Neuroradiology*, 2002; Arenson, 2006). In fact, they perform as well as most attending or private practice radiologists and are often at the level of interobserver differences among radiologists for significant misses. And the fact that another set of eyes will review the images the next morning should be more assurance to the referring physicians and patients.

Yet, more than once, physicians from the Emergency Department (ED) have stated unequivocally that they would prefer consistent readings rather than accurate ones! They really do not like to have to call patients they have discharged during the night and ask them to return to the ED for more studies or another follow-up.

While patient care is probably not compromised with residents providing first-line care, it is hard to defend when there is a miss at night by an individual who has not even finished the residency program. Then what is the answer?

At UCSF in the evenings, we have board-certified clinical fellows cover CTs and MRs until about 10 p.m. Most of these fellows act like super residents and simply provide wet readings to be reviewed by faculty the next morning. These recent graduates from residency programs read all cases other than Neuroradiology since they are still very familiar with all aspects of Radiology. Neuroradiology is covered by the Neuroradiology fellows and the cases are again checked the next morning.

In addition, we have subspecialty faculty available on-call for any difficult cases the residents or fellows may encounter. However, our experience is that these trainees will rarely call for help even when they should. We have given our referring physicians, especially those working in the ED, instructions that if they ever have a question or concern not addressed by the in-house resident or fellow, they can simply ask them to have a faculty review the images. Then the resident will call or page the faculty to review the case from home on the PACS. In our experience, this ability to reach an attending radiologist is very reassuring for our referring colleagues, yet is utilized infrequently.

Weekends are a different matter. We believe you simply can't allow cases to be wet read only for the entire weekend and then read on Monday morning. We have all sections covering their areas on both Saturday and Sunday. Faculty come into the hospital and read all cases available up until that time. For some sections, this may require only a couple of hours each day. Some sections spend most of each day reading cases and performing procedures. Interventional radiology and Neurointerventional Radiology are on-call twenty-four hours a day and the whole team, faculty, fellows, and residents respond whenever called. The ultrasound section also comes in on-call often due to the nature of their work and often the in-house residents are really not capable or comfortable performing the procedures alone with the technologists. The Pediatric Radiology faculty also comes into the hospital off-hours for procedures such as reducing intussusceptions.

Many institutions across the country have dealt with this problem by hiring a small number of general radiologists to provide coverage at night in-house. Obviously this approach is expensive, it can be hard to recruit participants, and does not provide subspecialty expertise. At least three radiologists are required to provide complete after-hours coverage and they usually demand a premium salary.

Some institutions, particularly those with Level 1 Trauma Centers, have created sections of Emergency Radiology. Often these sections provide after-hours staffing across a broader spectrum of Radiology. Daytime coverage often reverts to the organ specialties as appropriate, e.g., musculoskeletal, abdominal, etc.

Other institutions have hired "Nighthawks" (Bradley, 2007) or other services for hire whereby radiologists, usually General Radiologists, provide coverage by teleradiology from some remote site. These physicians give wet reads, not final interpretations, so this cost is incremental and usually paid by either the department or by the hospital. Certainly, if the hospital administrators demand this kind of coverage, they should pay for it. Some institutions make "Internal" nighthawk or partial nighthawk arrangements with junior or other interested faculty on an hourly or episodic based payment system.

Multiple studies have again shown that in-house residents perform as well or better than these nighthawk General Radiologists or the in-house hires. So once again, while solving some of the politics, patient care is not improved over resident wet readings. And the vast majority of residents consider this to be a significant component of their training and independent thought process.

All of this effort and success at UCSF, with resident wet reads and faculty backup, has not eliminated the interest of some parties to have faculty providing full services off-hours. This continued pressure has come more from hospital administrators than from clinicians. The chairs of Radiology in the University of California system hospitals, UCLA, UC Irvine, UC Davis, UC San Diego and UCSF, get together regularly to discuss common issues. One of the subjects discussed at many meetings is the possibility of providing subspecialty coverage across the institutions by pooling our talent and keeping the call burden under control because of the numbers of specialists in our collective departments. Although technically possible, there are a number of hurdles to overcome such as credentials at each hospital.

ACCESS TO CLINICAL SERVICES

One of the most fundamental issues confronting all radiologists is making sure patients have easy access to their services. Perhaps the biggest problem with either hospital-based practices or outpatient imaging centers is keeping up with the demand for services. If possible, the best strategy is to always have one more device, whether it is a CT scanner or ultrasound scanner, than is actually needed at any moment in time. In that fashion, you will always have the capacity to meet the demands of your patients and your referring physicians. We recognize that costs and space can constrain that attitude but it is worth it to plan ahead and try to stay ahead of the demand. This of course is assuming that current operations and equipment are run efficiently.

It is possible this philosophy may change somewhat if healthcare reform has as much bite as proposed, and you may not want to keep expanding services. As a department running clinical programs in four hospitals and two major outpatient buildings that are four miles apart, we recognize that great service can cause intra-department inefficiency. However, we believe that satisfying referring colleagues and their patients is key to continued success. Even when it is not as financially attractive to make it convenient for your patients, for example in terms of location or level of service (personnel), you should work in that direction. Most radiologist staffing inefficiencies can be managed by proper allocation of interpretive work via PACS.

This attitude also requires you to have a well-oiled scheduling process including schedulers who are both personable and knowledgeable. Obviously, they need an excellent scheduling system – usually part of the Radiology Information System (RIS) to be described more in Chapter 17 – and there needs to be commitment, whether from your department or others running a radiology call center, to achieve key metrics (time to answer the phone, time on hold, abandonment rate, and so on). Investment in call distribution technology is important, but we have found this investment often falls to the bottom of the hospital's list of needs.

At UCSF, what has worked is a conscientious dedication to metrics and leadership reviews of wait times for appointments on a weekly basis. We try very hard to notice long waits before they become trends. When we have failed to react quickly to the need to add equipment, we have lost business and have had to work even harder to get it back. Furthermore, we hold scheduling highly accountable; we have managers literally monitoring call volume trends in fifteen-minute increments and adjusting staffing as appropriate to better serve physician office callers and patients. We do all of this in the context of a heavily unionized work force, just to demonstrate its priority. Is this expensive – yes. Do we think it pays for itself in referrals – we also think the answer is yes. Much as we would like to think all the specialty practices are on the same side at UCSF, we know we need to provide this level of monitoring and oversight to be successful – otherwise referrals will go to our competitors in the community.

The authorization issues have already been discussed in Chapter 5 but need to be emphasized here. You must do everything you can to minimize the burden of authorizations for the referring physicians and their patients. This effort will require a lot of extra effort from your staff and they will need to coordinate their work with the referring physician's office and possibly the patient. It is unavoidable; if your competition handles these authorizations better than you do, you will lose referrals. Hospital-based, managed, and staffed imaging centers in general compare poorly to private practice managed facilities, which is another argument for a separate management structure and/or joint venture run by Radiology. As we mentioned earlier, it is important to check with your compliance officer before launching an authorization service, as there are strict rules around who may seek referral authorization for imaging.

Remember that the protocoling process by the radiologist must occur before you finalize the authorization since you will not otherwise know the exact procedure codes, CPT codes that will be eventually billed for that patient. It is worth the effort to redo work flow to improve the authorization process. Your collection results will be improved and referring offices will have greater satisfaction.

Prompt wet-reads for those physicians who desire to get them are essential for much of your outpatient business. You need to understand which physicians usually want such service and which do not. You should know which patients are returning to their referring physicians soon after the study is done and which physicians desire to get images via CDs or a secure web-viewing tool. These service issues can make or break an outpatient practice and attention needs to be given to these service aspects constantly. Such attention usually requires a practice manager or someone else capable of focusing the proper attention to these details.

These physicians are likely to expect prompt turnaround times on the final reads, often expecting them shortly after the procedure is completed. The best method for delivering these reports depends again on referring physician preference. Your choices, which can be set up in the physician directory of a good RIS, include telephone, fax, email, or inclusion in a CD with the images. If the latter, the report needs to be available before the CD is created which must precede the patient's discharge. Such prompt service requires immediate readings and voice-recognition (VR) transcription. Details about VR will be handled in Chapter 17.

These prompt readings require an online reading process that is easier to institute in a freestanding clinic than in the main hospital with resident and fellow teaching as well as many other distractions. This subject was partially covered above in the section on organization but needs emphasis here. Obviously this immediate reading is easier to accomplish with plain images, of extremities, abdomens or chests, and much more difficult with cross-sectional imaging such as CT, MR, PET/CT or ultrasound. Yet our referring colleagues and their patients expect the same service for these modalities. Therefore, the subspecialty sections need to think differently than the old-school approach of batch reading a couple of times a day. The reality is that faculty need to be present almost all day in the reading rooms with the residents and fellows and must attempt to keep up with the work as it is being done. Batch reading was related to the film era process of taking down and hanging studies by ancillary personnel, and has effectively disappeared with PACS and continuously updated work lists.

REPORT TURNAROUND TIMES

Below is a graph of the report turnaround times from our department at UCSF over a number of years (Figure 8–1). This graph takes a snapshot in time in October of each year to demonstrate the year-to-year variations. We choose to use median times since we believe this avoids the outliers that distort the averages. The graphs show both the intervals from exam completion to dictation and from report available to final signature. This latter interval avoids any transcription delays for the few reports not prepared by VR at the current time. That exclusion keeps the measurements confined to those activities directly attributable to the physicians. The improvements in turnaround time have been dramatic and are due to three factors:

1. Emphasis from the Chair and Vice Chair for Clinical Services
2. Daily email report showing all delinquent cases by practitioner
3. An incentive system with monthly listings of report turnaround times by MD

The daily emails show the physician's name and the number of reports that have not yet been signed within eight hours. This list is sent to all clinical radiologists. The monthly listing shows the physicians and their percentage of cases read within twenty-four hours as well as the percentage of cases over six days (gets after the outliers). The incentives – which are relatively small, $1000 per quarter – for those who qualify seem to be about right to alter behavior and these incentives were introduced six year ago. The faculty needs to have 80 percent within twenty-four hours from exam completion to final signature (less any transcription time) and they must have less than two percent over six days.

In an academic environment with trainees participating there really are three relevant intervals post procedure:

1. Time from completion of imaging to availability on PACS for interpretation (may be delayed by post-processing for example).
2. Time from availability to interpretation/dictation (continuous updating work lists, no batch).
3. Time from dictation to final signing. This interval should be zero if VR is used and faculty are working without trainees.

CRITICAL VALUES

The Joint Commission on Accreditation of Hospital Organizations (JCAHO), now called simply The Joint Commission, has long advocated for the adoption of a list of conditions that everyone agrees deserve special prompt communication. For Radiology, creating such a list of so-called critical values has been difficult for a number of reasons. First of all, we have long practiced the policy of calling the referring physician immediately about any case that has acute findings requiring prompt attention or demonstrates what we believe to be important new diagnostic information. But these critical values would prompt an "automatic" communication of some kind. Needless to say, such alerts are much easier for the clinical laboratory to define as a list of abnormal test results that could be life-threatening.

Examples for such radiographic findings include pneumothorax. However, as you well know, a pneumothorax may be followed by regular chest x-rays over several days and the patients' physicians already know about it. There is no reason to telephone a busy clinician to tell them that the known pneumothorax is responding well and has continued to decrease in size. In a similar fashion, do you call for every lung nodule detected on thin-slice CT? If so, our cardiac and pulmonary section radiologists would be calling multiple times every day.

Report Turnaround Times
October - Median Hours

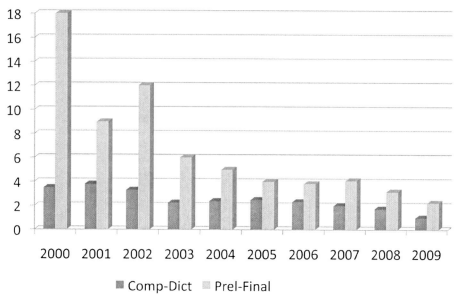

Figure 8–1. Hours for report turnaround.

Nodules over a certain size, say six millimeters, deserves a failsafe action plan. And some communication is necessary to assure proper follow-up even for those that are smaller.

This example of a small nodule deserves further discussion. How do you assure that follow-up actually happens? If you want another chest CT in six months, how do you make sure that happens? Let's take the case where a surgeon orders a chest CT for possible extension of an abdominal aortic aneurism, gets the wet reading and then operates on the patient. The chest CT report describes a small nodule of unknown significance and recommends another CT in six months. The radiologist did not copy the primary care physician since she did not know who it was and the surgeon never even read the report mentioning the nodule and did not accept the responsibility for follow-up. The surgeon was preoccupied with the immediate abdominal problem for the patient. Two years later the patient comes back with unresectable lung cancer. Obviously there are a number of unfortunate communication errors in this example. How could Radiology reduce the likelihood of this patient falling through the cracks?

One method is to flag in the RIS cases that need follow-up and then produce a tickler file for the flagged cases that encourages someone to take action when the appropriate interval has expired. Or, do so as part of a hospital-wide alert system, hopefully part of an Electronic Medical Record (EMR). One must be careful in designing these plans to distinguish between institutional referring physicians with whom tight electronic communications are possible, and outside non-affiliated referrers which present complex identification and communication challenges. Please see Chapter 17 for more information. We describe these cases as requiring follow-up or action by their referring physicians sub-critical findings but not as critical findings or problems that require immediate communication and intervention.

MANAGING MEDICAL CENTER RADIOLOGY OPERATIONS

What role does the chair or the other members of the Radiology faculty play in oversight of the clinical operations of the department? In most institutions, the operations of the technical aspects of the department officially report up to the COO and CEO of the medical center. The professional group – the faculty – usually does not have a direct responsibility over these operations. However, everyone recognizes, or should recognize, that the leadership of the faculty needs to be intimately involved with the leadership and management of the operations of the department.

Most often there is an administrative director of the clinical operations, or what we call Director of Medical Center Operations, and that individual usually reports to an Associate Clinical Director who reports to the COO. Sometimes the administrative director in Radiology reports directly to the COO, which can be viewed as an advantage but also could have two distinct disadvantages: either having other responsibilities assigned to him/her or being required to participate in administrative activities and committees, etc., that distract from attention to Radiology.

Regardless of the structure within the medical center, the chair must have some recognized authority and responsibility for the hospital operations. In some departments, this responsibility is very clear and well delineated. Sometimes there is a contract for certain director responsibilities and, of course, commensurate compensation. But whatever the arrangement, the administrative director in one way or the other must feel some obligation to the chair (or designee). Ideally, that individual would believe that he/she actually reports to the chair or at least feels equally attentive to the chair as to the medical center hierarchy.

At UCSF, we have a matrix structure that is well-developed and highly functional. Although there is not a direct line to the Chair, the Director of medical center operations reports weekly to the Chair and participates in all faculty/staff committees related to clinical operations, patient care, quality, and safety. The Chair also holds a monthly meeting with her and her hospital manager, the Executive Director for Ancillary Services, who reports to the UCSF COO. This monthly meeting, which includes others as well, is a good way to make sure department priorities are conveyed up the medical center chain of command. I would characterize Radiology's relationship to Medical center administration at UCSF as excellent, and these formal and informal methods of communication are extremely helpful.

At UCSF, there are two other key positions in Radiology leadership. We have a Vice Chair for Clinical Services who is our formal representative on institutional committees and task forces. He has an extensive job description and significant responsibilities. He meets regularly with key hospital staff including the operations director, head nurses, chief technologists, and so on. He is also responsible for educating section chiefs and faculty about policies or changes in practice. The Vice Chair for Clinical Services runs a biweekly Operations Committee that includes key faculty and staff leadership. He keeps a running issues list and makes sure concerns and problems are assigned and followed up. Minutes are kept and published; everyone in the group feels highly accountable.

The second key position is the Associate Chair for Quality and Safety, again with a formal job description and dedicated time. His job is to make UCSF Radiology the safest department in the country – it is a very simple goal! Again, we utilize extensive benchmarking and monitoring. He organizes and chairs a biweekly Safety and Quality Committee. He also participates in the department MR Safety Committee and a more recently formed Radiation Oversight Committee.

Both these positions obviously affect the technical and professional sides of the equation. Of course, Radiology is unique in that it has such a direct relationship between the radiologists and the hospital operations. And the chair is quite active in the medical center affairs, chairing a number of important committees as well as having served as President of the Medical staff. Likewise, the Director of Administration for the department who reports to the chair is also very involved in medical center affairs and, is in fact, supported in part by the medical center. So the entire professional department is closely linked with the medical center.

In some institutions, they have carried the relationship to another level in that they actually have financial incentives for the radiologist faculty based on the performance of the operations. These incentives should be based on metrics more than just the bottom line since continued improvement in that number is hard to sustain year after year.

REFERENCES

Arenson, R. (2006). Agency for healthcare research and quality morbidity & mortality rounds. *The wet read (spotlight)*. Accessed February 18, http://www.web-mm.ahrq.gov/case.aspx? caseID=121&searchStr=the+wet+read.

Bradley, W. G. (2007). Use of a nighthawk service in an academic radiology department. *Journal of the American College of Radiology, 4*(10): 675–677.

Radiology resident evaluation of head CT scan orders in the emergency department. (2002). *American Journal of Neuroradiology,* Accessed February 18, http://www.aj-nr.org/ cgi/content/full/23/1/103.

Chapter 9

TURF ISSUES

This subject is near and dear to radiologists all over the world. We are particularly vulnerable to having other physicians compete with us simply because we are physicians' consultants and, other than IR, do not have our own patients. If Vascular Surgeons start doing their own endovascular work rather than sending those cases to us, there is not much we can do, especially since we still need to get other referrals from them.

There are other reasons for our recent difficulties. We have been very fortunate in Radiology for decades now, enjoying new techniques and devices all along, earning very high incomes, and becoming more and more central and vital to care for so many patients. We have been recruiting the very best and brightest for our residency programs and the growth of radiologists in practice has been remarkable. The quality of images has become so much better that many of the cross-sectional studies appear easier to interpret. Even internists admit that cross-sectional imaging is so good that it has become an extension of the sacred physical exam (Goldman, 2004). One could argue it has been the "perfect storm" in that the convergence of these factors has made us an easy target for other physicians to want to take away some of what we do (Pressman, 2008).

Image-guided procedures have replaced many surgical techniques and minimally invasive surgery with imaging has become one of the dominant growth areas in treatments for so many of our patients. The scope of work of general surgery and vascular surgery is changing every day and they clearly feel both challenged and threatened by the successes in IR and they are eager to take this domain on as their own.

Historically, other specialties have been nibbling at our heels and slowly but surely have taken procedures from us over the years. One can create a long list of activities that once were completely in Radiology and now are often split among specialties such as cardiac catheterization, cardiac ultrasound, urologic interventions, obstetrical ultrasound, endovascular work such as peripheral stents and aortic stents, and neurointerventions such as coiling aneurisms. Other practitioners are doing more and more interventions such as thermal ablation of liver tumors.

Radiology as a specialty has grown and even thrived by staying on the forefront of technology and technique development. Academic institutions and industry partnerships with radiologists and radiology researchers have created significant innovations. Will this trend continue? We know of forces that threaten these developments. Legislation aimed at reducing healthcare costs is targeting imaging technology as a major contributor to those increasing costs. Will the pace of innovation continue in industry? Certainly a large reduction in profitability in the imaging device industry will put a damper on their investments in new technology (see Chapter 7). And the movement to discourage partnerships between industry and academia over potential conflicts of interest will further dampen these developments.

If we are no longer the primary force behind procedures such as obstetrical ultrasound, will the innovations continue at such a rapid pace? That is certainly the case in centers where radiologists are devoted fulltime to using these modalities. They are more likely to develop newer techniques then when physicians are seeing patients, doing a variety of procedures and performing imaging studies part time as well. Yet they know more about their patients and know more about the procedures they perform which imaging can assist.

In Chapter 2, we discussed the importance of establishing the rules of engagement concerning turf up front as part of the negotiations for the chair position. Obviously, the more support you can get at that time, the better. It is far easier to manage these issues with the support of the Dean and medical center CEO than to fight them alone chair to chair. At least get the agreement that such turf issues can be bumped up to the leadership of the school and medical center for help and that the Radiology Chair will have some support at that level. However, that support can change and decrease over time. And as new chairs are recruited in other departments, they are likely to insist on the same favored treatment by the Dean and CEO.

In our opinion, the biggest weapon in your arsenal for turf problems is your faculty's relationships with the referring physicians and the level of service your department provides every day to referring clinicians and their patients. The more referring colleagues appreciate the value we add to their clinical decision making, and the more that they work with Radiology faculty on research and training programs, the less likely significant turf issues will emerge. When you talk with your faculty about service, what reaction do you get? Do you feel confident that your section leaders and rank and file faculty put the best face on the department?

At UCSF, we had a very interesting blog article written about one of our reading rooms and it created some excellent discussion within our department. At the same time, we commissioned marketing research within our internal referring community. The marketing consultant conducted focus groups and we heard some very harsh comments (some very good ones too!) about openness, service orientation, reading room atmosphere, and so on. We were excited to try to change the culture to one of excellent clinician and patient service, but it has taken repeating the message to the department faculty and staff daily, weekly, monthly – regularly. We strongly advise you to take a walk through your reading rooms at noon, unannounced – what do you find? Are faculty there, ready to help? Do people turn around and greet whoever comes through the door? How would a clinician react to the radiologists reading heads-down and backs turned – would they find it intimidating? What about your report turnaround times? Do you know the names of your top twenty referring doctors and is someone in each section responsible for staying in touch with them?

Jump at opportunities to partner with referring colleagues and demonstrate understanding and a willingness to share. Look for those opportunities to expand business partnering with others, and grow a bigger pie together, rather than simply splitting the existing pie.

Service lines can work for or against Radiology with regard to turf (see Chapter 16). But one thing is for certain, you must be at the table in every service line that uses imaging, and that means practically all of them. In service lines, you should be able to get support from the other departments for protecting Radiology from too much cannibalization since they should realize the institutional importance of keeping Radiology intact.

An important point to keep in mind is that you must protect your core: those procedures that you consider vital to the future of the department. Your core procedures may differ from other Radiology departments but are likely to include MR and CT. Since procedures such as diagnostic MR and CT are so important to the department you should resist intrusion into that territory by others if at all possible. Of course, there are exceptions that might make sense such as MR guided neurosurgical procedures especially in the OR, or ultrasound guided OR procedures. For procedures like coronary CTA, sharing these cases may increase the number of referrals.

In fact, one general principle to follow is that using imaging for guidance in procedures is quite different than diagnostic procedures and it is the diagnostic CT and MR that needs to be protected the most. We should be able to hold on to the kinds of image-guided interventional procedures we perform now. However our opinion is that as image-guided therapies replace the work currently done by others, we will not be able to capture that business as our own.

Don't forget the requirements for training residents and fellows in Radiology. Just as other departments like to use the RRC requirements as an excuse to get involved in imaging, you can use the argument that Radiology can't give up certain imaging studies because of our training needs. Most of the time we have found that the RRC requirements that other departments speak about are exaggerated or misunderstood and that actual performance of these procedures is usually not required. The various specialty RRCs operate from the same parent organization, so it is helpful to bring conflicting requirements to the attention of the Radiology RRC for their awareness and clarification.

At UCSF, we have had very few outright skirmishes over turf and have always had the attitude that joining is better than fighting. In fact, over the years, we have trained obstetricians to do obstetrical ultrasound (still do), vascular surgeons to perform endovascular procedures, surgeons to use ultrasound in the OR, cardiologists to perform coronary CTA, and emergency physicians to perform a limited set of ultrasound procedures in urgent situations in the Emergency Department. We also have trained neurosurgeons to use endovascular introduction of coils rather than surgical clipping for aneurysms, but they are not currently practicing at UCSF. (See Chapter 13 concerning training other fellows.)

The more we train others, the more work we seem to do so the competition does not appear to hurt us. In ultrasound, the emergency physicians seem to need our confirmation in many cases, which can be a problem since we both bill for the studies (which does not appear to be a major problem since they are not using the same billing codes in most cases). In obstetrical ultrasound, we believe it is best for the patients to get follow-up examinations from the same group that performed the first exams, but that approach is not always followed. By design and with the support of the institution for completeness of the medical record, all of the images from Vascular Surgery and from Obstetrics are stored in our PACS so we have full access to them.

Other departments have a strong case to make if your department does not provide adequate service, with easy patient access and high quality subspecialty expertise. It is vital that your department provide twenty-four hour service as described earlier in Chapter 8 so that the referring physicians can not complain about inadequate service and use that as an excuse to branch out themselves.

Unfortunately, rarely is quality of patient care raised in these turf discussions. In fact, most often the real issue is money with control of patients and egos close second and third. In some cases, the bragging rights seem to dominate and when chairs from other departments at your institution go to their annual chairs' meetings, they are embarrassed when others claim to have taken this or that from their Radiology departments.

We believe that we in Radiology have done a terrible job documenting the importance of our work, and the value we add to the care of our patients. Outcomes studies demonstrating the importance of imaging are lacking and are difficult to perform. But more locally, we have done a poor job of showing through Morbidity and Mortality (M&M) conferences, tumor boards, and other quality assurance activities that we do a better job than practitioners from other departments.

REFERENCES

Goldman, L. (2004). *Celil textbook of medicine e-dition: Text with continually updated online reference.* Elsevier Health Sciences.

Pressman, B. D. (2008). Presidential address: Distinction or extinction, review article. *Journal of the American College of Radiology 5*: 1036–1040.

Chapter 10

FACULTY WORKLOAD

Determining the proper clinical workload for all radiologists – academic radiologists for the purposes of this text – is critically important for the chair and department. The balance between the clinical workload and academic time is very important to the success of the department both academically and financially. The other component in this balancing act is faculty salaries. The ideal scenario is to have faculty salaries slightly above the competition, workloads very near the averages across the country, high academic productivity, and the department financially sound. Is that scenario even possible, and is it sufficient? We mentioned the mantra of "can't live by pro fees alone" in Chapter 6 which described the importance of a joint venture or other source of revenue besides professional fees. We will delve into that issue more in this section.

WORK RVUS

Let's begin this discussion looking at the benchmarks for faculty work and the one most commonly used is the work RVU from the Resource-Based Relative Value Scale (RBRVS) system developed by the American Medical Association (AMA) and the Healthcare Finance Administrations (HCFA) and utilized by Medicare (AMA, 2011)

The RBRVS system provides a work RVU value for each billing code from the AMA Current Procedural Terminology (CPT), which is also used by Medicare and others. The work RVU is about half of the total RVU for each code. Some other components of the total RVU are practice expense and malpractice insurance. The RVU is adjusted by region of the country and then multiplied times a conversion factor to determine what Medicare will pay for each procedure.

The work RVU is supposed to be the same across all specialties and work RVUs for each procedure are to reflect the time required to perform the procedure. Unfortunately, the work RVU is not even consistent across subspecialties in fields like Radiology. The cross-sectional modalities have higher work RVUs than they should as compared to plain imaging like a chest radiograph or even ultrasound procedures or fluoroscopy. We have published several articles dealing with this subject over the years (see the list below) and those articles are the basis for much of this section (Arenson et al., 2001; Lu & Arenson, 2005; Lu et al., 2008).

Let's first look at the work RVUs, for the remainder of this section called wRVUs. If you look at wRVUs per clinical FTE or a fulltime radiologist, you will find major discrepancies based on subspecialty (Figure 10–1). This graph shows the average wRVUs per FTE in 2006 when the data was collected for each subspecialty. The data was collected from twenty-eight institutions, most of which were large university-based academic departments. And the data assumes that most academic radiologists have one-day per week, or 20 percent of their time, devoted to academic matters while working 80 percent clinically. The data is adjusted for those with significant (greater than 20%) activities that are not clinical.

As you can see, the average work RVU/FTE for Neuroradiology is significantly higher than for Pediatric Radiology, Nuclear Medicine, or Mammography. In the manuscripts mentioned, we also devised a concept of the adjusted RVU, aRVU, which took these variations among subspecialists into account and the average aRVUs/FTE were essentially equal across the subspecialties. The idea that no matter if a faculty had an unusual mix of procedures in his practice as compared to others in his subspecialty, one still could assess accurately how much work that faculty was doing compared to the others. Since this concept was fairly difficult for many to grasp and since Deans and schools of medicine are using work RVUs for measuring a variety of activities, we have mostly concentrated on the wRVUs but we have been looking at subspecialties separately.

How should one use the wRVU/FTE data? It is important to understand that this data should not be used alone. Many factors go into actual workloads such as clinical sites that must be covered, the number of faculty needed to provide the 24/7 coverage for a small section and situations where faculty work in more than one subspecialty. Although not common, there may be large variations in the case mix in a particular section compared to other institutions. One example of that phenomena would be the UCSF Outpatient/Mt. Zion section consisting of General Radiologists. Since they mostly read plain images, they do not compare well in wRVUs/FTE to similar radiologists in other institutions who also perform CTs and possibly MRs as well. These local variations must be considered when analyzing this data for your department.

Work RVU's / Section

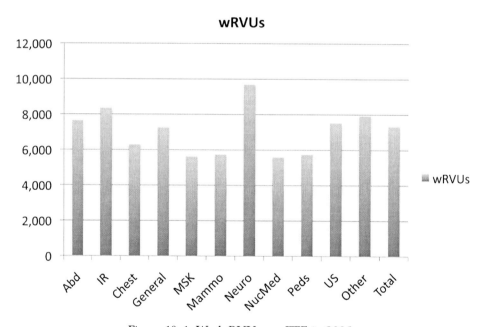

Figure 10–1. Work RVUs per FTE in 2006.

Having provided the provisos above, we will now argue that this data is most useful to determining when to hire the next radiologist in any section. If their workload is at or below the national averages, you can resist the desires of a section to add another faculty member.

Likewise, you may want to add another faculty member in a section that is considerably over the average for that subspecialty. Local variations will likely be argued but keep in mind that reimbursement follows wRVUs fairly well and adding faculty if the wRVUs do not support it would not be justified.

In addition, the wRVUs/FTE can be a signal for difficulties in work efficiency that need to be examined and rectified, if at all possible. Keep in mind that PACS, which will be described more fully in Chapter 17, significantly improved radiologist productivity, perhaps as much as 30 percent (Mackinnon, 2008). That increase in productivity mostly affected those radiologists who were performing CTs and MRs. This improvement in productivity has further enhanced the differences between the productivity of those performing these cross-sectional studies and those who do not.

The AAARAD has picked up the responsibility from the SCARD and from our department to regularly update the workload data from institutions across the country. In fact, they have been much more successful in getting departments to participate than we were and now produce annual survey data and present it at the SCARD/AAARAD meeting each year. One of the reasons for their success, besides tenacity and hard work, is that they refuse to give the results to any department who has not participated in the survey. But with their permission, in Figure 10–2, we are showing the AAARAD 2010 mean wRVUs/FTE along with the SCARD 2006 data already shown in Figure 10–1 for comparison. The volume of work per radiologist has been climbing for a number of years, with the most notable increase occurring in association with PACS. As you can see from the figure below, Musculoskeletal has seen the largest increases followed by Breast, Neuroradiology, and Ultrasound since 2006.

The AAARAD data includes subspecialties not separately listed in 2006 and did not include the category "other." Therefore, these data are not exactly categorized the same.

Let's get back to the question about being able to live on the professional revenue generated by an average workload. Figure 10–3 shows the salaries that can be generated from overall reimbursement as compared to Medicare, based on assumptions for workload per radiologist and academic and practice expenses. Those assumptions are the following:

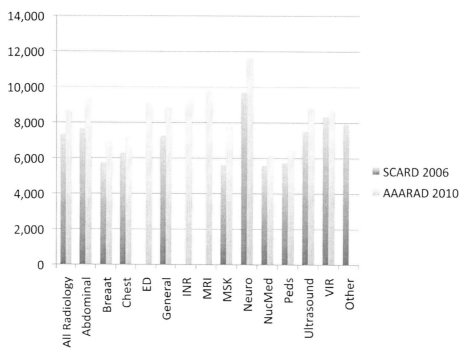

Figure 10–2. Mean RVUs per FTE for subspecialties in Radiology, 2006 and 2010.

- Dean's Tax/Medical Group/Billing = 14%
- Department Admin/Education/Overhead = 12%
- Salary Benefits = 18%
- $/wRVU based on 100% Medicare ($57) or higher %

You should adjust these figures based on your own experience, but the results are not likely to be very different. As you can see from this data, it is difficult to support competitive academic salaries for diagnostic radiologists unless you are both achieving reasonable levels of faculty productivity and have very good reimbursement.

Depending on how senior your faculty are, you can quickly see the required workload on average that your faculty needs to produce in order to support their salaries. As you can see, even with reasonable reimbursement, it is not possible to cover salaries, benefits, and other academic expenses, especially high Dean's taxes. Again, the same assumptions apply and it is important for you to substitute your own data such as Dean's tax and medical group tax, if any. Also, you need to substitute your own information about the department overhead

Supporting Salaries

% Medicare	WRVUs / FTE	$ / wRVU	Salary
100%	7,330	$57.00	$267,965
130%	7,330	$74.10	$348,354
160%	7,330	$91.20	$428,744
190%	7,330	$108.30	$509,133

Dean's Tax / Medical Group / Billing - 14%
Department Admin / Education / Overhead - 12%
Salary Benefits - 18%
$ / wRVU based on 100% Medicare ($57) or higher %

SCARD Survey, JACR, 2008

Figure 10–3. Salaries supported by various levels of reimbursement.

Revenue Required for Salaries

Average salary	With Benes	W Dpt OH	W Dean / MG	$ / wRVU	wRVUs / FTE
$250,000	$295,000	$330,400	$376,656	$57.00	6,608
$300,000	$354,000	$396,480	$451,987	$57.00	7,930
$350,000	$413,000	$462,560	$527,318	$57.00	9,251
$250,000	$295,000	$330,400	$376,656	$65.55	5,746
$300,000	$354,000	$396,480	$451,987	$65.55	6,895
$350,000	$413,000	$462,560	$527,318	$65.55	8,045

Dean's Tax / Medical Group / Billing - 14%
Department Admin / Education / Overhead - 12%
Salary Benefits - 18%
$ / wRVU based on 100% Medicare ($57) or 115% ($65)

SCARD Survey, JACR 2008, 7330 wRVUs / FTE

Figure 10–4. Revenue required for salaries.

and other expenses. But in the end analysis, you are likely to find that in order to keep faculty working at a reasonable level, you need to have other sources of revenue which usually means technical fees, such as in a joint venture.

Another way of looking at this data is as shown in Figure 10–4 below.

REFERENCES

AMA. (2011). The resource based relative value scale. Accessed of February 5. http://www.ama-assn.org/pub/physician-resources/solutions-managing-your-practice/.

Arenson, R. L., Lu, Y., Elliott, S. C., Jovais, C., & Avrin, D. E. (2001). Measuring the academic radiologist's clinical productivity: Applying RVU adjustment factors. *Academic Radiology, 8*: 533–540.

Arenson, R. L., Lu, Y., Elliott, S. C., Jovais, C., & Avrin, D. E. (2001). Measuring the academic radiologist's clinical productivity: Survey results for sub-specialty sections. *Academic Radiology, 8*: 524–532.

Lu, Y., & Arenson, R. L. (2005). The academic radiologist's clinical productivity: An update. *Academic Radiology, 12*: 1211–1223.

Lu, Y., Zhao, S., Chu, P. W., & Arenson, R. L. (2008). An update survey of academic radiologists' clinical productivity. *Journal of the American College of Radiology, 5*: 817–826.

Mackinnon, A. D., Billington, R. A., Adam, E. J., Dundas, D. D., & Patel, U. (2008). Picture archiving and communication systems lead to sustained improvements in reporting times and productivity: Results of a five year audit. *Clinical Radiology, 7*: 796–804.

Chapter 11

BUILDING RESEARCH

One of the most important aspects of a successful academic department of any kind, including Radiology is research. Research can take different forms but generally refers to manuscripts produced by the faculty and research grants supported by outside entities. Publications are most important if they appear in peer-reviewed journals, especially the most prestigious journals in a specialty or in medicine in general. In Radiology, the premier journals are *Radiology*, *Radiographics*, *Academic Radiology*, and the *American Journal of Roentgenology*. The *Journal of the American College of Radiology* and the *American Journal of Neuroradiology* are also considered important journals. One measure of the importance of a journal is the impact factor that is determined by the number of citations a paper gets in other peer-reviewed journals. *Radiology* has the highest impact factor of Radiology publications except for the *Journal of Nuclear Medicine* which has a small but dedicated following and lots of review articles.

One so-called "throw away" publication that has a very wide distribution is *Diagnostic Imaging*. This journal is called a throw away because you do not pay a subscription and it is not peer-reviewed. The only reason to mention it here is that the circulation is very wide with a very large number of readers and can have a bigger impact than some of our peer-reviewed journals. However, one does not get academic credit for publishing in such a throw away journal.

Publications outside of Radiology that are highly regarded include the *Journal of the American Medical Association*, the *New England Journal of Medicine* and the journal *Nature*. To have a paper published in one of these journals is particularly impressive. Publication in a journal outside of Radiology is also quite useful to reach an audience of our referring colleagues rather than radiologists. Reaching other physicians is particularly important for subjects related to which studies to order or for conditions for which new imaging approaches are possible.

The next issue is the type of publication, which could be new scientific information, a review of current techniques or diagnostic approach, or some kind of outcomes analysis perhaps resulting from a clinical trial. All of these publications are of value but the most valuable from an academic point of view are those that produce new science and information never presented before. Those articles that introduce new scientific information that also have a large impact on society are especially valuable and they are often published in the most prestigious journals described above.

Several reviewers, usually "blinded" to the identification of the authors or their institutions, review peer-reviewed articles. Of course, it is not always possible to redact articles enough to prevent identification of the source, but every effort is made to achieve that goal. In that fashion, the publisher and journal editor achieve as unbiased a review as possible. Reviewing articles for journals is an important academic exercise that every academic radiologist should participate in. Until individuals start publishing and become fairly well-known, they are not likely to be asked to be a reviewer, unless recommended by their chair or other senior and well established faculty member.

Obviously the old saying "publish or perish" has some merit and no matter what academic track you are on, it is important to publish and the more new works and new science the better. In clinical-educator tracks, where there is as much or more weight placed on quality teaching rather than research, publications about teaching methods and review papers are just fine. But to get promoted, you should plan on three or more peer-reviewed publications each year and the more papers on which you are the first author the better. Later in one's career, being the last author is probably better since it reflects the mentoring nature of the contributions usually for more junior authors who are the first or second authors.

NIH RESEARCH FUNDING

Getting funding from entities outside of the institution, especially government entities is viewed as the most important accomplishment in research. The independent investigator initiated R01 grant from the NIH is the absolute gold standard. Getting one or preferably a couple of these over a number of years almost guarantees promotion in any institution. Of course, this promotion assumes you are also publishing as described above. Getting such grant funding is practically impossible without adequate publications, demonstrating that you are really knowledgeable and capable of performing the work under the grant.

It is also practically impossible to get such funding unless you have done significant pilot work and published the results. Some would argue you have to do much of the work of the grant first before sending in the application to demonstrate you can actually achieve the specific aims you are proposing.

In order to have the time and resources to get such pilot data, you need to have a very supportive chair and a department that has the financial resources to support you. And for the chair to use the department's resources in that fashion requires a culture in the department that values such research. That culture does not happen overnight, and, in fact, is relatively rare in academic Radiology departments. Seven departments have over 50 percent of the funding from the NIH in Radiology and in these departments, you can be sure such a culture exists (see Figure 11–1). Even in these highly research-focused departments, there are a number of more clinically-involved faculty who would rather get the additional revenue in salary support. Balancing those competing interests is the job of the chair and senior leadership in the department.

Academic Radiology departments and their chairmen are measured by a number of parameters to determine their standing among their peers. One of the most important benchmarks is the ranking of the NIH research funding. The chart in Figure 11–1 comes from the Academy of Radiology Research (2010) and includes those institutions such as Massachusetts General and Brigham and Women's Hospital that are excluded from the NIH published data since they are not universities by themselves. This data also includes the funding of faculty in academic Diagnostic Radiology departments who happen to channel their funding through other mechanisms such as a Veterans Affairs foundation. Radiation Oncology funding, which is included with Diagnostic Radiology as listed by NIH, are excluded in these numbers so that we are looking at Diagnostic Radiology alone. The full listing can be obtained from the Academy and is available on their website

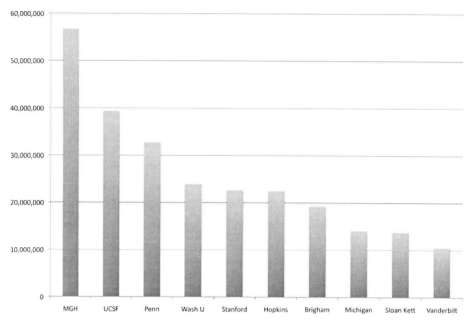

Figure 11–1. Diagnostic Radiology NIH Funding 2009.

at http://www.acadrad.org/.

The chart above simply shows the top ten in NIH funding and these figures include the American Recovery and Reinvestment Act (AR-RA) funds that will expire in 2012. These funds were part of the Stimulus funds that the President and Congress enacted to give the economy a push. We are all hopeful that additional new funding will be available after that time, but many of us view this as a "cliff" we will fall off of in less than two years.

The faculty and departments at the top of this list should be very proud of their research accomplishments. Although the top ten or so have been relatively stable for a number of years, there are a few exceptions. Figure 11–2 shows the percentage of change from 2006 to 2009 and from 2008 to 2009 in total NIH funding by department (only the thirty departments that receive the most funding are listed) (Academy of Radiology Research, 2009). Actually MD Anderson had the greatest increase, from zero to almost $7 million and the University of Texas at San Antonio increased by 730 percent since 2006. These two would have obviously made the graph unreadable so we deliberately left them out. If you look at the departments that are at the left end of this chart plus these two, those departments enjoyed the

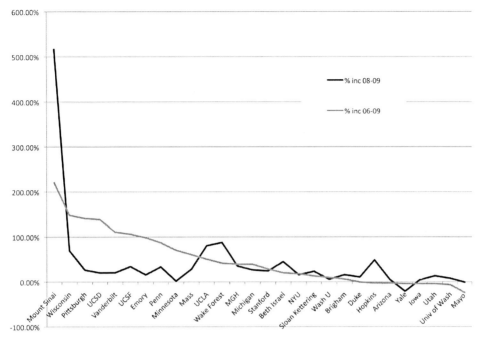

Figure 11–2. Change over past few years in total NIH funding.

greatest gains in these last few years. Do keep in mind that substantial research goes on at all of these institutions that is not reflected here since the principle investigators (PIs) are in other departments.

We will delve into how these departments have achieved this success later but there is another piece of important information to consider in analyzing this data, namely how the departments' ranking compares to the overall institutional ranking. As we will discuss more later, it is very difficult to have a very large successful NIH funded research operation if the culture and emphasis of the institution does not match. Figure 11–3 shows the difference in department rank as compared to the institutional rank for NIH funding. Let us explain by a couple of examples. First, take a look at number fifteen, which is NYU. You will note that they are plus twenty-one which means that the department performed substantially better than the university overall. Whereas, number sixteen, who will go nameless here, is eleven behind the overall campus rank.

A number of departments have far exceeded the institutional ranking such as NYU, Utah, Iowa, Minnesota and the University of Texas at San Antonio. They should all be congratulated for performing bet-

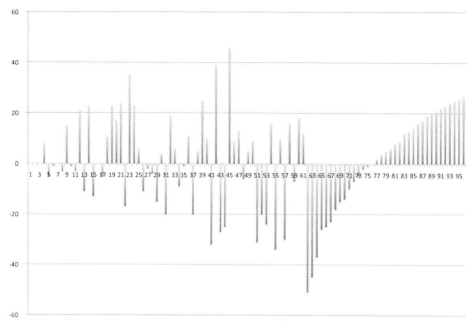

Figure 11–3. Difference in NIH ranking between department and institution.

ter than their institutions and that is a significant accomplishment. For those departments listed at the end of the chart from around sixty-three on, please note that these departments had no NIH funding and we assigned an arbitrary number of sixty-eight to each (we have sixty-seven departments with some NIH funding in Diagnostic Radiology). Those with the greatest negative numbers are farthest from their institutional rankings. Those with positive numbers simply reflect the fact that their institutions are below sixty-eight in the institutional numbers. The Radiology departments at those sites should not be expected to have much funding since the institutions do not either.

STARTING A RESEARCH PROGRAM

A department that has little or no funded research going on is at a distinct disadvantage compared with the others. The cultural issues are profound and a new chair will be most successful if there has been a clear mandate by the Dean that he/she build a research program. Hopefully, new funds have also been allocated to get such a program off the ground. The best way to get started is to assess the strengths of other departments around you. Determine where collaborations would be most fruitful and start there. And then think strategically about the kinds of programs you want to build. You are more likely to be successful if you can identify a few areas for strong translational research programs. Hire a few PhDs into Radiology for these areas, preferably with joint appointments or at least joint recruitments with basic science departments or other clinical departments with strength in PhDs. These individuals will want to affiliate with others like them and will feel more at home if they have such relationships.

Then build your programs around these key researchers. You should try to identify radiologist faculty who are likely to partner with these new PhDs in the appropriate areas. You certainly want a neuroradiologist to work on a program in brain MR, for example. These PhDs who are hired to be the leaders in key areas need to be more senior or at least come with demonstrated grant-getting ability and be able to lead a program that grows over time. These recruitments will not be easy since you do not have a cadre of similar PhD faculty already in the department. The start-up packages need to be substantial enough to get them to come (see Chapter 14). Over time, as the culture in the department changes and as you recruit new young, more research-focused radiologists, then grants can be expected from radiologists as PI in addition to those with PhDs as PI. But keep in mind that your PhD faculty will always conduct most of your research, as is the case in most clinical departments today.

RESEARCH COSTS

What does research cost? The first important lesson is that you cannot make money on research, especially government-supported work. The best you can do is break even. That general rule is true since you basically can get your expenses paid by the federal agencies, but you can't charge them anymore than that. Of course, your institution has an overhead rate, negotiated with the federal government each year. This overhead rate is also called an "indirect" rate or facilities and administrative (F&A) rate. That indirect rate covers facilities depreciation, utilities, building maintenance, and central and departmental administrative costs. A special ruling called Circular A–21 from the

Office of Management and Budget (Office of Management and Budget, 2004) prohibits institutions from directly charging certain administrative costs to grants. This circular was last updated in 2004. Basically A–21 prevents you from getting reimbursed for administrative personnel working on your grants. But allows your institution to recover some of these costs as a percentage of each grants direct expenses. Most institutions retain some of the indirects to cover building depreciation, utilities, and central administrative units, but your institution should be passing to your department some of the indirects they collect to cover departmental administrative costs. However, we do not know of a single institution that passes enough back to cover all of the costs.

Indirects are substantial amounts, often more than 50 percent of the direct costs. Many of our institutions depend on these funds to support the infrastructure of the campus. In the University of California system, some of the indirect funds are used to support the central administration of the system and do not get returned to the individual campuses. The more research-intensive medical campuses, UCSF, UCSD, and UCLA often complain that too much of the indirects generated by their campuses are siphoned off for the other schools or the central administration. For UCSF, after the Office of the President and campus administrations take their share, little is left for the department, which basically gets about nine percent of the indirects generated back to cover its research-related administrative expenses. At UCSF, we focus on generating financial reserves primarily to help fund this gap.

At UCSF, the cost for facilities and administration related costs for research on-campus is around $160.46 per square foot. Unfortunately, the federal government does not pay that amount in the indirects since they cap the administrative costs at 26 percent of the direct costs. The actual costs for research are considered substantially more than that figure with a number of costs not allowed to be reimbursed by the government. It is not unusual for research administration costs to be twice the amount of indirects that the campus returns to the department. The rationale for calculating the indirects by square foot will be discussed later.

RESEARCH SPACE

For Radiology, we do not have the same requirements for space as basic science departments or even other clinical departments. Typically we need so-called dry bench space, which is usually for computer-intensive work, and for imaging equipment with associated offices. We have the added expense of purchasing research equipment such as MR scanners. For animal research, we need animal imaging equipment and animal holding facilities as well as an animal surgical suite. You can depreciate these costs as part of a recharge rate applied to the facility and equipment, as we will explain later. In other departments, one often equates researchers into the number of benches that are needed in a wet laboratory. The typical starting researcher often gets around three benches. These are associated with faculty offices and common spaces such as conference rooms and kitchens along with administrative space for personnel offices and file storage areas.

UCSF CHINA BASIN RESEARCH FACILITY

In 2002, Radiology at UCSF was desperate for additional research space and no space seemed available on campus. At the same time, the dot-com bust was occurring and a lot of new commercial space had been built with the anticipation that new dot-com demand for space would be coming. So millions of square feet of commercial space became available and the prices fell precipitously. At UCSF, rent for off-campus space had to be considered a direct charge to grants since such rent was not negotiated into the indirect charges. Some institutions have gone the other route. It became apparent to us that we could move funded work from the on-campus rate of 52 percent to off-campus at 26 percent and use the difference – with NIH permission – to fund the rent plus have a little available to fund more of the science. So we signed a long-term, fifteen year lease with a facility near our Mission Bay Campus, where many of the UCSF basic scientists are now located.

The China Basin facility was somewhat risky in that we needed to rent more space than we could guarantee with current funds and we could not be sure the funding we had would continue. And we had to build out that space for MR and CT scanners as well as animal facilities and equipment. The construction costs were largely covered by the tenant improvement allowance we negotiated with the landlord. Please keep in mind that the big loser in this proposition was the campus in that we were only able to generate half of the indirects that we could get if we remained on campus. The university went along with us simply because we had no room to grow. Our Dean actually made us put $1 million plus into an escrow account to protect him from our financial folly if we could not make a go of this venture. The Dean that succeeded him paid us back.

Judging by our success in research funding, obviously the gamble paid off and we have been able to grow our research enterprise partly because of the additional space available at China Basin. However, we also built an outpatient imaging center there with the medical center. By having the clinical and research spaces adjacent to each other, we have been able to share expenses and utilize personnel for both activities. The advantages for our research-focused radiologists should be obvious for they can do both activities at the same site.

CALCULATING SPACE ALLOCATION NEEDS

Many institutions struggle with space allocation all of the time. How does a school or campus decide on the space needed for a new recruit or what to do when a department's faculty loses funding after getting substantial space for it? The most common method for determining space allocation is some variant of dollars per square foot of grant support. Some campuses use only indirect funding in the calculation to avoid giving credit to grants without adequate indirects. This underfunding of indirects can occur with some foundations that refuse to support infrastructure and a number of contracts. One way to strongly discourage applying for such awards is to charge the recipient faculty or departments with the indirects which they must fund from discretionary sources or by using some of the award's direct funding.

In fact, some institutions now charge "rent" to the departments for all of the research space on campus and pass a large portion of the indirect recovery back to the departments. In that fashion, it is the department's responsibility to manage those expenses and the indirect revenues. There is a strong incentive for a department that loses funding to pass the space back to the Dean or another department rather than holding on to the space and subsidizing the cost for that space. Obviously, one of the major resources a Dean can hold is space, available for recruitments of either department chairs or key recruitments for the campus. Without some mechanism for getting space back from departments, the Dean has little ability to offer space to new recruits after others have left.

Other campuses use the indirects generated by departments based on square footage to determine the distribution of the space and reallocation accordingly. These campuses usually have a committee that periodically reviews the calculations per square foot for each department to see changes over time. At UCSF, the SOM calculation was around $120/sq. ft. on average which is substantially below the $160/sq. ft. figure cited above. But a handful of departments found themselves below the $120/sq. ft. figure and they were forced to give up space unless they could increase their indirects fairly quickly.

When our Mission Bay Campus opened, many basic science departments jumped at the opportunity to have more space per investigator. Perhaps some of these departments took on more space than they could justify and are among the departments now facing indirect $/sq. ft. well below the average. But some of these departments also argue that one must consider shared spaces, shared equipment facilities, and similar calculations that affect the space figures.

CAMPUS CORES

To renovate space and equip it with expensive scanners for either human or animal research is very difficult for departments to achieve without help from the school or campus. Most institutions consider imaging vital to research on campus and usually provide funding for such imaging cores. They usually turn to Radiology to manage such facilities or at least they should. Sometimes these cores are instituted by the department and are sometimes part of a recruitment package for a new chair. The department may end up responsible for the finances of these cores after they are initially funded by the campus and it is critical to develop a user community that will pay for use of the equipment installed. The most common mechanism for funding these operating costs, and possibly rent, is the recharge process. Keep in mind that the campus can collect, through the indirect rate negotiated with the government, reimbursement for investments in research equipment and renovations, including scanners. Some campuses have avoided this issue, such as UCSF, by declaring that such equipment will be purchased by departments and they do not seek payment through the indirects.

RECHARGE RATE

As mentioned above, one of the best mechanisms for recovering expenses for imaging research facilities is the recharge rate. This rate is set each year by predicting the expected use of a facility and determining the cost rate that would cover the legitimate expenses for that operation. Keep in mind that at best you can break even since this covers actual costs, and profits of any kind are not allowed. For an imaging room, those expenses can include the technologist, maintenance of the equipment, supplies such as contrast, and computer expenses allocated to that room (PACS, network), and associated administrative expenses for scheduling, setting rates, and billing users. If the facility is in rented space, that portion of the rent allocated to that room could also be charged. As long as the equipment was not purchased with federal grants, the cost of the equipment can also be included as a depreciation expense. For expensive equipment like MR scanners, you have to be careful since adding such an expense could make the recharge prohibitively expensive and investigators may be unable or unwilling to charge those expenses to their grants. Of course, the investigators need to know in advance how much to put into their grant applications for the number of scans they expect to use.

The depreciation amount can be stretched out over a number of years, such as ten, even if the payments for the scanner are finished in five years. The uncovered payments end up as a deficit for that account and would theoretically get paid off over the ten years. By spreading out the depreciation allocation, you can keep the recharge rate down, but you run the risk of needing to replace or seriously upgrade the equipment before the full depreciation period has run its course.

Obviously, if you can get the campus to buy the equipment and pay for installation, then the recharge rate can be kept within reasonable levels, even including some of the costs for depreciation so that a fund is established for eventual upgrades or replacement. For equipment which is not purchased by the university but is funded from federal money, the cost for depreciation must not be included in the recharge. Gift funded equipment can be depreciated, however. Once again, keep in mind that the campus can include the cost of purchasing and installing such equipment as part of the indirect calculations. And that cost is in the facilities portion which is not capped as is the administrative portion.

Clinical patients can be scanned on such research equipment if the recipient of the technical fees, usually the hospital, pays the standard recharge rate. The medical center will actually get a break since the recharge by definition can only break even and they often collect more than that for the technical fee reimbursement. One thing to remember if you plan for the medical center to be a user of research equipment in this way is to be sure to set rates to recover all of your costs. It makes no sense to subsidize clinical use of the equipment from departmental discretionary dollars when the medical center could make a substantial net from the technical fee reimbursement.

You do need to be a little careful with equipment "donated" by vendors or substantially reduced in price for a research partnership. With such equipment, scanning clinical patients can be problematic since the technical fees paid most often include a component covering the expected costs for the equipment. This subject is a complicated one and you will need to consult with the experts at your institution since some of the equipment depreciation expenses are handled in the annual cost reimbursement negotiations with the government. The subject of partnerships with industry will be further explored in Chapter 21.

Please note that there are a few highly financially successful recharge activities that are very creative in picking up costs associated with "research and development" of new imaging techniques. If such activities are able to keep operating costs plus depreciation at a reasonable level resulting in rates that are at the low end of what is acceptable to the research users (i.e., are similar to rates charged for the same service at other institutions), then there may be room in the rates to add costs for postdocs or SRAs who are helping to advance the techniques in use on these scanners. This is possible only in situations where there is a high volume of activity so that large fixed costs for equipment depreciation can be spread across a large user base. It is very unusual to be able to include such costs, since few activities have a sufficiently large user base; thus recovering basic operating costs and depreciation often produces rates that are at or above the highest level that users (and funding agencies) will find acceptable.

Recharge activities must be managed very much like small businesses to be successful. Marketing is a consideration. Potential users need ways to learn about department facilities, and websites can help with this. You might also consider having Masters or PhD staff who can hold grand rounds to demonstrate uses of imaging techniques and help get the word out to potential users. The level of service is important to users, particularly those who are outside the department and may not be familiar with imaging techniques. In some cases we have rates that are "unassisted" and those that are at a higher "assisted" level, to provide the additional support necessary to support a non-imaging-conversant user. This may be one way to grow a user base for the equipment. Another way is to subsidize pilot studies for internal and/or external users to familiarize them with imaging techniques and show them the advantages of a particular technique to their studies (while also getting the preliminary data for grant applications). In this way, users see that they are paying a reasonable recharge rate, but the pilot funding lowers the initial cost hurdle. It is also a good way to show users that the department is supporting their needs – department support that is simply buried in a subsidy to a recharge activity is invisible to users.

COMPETITION FOR RESEARCH FACILITIES

On campuses, which have invested in imaging cores, and where these investments are managed centrally, having competitors install such duplicate equipment is not much of a problem. Otherwise, such competition can be a large problem. On our campus at UCSF, we have a small number of examples, but important ones, where other departments have managed to get equipment purchased with funds from grateful patients. These facilities do offer some distinct services, but in general are duplicative of our imaging facilities. From a campus perspective, having two MR scanners in use half of the time is certainly not as attractive as having one scanner, shared, and used all of the available time. Unless the institution manages such purchases and installations, none of the facilities will be financially sound.

We now have some new research buildings being constructed at Mission Bay that have substantial space reserved for imaging, including MR and PET/CT. If they are allowed to install competing scanners, even if reserved for research patients, we could be in trouble. We are hoping for an agreement that they cannot install such systems unless we are near capacity with the existing ones. And, of course, we want to be actively involved in any of these imaging systems installed in these new research buildings.

RESEARCH INTEREST GROUPS

A couple of years ago, we realized that more revenue was coming to the department from research than from clinical work. Keep in mind that research does not pay for itself since the expenses are higher than the revenue and, in fact, is subsidized by the clinical revenues. At the same time, we also realized that almost half of our faculty were not physicians but scientists. We decided, at that time, we needed to change some of the leadership organization of the department and our name to reflect what we were. So our department's name was changed from Department of Radiology to the Department of Radiology and Biomedical Imaging. We also appointed one of our leading PhD faculty as the Vice Chair for Research.

Perhaps the most novel change we made was in the organization of our research activities. We had a large number of semi-independent laboratories, each managed by a separate PI, some with overlapping areas of focus. And there was really no coordination or organization to these labs. We created a select committee to decide on a different strategy and they developed the concept of the Research Interest Group or RIG and the SRG.

All of the RIGs and SRGs are led by an MD and a PhD to help facilitate the interaction of these two groups. The RIGs are more focused on individual diseases, that often match the various institutes at the NIH and the SRGs are more focused on techniques and infrastructure. Although the SRGs are often supportive of the RIGs, they also have substantial research conducted by their own PIs, usually not primarily involved in any particular disease or organ system.

Our initial group of RIGs include:

- Brain Behavior
- Brain Cancer
- Breast Cancer
- Musculoskeletal and Quantitative Imaging
- Neurodegenerative Diseases
- Neurovascular/Neurointerventional
- Pediatrics/Fetal
- Prostate Cancer

The Specialized Resource Groups (SRGs) include:

- Biostats/Outcomes
- Informatics and Image Processing/Display
- MR/CT Contrast Agent Development
- MRI/MRS
- Nuclear-Optical Imaging

The RIG leaders participate in a committee called the Executive Research Council that is chaired by the Vice Chair for Research. This Council meets monthly with the Chair and the Executive Vice Chair of the department as well as with key administrators. RIG leaders participate in faculty evaluations at the end of the year, and are held accountable for their RIG members' support of department activities including use of recharge facilities and space. We also used the RIG, SRG, and Executive Research Council structure to dramatically improve our PhD recruitment policies, moving away from easy fixes with existing post-docs, to one of searches for open positions and careful, strategic review of requests for new PhD slots. The Executive Research Council helps department leadership to identify gaps in our research portfolio, and helps us make key decisions around equipment purchases and upgrades as well as outreach to non-radiology investigators on the campus.

Although still new, this organization has already demonstrated success in the coordination and facilitation of major grants including the ARRA funding that we are currently engaged in.

REPORTING ON PATIENT RESEARCH STUDIES

One of the most challenging aspects of performing imaging on patients in research studies is the issue of how to handle incidental findings. Usually the informed consent documents attempt to make it clear that the results of the imaging studies will hopefully benefit science, not the individual patients participating in the study. No matter how carefully this fact is stated, patients expect to hear if they have findings on the images that might be important to them. In addition, investigators have an obligation, even if not stated, to provide their research subjects with any information that would be important for their care.

If we are performing, say CT scans on research subjects, do we expect radiologists to read the scans and pass any findings on to the patient or that patient's referring physician? Or do we expect the information to only be given to the PI? Do the PIs include radiologists as investigators on their grants in the first place? And are the radiologists paid for their professional services?

These questions all need to be addressed up front when research studies are being designed. In addition to the costs of the scans themselves, if radiologists are going to be expected to offer interpretations, their time and effort must be budgeted somehow. Either they can be included as part of the research study, for a portion of their salary as an investigator or be paid a fee-for-service payment as part of the cost per scan. Often neither method is budgeted and the PI approaches the department for the first time after getting the award.

Even when a radiologist is included as an investigator, be careful that the percentage of time is sufficient to read all of the imaging studies planned. Often a radiologist will be included as a very small percent effort yet be expected to read a large number of scans. Or the radiologist's percent effort will be cut dramatically when the overall funding is reduced.

So how big is the problem of incidental findings? Illes published articles (see list below) in which she found that overall incidental findings occurred in 18–20 percent of studies whereas only two to eight percent were significant clinically. What to do with positive findings is the question. The first issue to resolve is who is responsible for communicating with the research subject, the patient, and with the patient's physician? The individual responsible could be the PI or the radiologist directly. This information should be included in the informed consent. But who will pay for any follow-up studies needed? If the individual has health insurance that will cover the procedures and interventions required, then fine. But what do you do if the individual is not insured? Does the investigator have any obligation in this regard?

If a radiologist is not involved in the study, which is often the case to reduce expenses, does the PI have the expertise to identify these incidental findings? A physician, as PI, may be very familiar with the manifestations of the disease under investigation, but may not be very familiar with other conditions. Does that investigator have any legal responsibility if incidental findings that are missed turn out to be a problem? Does a disclaimer in the informed consent suffice to protect the investigator? There are differing opinions on that topic but the answer most likely depends on the tort laws in the state in which the individual lives (Glover & Atlas, 2004; Illes et al., 2004; Illes et al., 2006).

RESEARCH TECHNIQUES RAISING EXPECTATIONS

One other problem we face with research studies that are successful is that they often demonstrate a clinical utility for a new technique that is not yet reimbursed by insurance companies. The referring physicians become quite excited about the new imaging studies during the investigation and grow to expect that these new techniques will be available for their patients going forward. But the reimbursement process takes time and is often political and not necessarily guided by what is truly the best approach for patients. The referring physicians and their patients get angry when such studies are denied or they are expected to pay out of pocket. This is another area where a strong relationship with referring colleagues, other chairs, and the medical center is important. For example, at UCSF, we developed some excellent 3D imaging and post-processing techniques through a research program. The neurosurgery chair, who participated in the original research, began using the techniques regularly both before and after surgery and was very irate if a patient went to surgery without these 3D images. Yet, there was no reimbursement for the studies. Because of his interest and support (demands perhaps) our hospital administration was willing to provide strategic support for the staff and equipment required to support these surgical cases. Over time, this program has evolved into its own research lab and recharge activity, but we still count on hospital support to satisfy referring clinician demands, as opposed to providing the service on unfunded research time. And the medical center can use these efforts as a marketing tool to show that we are cutting-edge.

REFERENCES

Academy of Radiology Research. (2010). NIH total awards (excluding contracts). Accessed February 22. http://www.acadrad.org/nih-rankings-grants/NIH-Rankings-2009.pdf.

Glover, G. H., & Atlas, S. W. (2004). Discovery and disclosure of incidental findings in neuroimaging research. *Journal of Magnetic Resonance Imaging, 20*: 743–747.

Illes, J., Rosen, A. C., Huang, L., Goldstein, R. A., Raffin, T. A., Swan, G., & Atlas, S. W. (2004). Ethical consideration of incidental findings on adult brain MRI in research. *Neurology, 62*: 888–890.

Illes, J., Kirschen, M. P., Edwards, E., Stanford, L. R., Bandettini, P., Cho, M. K., Ford, P. J., Glover, G. H., Kulynych, J., Macklin, R., Michael, D. B., & Wolf, S. M. (2006). Ethics. Incidental findings in brain imaging research. Working group on incidental findings in brain imaging research. *Science, 311*: 783–784.

Office of Management and Budget. (2004). Accessed on February 5. http://www.whitehouse.gov/omb/circulars_a021_2004.

Chapter 12

BUILDING A STRONG
RESIDENCY PROGRAM

O ne of the most competitive activities we are engaged in is getting the best and brightest resident candidates into our program. There are a number of approaches to developing a strong program that we will explore in this section. Perhaps the most important ingredient is reputation. How do you build your reputation? It is far easier to develop a bad reputation than a good one and bad news seems to travel through the resident applicant pool amazingly fast. Certainly "Aunt Minnie" and other chat rooms on the web facilitate such news getting around quickly. A good reputation is usually developed over many years and depends on many factors.

Perhaps the most important contributor to reputation is the overall morale among the residents. Overall morale of the faculty, fellows, and staff also contribute. Happy residents will attract other residents. To keep your residents happy requires giving them an environment in which they can thrive, which is not the same as giving in to every request. In the sections to follow, we will explore the components that we believe are important for the supportive environment that is needed.

Reputation is also a function of the institution around you. Just as it is difficult to achieve major NIH funding without a strong successful research environment surrounding you, the same applies to residencies. It is important to focus on the kind of program you want to build. If you are a research powerhouse, then attracting future researchers is appropriate. On the other hand, if you are a very good clinical department, you might want to go for the strongest clinical residents you can attract.

RESIDENCY PROGRAM DIRECTOR (PD)

Choosing the right PD is obviously an important component of building a strong residency program. Who would be the best PD in your department? You will probably want to choose someone who the residents like but more importantly someone who will be a strong advocate for the residents with the other faculty and with institutional leadership and with referring physicians as well. You need someone who will be able to successfully lead the Residency Review Committee (RRC) site visits and who can put together the documentation required for that process.

Although preparation for the site visit is a mammoth task, the requirements, evaluations, and documentation is a continual process with the program coming under annual scrutiny through the ACGME resident survey. The survey requires at least 70 percent completion in order for the PD to receive the results. Issues of trainee satisfaction with the program that arise through the survey should be discussed with the teaching committee and an appropriate plan of action for areas of concern should be outlined and implemented and the subsequent progress reviewed. A key aspect of trainee satisfaction is effective communication. At our institution, the PD meets every two weeks with the chief residents, with each class every four months, with each resident every six months (the associate PD may have to assist with this process for large programs), with the whole program every four to six months, and with residents at each major hospital rotation every month. In addition, we maintain an open door policy for resident communication with the PD, associate PD, and chairman.

The Program Director usually is someone slightly more senior but not so far out from their own residency in order to be able to identify with some of the residents' issues. You do not want to pick a very junior individual, even one who meets the criteria for appointment to this position according to the RRC. And you have to provide dedicated time for the PD's efforts. Larger programs require substantial PD time, on the order of two to three days per week whereas smaller programs may only need a day per week, or 20 percent dedicated time. Larger programs – over thirty-two residents or so – should also have associate PDs that may have limited (half day to one day per week) or no dedicated time.

Obviously, you want someone who views resident education to be most important and someone who knows a good teacher when they see one. The most important ingredient is dedication to the tasks at hand and a willingness to go after the serious issues facing the program. It is important to recognize that as a resident advocate, the PD may at times be at odds with the interests of section chiefs and must be able to negotiate potential conflicts of interest between the educational program and service needs.

A strong staff residency program coordinator, responsible for the day to day running of the program, is critical. This individual will probably be fulltime and has to coordinate the applicant interview process in addition to keeping the records for the residents. An enthusiastic coordinator who gets along well with the residents is very important to the success of the program.

Both the PD and the coordinator should be active in the national scene. These individuals should meet with their counterparts at the annual Association of University Radiologists (AUR) meeting and should become involved in their groups within the AUR. In that fashion, they can compare notes and learn best practices as well as share their knowledge and approach.

MENTORING

One aspect of the residency program that often is overlooked or given low priority is a mentoring program. First year residents are often overwhelmed by the sheer volume of information they are expected to master in just a few years. They can be far from home and family and in unfamiliar territory in many ways. It is not at all unusual to have normal life issues – marriages, relationships, finances, housing, etc. – contribute to residency stress. Residents may also be having difficulty with particular subject areas or problems with certain faculty or fellows. They may be having trouble with fellow residents or even in their personal relationships. They often have individuals they can trust to speak with about these issues, but sometimes they do not. Of course, you would hope they are comfortable talking with the PD or coordinator or even the department chair, but sometimes they are intimidated by these individuals and do not feel comfortable approaching them.

Having a mentor assigned to each resident especially in their early years can be very helpful to address the kinds of issues mentioned above but also to keep a more personal eye on individual residents. Monitoring their progress during each rotation and recommending additional reading or other activities as appropriate early on when problems are first appearing can be very valuable.

Who is the best person to be chosen for one's mentor? Obviously, you want to pick individuals who will be respected, inspirational, and trustworthy. You want to pick those who have demonstrated an interest in residents and are willing and able to lend the attention needed. If you have junior faculty, recently out of their own programs, they may be useful since they can relate to the residents in a more personal manner. If they are most interested in Neuroradiology, you might want to pick a neuroradiologist as a mentor. And if the resident is heavily involved in research before the residency program, you should try to pick a mentor with similar interests.

The mentoring program needs some structure and we recommend a written "contract" where expectations are clear and documented. The agreement should cover the expected frequency of face-to-face meetings, the expectation of dinners or other social interactions and the specific duties of the mentor regarding evaluation of the resident. If you expect the mentor to meet with the resident after every rotation, make it clear in the contract. It is also important to make sure the mentee – the resident – understands his or her role in the relationship, with goals or objectives to work on and a clear understanding of what will be discussed. The resident should also have an "out" if after a period of time, the relationship doesn't work or there is no rapport. When this happens, it does not reflect poorly on either party; it's just a normal part of these relationships, and it important to have enough depth among mentors to allow changes if necessary. Mentors are supposed to be helpful, so be prepared to take action if some faculty simply are not cut out for the role and make sure the residents are not fearful about speaking up about whether they are getting what they need from the program.

INTERVIEW PROCESS

How applicants are interviewed in your department can go a long way to determining the candidates' impressions of your program. You must choose faculty who can interview effectively, yet make every applicant feel comfortable. These interviews are stressful for the applicants under the best of circumstances and anything that the interviewers can do to help them relax is greatly appreciated. And the interviews will likely be more productive if the applicants are more comfortable with the process.

Of course, prior to the interviews, the applicants must be selected for interviews. And even before that selection can occur, information about the program must be available for potential applicants. The department's website is critical to that process. The potential applicants should believe they have most of the information they need simply by visiting the website.

After they have applied, you need dedicated individuals, often in addition to the PD, who can devote their time to reviewing the applications from the ACGME website. The program coordinator should be the one responsible for gathering the information for review on all of the applicants. This review is critical to identify, from among the many applicants, the subset that can be interviewed. You have to rely on the letters of recommendation, the Dean's letter, and the school transcript for much of the data on which to make a decision. You have additional information in the individual's statement and, of course, you have the board exam scores and the applicant's curriculum vitae (CV). It is very easy to overlook a strong but not outstanding candidate on paper who may turn out to be the next Nobel laureate. Individuals who are characterized as "quiet" are at a distinct disadvantage in this process, as well as in life in general. One could argue that such quiet individuals may not make great radiologists anyway if they lack interpersonal communication skills, but there are quiet effective communicators as well.

You should decide in advance the criteria for selection for those you want to interview. Are you going to emphasize grades, board scores, or extra-curricular activities? Do you want to give those with research experience extra credit? Are you looking for those in your geographic area already? Whatever you want to emphasize should be clear to those who are helping to select the candidates.

Once you have picked your interviewees and they have agreed to come, then you must plan the activities for the interview days. At UCSF we have chosen to interview up to eight candidates on each interview day so that we can concentrate our attention to just a few at a time. Since we interview a little over fifty applicants for our thirteen slots per year, we need seven or eight interview days. Although taking out eight days for interviews and carefully reading each packet is very time-consuming, we attempt to have the same interviewers for all of the days. In that fashion each faculty interviewing has the opportunity to see a reasonable number of applicants to compare with each other.

Other departments have chosen to interview all of their candidates on the same day, bringing in a large number of faculty to interview but getting it done quickly. They often have a large dinner the night before for all of the candidates. This approach is certainly more time efficient for the faculty but we believe it is less personalized than our approach.

We also make sure that several of our residents help with the interviews and we have found that they often have insights about these candidates that the faculty seem almost oblivious to. Of course, we have them attend one of our daily conferences, provide the opportunity for them to have time at lunch with some of our current residents, and we have a small informal gathering at the end of the day. At that reception, we invite all of our residents and faculty, although by the eighth interview day, we are lucky to have a handful attend. We attempt to coordinate interview days with Stanford and other West Coast institutions to make it easier for applicants from the East to group West Coast trips together.

We have an elaborate scoring system that attempts to provide a ranking by each person interviewing. These scores are combined with each other as a starting point for our evaluation discussion, which occurs one evening and often goes on for hours. All of the interviewers meet together to discuss each candidate and their records are reviewed one last time. Although it may not be terribly efficient, we believe that it is as fair a process as we could create. The final rank list is then sent into the national match process.

A few comments about diversity are appropriate here. Of course, we look for qualified candidates who come from under-represented minorities. We openly discuss these candidates at our evaluation meeting. We actively push for women, who overall in this country are not well represented in Radiology. We feel this is a big mistake and we encourage women medical students to consider Radiology as a specialty. Often women shy away from Radiology because of the physics required, but we have found little difficulty for women because of the physics. Our experience with under-represented minorities is that not only do these individuals perform well, but they add exciting diversity into our program and department.

A number of points should be made about the interviews. It is very important to instruct those faculty and residents who perform the interviews that these interactions should serve several different purposes. Not only are we attempting to learn about a candidate's achievements, but also we are assessing their "fit" with our program. Will they be team players and help out their fellow residents? Will they be able to handle the workload? Will they be happy? We are also in the job of salesman and we attempt to convince all of our candidates that this institution is clearly where they should want to be a resident.

Although we do not rank individuals based on their preferred subspecialty areas, if we have too many interested in the same subspecialty area, we view that as a potential problem. As we will mention later, practically all of our residents choose to stay on at UCSF for fellowships so that if we have too many going into a single subspecialty, we could have conflict.

After we have submitted our rank list and after the applicants have done so as well, we ask all of our interviewees to fill out a brief questionnaire about the interviews and about our program. We have been conducting such a survey for many years and find the results to be very helpful in refining the interview process. The match results as well as this survey provide us with important feedback concerning our competition. We are constantly assessing our performance with those we consider our peers.

FINANCIAL PERKS FOR RESIDENTS

Because UCSF is located in one of the most expensive areas in the country, we are constantly looking for ways to make ourselves more competitive when it comes to salaries and living arrangements. Our salaries are more than competitive but not high enough to offset the higher cost of living. We have been able to offer a substantial housing allowance, thanks in part to the medical center. We also offer a book allowance and travel expenses to national meetings for presentations. We provide a laptop computer to incoming residents. We support our residents' attendance at the Armed Forces Institute of Pathology (AFIP), which is considered a very worthwhile rotation by our residents. As will be explained later, the alumni association for our department, the Margulis Society, covers much of the expenses for the AFIP.

RESIDENT ROTATIONS

Our residents have thirteen, four-week rotations each year. These rotations are through each of our subspecialty sections based on the core curriculum that we have devised. Our residents rotate to the Veterans Administration Medical Center (VAMC) and to the local county hospital, San Francisco General Hospital (SFGH), which are completely staffed by UCSF faculty and trainees. First year residents, in fact, spend most of their first year at SFGH since so much basic training is centered there. The residents learn about diseases that are much more common in patients cared for at these two sites. The VAMC rotation focuses on Alzheimer's and other neurodegenerative disorders common in the elderly population it serves, as well as the fallout from tobacco and substance abuse. SFGH is the major trauma center for the San Francisco area, and our residents are well immersed in trauma there, as well as gaining exposure to patients with AIDS, hepatitis, brain injuries, substance abuse and psychiatric issues, tuberculosis, and other diseases prevalent in a low-income, densely populated community. We do not allow rotations at institutions other than those directly affiliated with UCSF, such as the VAMC and SFGH.

Our core curriculum is basically three years in length, fitting nicely with the new format of the residency structure being instituted by the American Board of Radiology (ABR). This three year curriculum leaves a full year for electives including research. We have a NIH Institutional Research Training Grant (T32) in which four of our residents (or others) can dedicate a full year to research, usually in their third year. We will push that back to the fourth year with the new ABR format. In addition, residents who choose not to undertake the twelve months of T32 training may submit proposals to the program director for up to a maximum of six research rotations during their residency.

As you probably are well aware, the new format provides a qualifying examination, computer-based and case-based, at the end of the residents' third year. This exam combines physics and the prior written exam and has a number of components that all must be passed. The final certifying examination may be taken fifteen months after completion of the residency program. This final exam is also computer-based and case-based and will be weighted toward the practice experience of the examinee. If someone has taken a subspecialty fellowship and is specializing in Abdominal Imaging, the exam will be weighted toward that subspecialty, but will also cover other aspects of diagnostic radiology so that successful completion of the process will allow for certification in the entire specialty.

We encourage all of our residents to take elective time for research, from a few months to twelve months as described above. We expect each resident to present their work at national meetings or submit material for publication. We emphasize that research is part of the education process, including understanding outcomes research, research methodology, and critical thinking. Although a number of our residents will end up in private practice, we pride ourselves in producing some of the next generation of academic leaders in this country. We believe that we, along with other research-intensive departments, have a special mission to create these future academic radiologists. Our recent track record, including the number of our own residents who have joined the UCSF faculty in the last two years (more than seven people), would suggest that we are achieving our goals in this regard.

RESIDENT CALL AND NIGHT FLOAT

Our residency program is fairly flexible and we have created special rotations based on resident desires and needs. Our chief residents are responsible for making the rotation schedules but they consult with the PD for any rotations that are unique or unusual. We recently created a night float call system whereby the residents on-call at night take the bulk of their weekday calls in blocks one to two weeks at a time. They are on duty from late evening until early morning and are off duty for the remainder of each day. In this fashion they keep within the ACGME guidelines for work hours and get much of the call burden out of the way. The continuity each night with the technologists and referring house staff are added bonuses.

Resident call has been the subject of much debate. Many academic leaders in Radiology believe that the night call for the residents is an extremely important learning experience in which they develop the ability to "think on their feet" and gain confidence in their independent assessments. Others believe that it is not appropriate for second or third year residents to shoulder the responsibility of determining patient care in the middle of the night. We continue to believe that residents taking night calls with appropriate and responsive attending back up from home works very well to take care of our patients and satisfy referring physicians. We covered this subject in Chapter 8 in some detail.

TESTING AND EVALUATION

How frequently should residents be evaluated? How often should they be expected to take some kind of examination? Obviously there is no single answer to those questions, but some formal evaluation process is necessary, not only for the RRC reviews but for the sake of the residents' progress throughout their residency. And the residents do need to practice somewhat for the exams that they must pass in order to become board certified. To this end we have introduced end of rotation and end of year online testing as discussed below.

The e*value system (e*value, 2011) is used by many institutions and is used by UCSF. All residents are evaluated at the end of each rotation and they, in turn, evaluate the faculty – anonymously of course. We were amazed at the difficulty we have encountered at-tempting to get honest evaluations of residents by faculty. The faculty are quite nervous about giving a resident anything other than an excellent evaluation, concerned that the resident will be upset. Why these faculty who are clearly in the power positions in relationship with the residents would feel this way is hard to understand. However, because of this fact and in order to make the evaluation of residents as unbiased as possible, we have instituted a composite evaluation at the end of each rotation where the faculty create a collective evaluation rather than individual ones.

The residents, likewise, are reluctant to write down anything negative about a faculty member, in fear that the individual being criticized will somehow figure out the source of the critique. We go to great lengths to protect the residents from any repercussions from their honest assessments, but we still do not believe we always receive the full truth. The important thing is to continuously reinforce with the residents that their evaluations are anonymous and their comments are taken seriously by the PD and department leadership. At UCSF, we have taken action when resident comments about a faculty member are consistently negative. We want to make sure that if residents are willing to take a risk and tell the department about a problem, that they see concerns taken seriously.

We have given the residents the ACR in-service examination for years and find that to be somewhat useful. Obviously, much depends on the actual rotations that a resident has completed and the residents consider the exam to be a nuisance more than a helpful analysis of their performance. Recently we have decided to institute more formal written exams at the end of each rotation to provide more immediate and concrete feedback concerning the resident performance. The end of rotations exam takes the form of an online case-based test module. This serves the dual objective of providing an opportunity for verbal feedback to the trainee by faculty reviewing the test and also providing residents a concrete assessment of performance development during their training. Similarly, we have instituted an end of year exam designed to be a clinically applicable case-based review of all subspecialties. The residents seem very supportive of this change.

CHIEF RESIDENTS

The choice of chief residents is very important and selecting those individuals who are not only popular and respected among the residents but also capable of handling the many tasks assigned to the chiefs can be a challenge. We start with a vote by all of the residents for anyone in the third year class. Our chief residents serve from the middle of the third year to the middle of the fourth year, although we may change this with the new resident board examinations. The faculty teaching committee, which also has the current chief residents on it, takes the vote from the residents as the starting position and then decides on the next chief residents. Most often we are in agreement with the residents' choices but sometimes there are very close votes and the committee chooses one slightly lower in votes than the other, often considering gender and personality as factors.

The chief residents not only create and manage the complex resident rotation schedules, but they also manage the call schedule and a variety of events for the residents. They plan and execute the resident picnic, a variety of sports competitions against the Stanford residents, and the Minagi golf competition, named after one of our most illustrious emeritus professors, Hideyo Minagi, who is a legend himself and an avid golfer as well. We have three chief residents and try to schedule them so that one is located at each major site each rotation. However, this arrangement is not always possible, therefore, the chief residents select a site representative for each major site location to lead the day to day responsibilities and act as the go-to embedded senior resident. The three chiefs generally divide up the work so that one is primarily responsible for the rotation schedule, one is responsible for call, and one handles all leave requests (vacation, sick, etc.). We also ask the chief residents to participate in the Department Operations Committee and the Department safety committee, and their input is always valuable.

We have found chief resident involvement in the residency program invaluable not only for facilitating communication (town hall meetings, direct resident feedback, meetings with the class representative, meetings with PD) but also in term of innovative ideas. We encourage each group of chief residents to develop a legacy for their term. Such projects have resulted in the development of the "Brant and Helms" study groups for first and second years, development of an online conference evaluation and attendance system, revamping of the core curriculum, introduction of audience response systems, and development of the end of rotation and end of year case-based teaching modules. Empowering the residents has been rewarding in many ways and has resulted in a tremendous effort on the part of the trainees to assist the PD in continuously improving and revamping the training program with the needs of the residents.

ROBOTICS AND SIMULATION SYSTEMS

Robotic systems are heavily used by surgeons and surgical training programs. Simulation systems are often used by Anesthesia and by

Surgery but Radiology has not widely adopted the use of simulation systems as of yet. For surgeons, they are necessary for training in robotic surgery and in endoscopic surgery.

Simulation systems are widely used by medical students or interns for learning basic concepts such as chest tube insertion, retinal exams, and pelvic exams. Dedicated simulators for prostate lesions and breast lesions can provide the trainees experience before touching real patients.

These systems allow trainees to practice without possibly hurting patients, much like the pilots learning tricky maneuvers for aircraft without endangering passengers. Mannequins have been used for years for basic and advanced CPR training. These systems are also useful for team building such as the code team or operating room teams.

For Interventional Radiology, several systems have been developed by companies such as SimSuite. Their mannequin teaches a variety of endovascular skills for Cardiologists, Vascular Surgeons, and Radiologists. Not only do these systems provide the opportunity to learn how to conduct procedures with catheters and guide wires, but also teach how to deal with unexpected reactions and drug interactions.

Although these systems are best at teaching basic skills, they are getting better all the time. The JCAHO and other organizations are looking to simulators as an excellent way to assure a basic level of competence and will probably start insisting on their use for credentials, privileges, and certification in the near future.

CHAIR INVOLVEMENT

The department chair must be actively involved in the residency program. Although fellows are very important, as will be discussed next, the residents are the jewels of the department, are around for at least four, usually five years, and are the prime source for future faculty. They are also the ambassadors for the department no matter where they go. The department chair should be actively involved in the resident interview process and the selection of the next residents. He/she should meet with the residents regularly and should work closely with the PD to assure that the residency experience is as good as possible.

At UCSF, the chair meets with the residents for lunch monthly at each major site, Parnassus, VAMC, and SFGH. He reviews with each resident the current or last rotation, the good and bad. They soon learn that the chair takes what is heard at these meetings very seriously. He tries to wait, look for trends, and attempt to delay any feedback to the faculty in order to protect the identity of the source information. The PD or associate PDs often attend these meetings as well. Some of the faculty have suggested the chair listens more to the residents than the faculty. Frankly, he finds what the residents have to say is usually accurate and not based on possible personal gain.

The Program Director involves the chair with any disciplinary matters regarding the residents and informs the chair of any outstanding issues that have not been adequately addressed without the chair's involvement.

REFERENCES

e*value. (2011). Accessed February 5. https://www.e-value.net/.

Chapter 13

FELLOWSHIP PROGRAM

The clinical fellowships are usually one year in length and are organized most often to coincide with subspecialty sections. Some of these fellowships are ACGME approved programs, with Certificates of Added Qualifications (CAQs) and others are more ad hoc. The ACGME approved programs are very similar to the residency programs in that they have a review cycle and get approved for a set number of years, they have similar requirements for documentation, and most importantly, the fellows are considered house staff and cannot bill for services. The medical center hopefully pays their salaries and can claim them on their cost reports. However, they only get reimbursed for half of the amount they normally collect for residents. And they are subject to the same caps on numbers of slots as residents. If a medical center is over the cap, the support for fellows is often the first to go.

The non-ACGME fellows are really clinical instructors or junior faculty and they can bill independently. They can be used for moonlighting or evening coverage and actually can dictate, sign, and bill for their work. They can also oversee and monitor resident work and can sign off on dictations by the residents. ACGME fellowships are common for Nuclear Medicine, Neuroradiology, Pediatrics and Interventional Radiology, but also exist for Abdominal Radiology, and a couple of other subspecialties. Most departments have chosen to keep the abdominal fellowship or others in the non-ACGME category because of funding and because the ACGME fellows can't work independently.

At UCSF, we have fellows in all of the sections listed in Chapter 8 with the exception of the Ambulatory General Radiology group. We have a large number of clinical fellows – around twenty-eight – and we are always concerned that this group of trainees might be competing with our residents for interesting cases. Occasionally, especially early in the academic year, the residents will mention in our luncheon meetings that they are having a problem with aggressive fellows. So far, we have managed to keep this issue under control. Obviously in Neuroradiology and Interventional Radiology, this kind of competition with the residents could be a problem. Yet residents are not expected to do complex IR or Neuro IR cases. The residents rotate to the Mt. Zion Hospital for basic IR where they are able to perform simpler procedures with the attending and no fellow. The same is true for the VAMC and SFGH so they certainly get ample opportunities to perform procedures.

We often tailor our fellowships for our own resident graduates. These are sometimes combination fellowships for ultrasound and women's imaging or ultrasound and Abdominal Imaging. And recently we have started to rotate our fellows in certain sections to cover part of the year at either the VAMC or SFGH. Fellows, like faculty, rotate to both Mt. Zion Hospital and to our China Basin Outpatient facility on a regular basis.

Our IR fellows rotate through Vascular Surgery and their fellows spend time rotating in IR. Likewise, we have Obstetrical fellows spending time with our ultrasound faculty, limiting their instruction to obstetrical and gynecological studies. And we train Cardiology fellows in coronary CTA. We also have an occasional fellow from other services rotate on our services primarily to get exposure to our imaging to meet their RRC requirements.

A number of years ago, the Society of Chairmen of Academic Radiology Departments attempted to organize a fellowship match process similar to what is in place for residents. Most departments realized that such a match would allow interviews to occur much later, as late as the end of the third year of residency, and would relieve the pressure on applicants to decide immediately after an interview if they would accept a position. Often less desirable fellowships would land applicants early and these individuals would miss out on the opportunity to train at an institution they would prefer. Needless to say, programs that were not as attractive were concerned with this match process.

If the number of residents applying for fellowships was equal to or exceeded the number of fellowship slots, then the match would have continued to be attractive to most involved. But many fellowship positions historically have gone unfilled, creating pressure for some programs to ignore the match rules and offer positions outside of the match. A few prestigious programs broke rank and the match quickly unraveled. The ACGME fellowships continued with the match since they had the support of their society organizations as well as the teeth of the ACGME accreditation process, just as the residency match does.

Since then, residents have learned that they must apply to more programs earlier in their residency in order to secure a desired fellowship program because the programs start interviews earlier and earlier. One could argue that this dilemma is just one example of the utility of having all fellowships, or most of them, within ACGME programs. The added benefit would be the avoidance of much of the turf issues since Certificates of Added Qualification (CAQs) would be required for credentials in subspecialties and each specialty could not develop their own ad hoc criteria for such credentials.

During the 2011 AUR annual meeting, the subject of a SCARD session was the fellowship match once again. Many chairs spoke of the problem of competing fellowship programs offering candidates jobs as early as the beginning of the third year. They also mentioned that a number of candidates were reneging on commitments to begin fellowships in their departments, either because of changes in their lives or a better offer from another program. Of course, changes in the applicants lives are more likely to occur if significant time elapses between commitment and the start of the fellowship. The early start dates seemed more of a concern than the fairness of the match process, but both were discussed.

There was general consensus that something had to be done and a task force was created to study the problem and bring recommendations to the fall, 2011, meeting of SCARD. There was optimism expressed for two reasons. The new qualifying examination for the resident boards at the end of the third year would discourage residents from interviewing earlier than the examination since they would probably be studying. Also a website, possibly organized by SCARD/RSNA could be used as a clearinghouse for fellowships and chairs of departments would have to sign a pledge of professionalism to abide by the rules or else be banned from the website. If candidates for fellowships used that website to find programs of interest, the department chairs would be reluctant to try to attract applicants on their own.

Chapter 14

FACULTY RECRUITMENT AND RETENTION

One of the most important aspects of departmental leadership is the recruitment and retention of faculty and staff. We will discuss faculty for most of this chapter and will deal with staff at the end. Each faculty recruitment should be viewed as a once in a lifetime opportunity, which is not to be squandered. As a chair, it is critical to resist getting the next warm body to fill a clinical need. In general, when in doubt about hiring someone, don't – it is much easier to hire someone then to get rid of them if they do not work out. We can assure you that one of the most satisfying aspects of the chair position in an academic department is the cadre of new faculty that have been hired. Department chairs can take pride even in those who have left, if they went on to important academic positions and became leaders in their fields. Because such recruitments are so precious, we will examine some practical aspects of recruitment and how to assure yourself that you are indeed looking for the best and brightest possible candidate whenever you recruit. The textbook, *Good to Great* has a number of important lessons to apply to department leadership, including recruitment. Let's examine some of those lessons now.

LESSONS FROM *GOOD TO GREAT*

Primary lessons from the text *Good to Great: Why Some Companies Make the Leap...and Others Don't* (Collins, 2001) are the concepts of discipline and "getting the right people on the bus." If you have not read his book, we recommend it highly. This text was the product of a research project in which the author and his research team studied why certain companies had sustained success while others in the same industries did not. They looked for common ideas across these successful companies that were lacking in the others. Jim Collins goes to great length to develop the idea that discipline is critical in everything about each of these companies. He describes disciplined people, disciplined thought, and disciplined action.

Disciplined people are the heart of successful companies. If you are able to recruit disciplined leaders in your department, your job as chair is made considerably easier and you are more likely to be successful. Which gets to the next basic principle in Collins's book that you need to "get the right people on the bus, and the wrong people off." It is very difficult in the UC system, and in most academic environments, to remove faculty who are not performing well. It is essential to make appointments that are clearly the best person for a given position. As Collins later discusses, if you hire self-disciplined people, they will not have to be managed and you can devote your attention to managing the system.

Collins also describes the level five executive, the highest level, as someone who is not a desk-pounding bravado but rather a "self-effacing, quiet, reserved, even shy" individual who will put the needs of the company before their own needs and desires. These individuals are often insiders rather than recruited from outside and are a blend of humility and determination. Although this discussion was related to the company CEO and is best applied to the traits needed for an outstanding chair, we are presenting it here to consider for all recruits especially section chiefs.

The next idea is not from *Good to Great* but a concept that we have utilized at UCSF over the years which we call the Race Horse Theory. We believe we need to hire young unproven racehorses who have great potential but are not yet fully grown or developed. We need to be able to pick out those who are likely to be future leaders by looking for traits such as discipline, enthusiasm, creativity, initiative, and general wisdom. They tend not to have great fear of the unknown. And they need to be street-savvy and understand the academic race well. Often highly successful academic faculty, whether physicians or scientists, are not really "team players" and often build their own laboratory teams without playing well with others. Although these individuals can be successful and you definitely can benefit from having them on-board, they will usually not be the greatest leaders and will not likely develop the next generation of outstanding individuals. And they may not share your vision of how the department needs to grow.

These young racehorses then need to be nurtured, trained, "fed" if you will, and developed into the future great racers that will out-perform the others. The infrastructure of the department and the mentoring program has to make sure they are properly developed.

Another concept from *Good to Great* is the idea of "First Who, Then What." Collins argues that you first need to get the right people on the bus, and then worry about building the program or making other changes. You want to develop your core team first before developing the strategy or vision for the organization. You need your core team to help you develop that vision and be fully engaged in it.

The last concept from *Good to Great* that we would like to discuss here is the "Hedgehog Concept." This theory is based on the essay from Isaiah Berlin, "The Hedgehog and the Fox" in which he divided the world into hedgehogs and foxes. "The fox knows many things, but the hedgehog knows one big thing." The Hedgehog concept is the understanding of what it takes to be the best at whatever you are doing rather than having a plan or the intention to be the best. You have to have a firm idea of what your overall goals are and you must keep that in mind whenever you are making a decision or hiring the next person. That understanding must color every move you make and never be forgotten.

RECRUITMENT PROCESS

Now we want to discuss some down to earth, practical aspects of recruitment. The first task is to determine the type of candidate to be sought and to establish the search process. The reason for the recruitment should drive this planning process so that you can find the individual that best fits the department's need.

Academic Series

The first thing is to establish the proper academic track for the individual. Is this person going to be a heavy researcher or mostly clinical? If mostly clinical, do you expect them to publish very much or teach residents? Or are they going to be in the reading room all the time? At UCSF, we have the in-residence and the ladder ranks that are the most academically challenging and have an expectation for extramural funding and significant paper production. Both series have a strong expectation for quality teaching. The clinical X series is less demanding for research grants but has similar expectations for manuscripts. The clinical X papers can also be more clinically focused and commonly involve analysis of clinical trials as well as outcomes studies. The clinical X has high expectations for teaching and is comparable to other institutions' clinician-educator tracks. The clinical work has to be strong.

Our clinical series has an expectation for excellence in clinical work associated with some teaching and paper production. These manuscripts could be more descriptive case series or similar work as is commonly in the Radiology literature. The clinical series faculty are not in the academic series and do not have a variety of benefits of the academic tracks.

At UCSF, we have multiple steps within each rank of assistant, associate and full professors. Generally speaking, we determine the appropriate rank and step for an appointment based on the years of experience since completing residency and fellowship. However, a radiologist who has also obtained a PhD or spent considerable time doing research in a laboratory may have multiple manuscripts to weigh into the determination of the starting appointment. When there is doubt, we ask for advice from the Dean's office. If we follow that advice, we are not likely to have difficulties getting approval for that rank and step.

So in establishing the proper startup package, you first have to decide on what you need. If it were strictly someone who will be a clinician with only moderate requirements for manuscripts or teaching residents, then perhaps the clinical series would suffice. If fresh out of fellowship, then assistant clinical professor step 1 (or the equivalent junior level in your own institution) would be appropriate. If you are looking for a radiologist with experience and current NIH funding at another institution, then you might start them off at a much higher level and in the in-residence series.

For PhD scientists who will be fulltime researchers and educators, we usually expect them to be in the in-residence series. Yet we have a number of such individuals in the adjunct series at UCSF who are strictly focused on research, have funding or are expected to have it, and who do not get very involved in teaching. They tend to be part of a larger group such as the RIGs as we described in Chapter 11. Adjunct faculty do not have all of the privileges of in-residence faculty such as not being able to be the thesis advisor for graduate students. Also the requirements for advancement for adjunct faculty typically do not include the breadth of activities (teaching, research, and public service) that is expected of the in-residence or ladder rank faculty member. For this reason, many such faculty want to switch to in-residence after they obtain grant funding. The department must resist "rewarding" adjunct faculty with in-residence appointments simply because they are doing well. The appointment for in-residence researchers must be based on a significant need for the department and the selection of the person to fill such a position should be based on a national search. The very best candidate who can be identified that fits the job description should be sought for such a position.

So what are the criteria for adjunct faculty? Often post-doctoral fellows are successful, obtain their own funding, and are an integral part of the team in a RIG or lab. They then get appointed in the adjunct series in order to have a faculty appointment. This is a natural stepping-stone and a number of our graduate students earn such appointments. Or they may be recruited as a needed member of the team from another institution and often a faculty appointment is necessary to get them to come to us. And we sometimes need to make such an appointment to retain someone who we would like to consider for a long-term relationship.

Some departments at UCSF and a number of departments elsewhere use the series like the adjunct series as an entry into the faculty. Once they are established, then switching to the in-residence, or equivalent, track is considered. In this fashion, risky appointments can be made with the idea of letting go those who do not make it. We prefer to select individuals up front based on our needs, and based on what we can learn about the candidates, but riskier appointments are less attractive with this approach.

Recruitment for Radiologists

As stated earlier, we usually decide to recruit a radiologist to fill a clinical need. As mentioned in Chapter 10, we use analysis of our

RVU workloads to help determine when we need to add another sub-specialist in any particular section. As we discussed in the previous section, you first need to decide on the kind of recruitment you wish to pursue. The most common recruitment is for someone to work clinically about 80 percent of the time and to have one day per week, or 20 percent, for academic pursuits. At UCSF, we do not often recruit for someone to be overwhelmingly clinical, although we have a number of very important members of our faculty who are in the clinical track. Since we are mostly interested in someone to fill the clinical void, we usually advertise and pursue candidates by seeking individuals who could fit in the clinical X series or the in-residence series depending on their background and interests. We want to find the best possible candidate for our clinical needs and then see how they fit academically. Of course, we are always seeking the strongest academic candidates but usually confine the search to the area or subspecialty needed clinically.

Recruitment for PhD Scientist

We periodically examine our research strengths and weaknesses, usually at the Executive Research Council (described in Chapter 11). When we identify gaps and opportunities in important research areas, we often target those areas for recruitment. Often radiologists need scientist partners to be successful in their pursuit of particular research areas. Or other departments approach us about a possible joint recruitment in areas of scientific overlap, often where they need imaging expertise. And we may identify an area of vulnerability in which other departments may be tempted to fill the imaging void.

Search Committee

The next step is to put together the search committee. For radiologist searches, we commonly put on search committees at least one member of the primary referring department. We often have the section head of the subspecialty to which we are recruiting to serve as the head of the committee. For PhD searches, we include the RIG leader or head of the laboratory. And we always include our Vice Chair for Academic Affairs as an ex-officio member of the committee. Then we put together the appropriate job description, which is used to write the formal request to the Dean's office for approval of the search as well as for the necessary journal advertisements. We usually advertise in *Academic Radiology, Radiology* and the most prestigious pertinent subspecialty journal or related scientific journal for PhDs. We do not often get great candidates from such ads but on occasion we do.

We have not often used a search firm or headhunter for these searches but on occasion, when we are having difficulty finding the right individual, we will do so. Our experiences with such recruiters have been mixed and we are not sure it is worth the expense. No matter how one conducts the search, it is very important to reach out to contacts in other departments to see if they know of individuals who might be interested in such a position. For starting radiologist's positions appealing to radiologists right out of fellowship, contacting section chiefs in other institutions is likely to find good candidates. These section chiefs are often friends with your faculty in the subspecialty in which the recruitment is being conducted through one society or another. For PhDs, finding post-doctorates who have started to establish themselves with grant funding, significant publications, and national exposure is the best approach.

Once you have identified the best candidates, your search committee has to begin the selection process by first getting the CVs of those who are interested. In addition to the names obtained by contacts elsewhere and, of course, any viable internal candidates, the committee needs to seriously look for minority candidates. Although it is important to maintain the highest standards, the committee must make extra effort to find suitable candidates who are from under-represented minorities. This pursuit for minorities is not only morally responsible; it is really healthy for the department and the school. Having a diverse faculty attracts diverse residents, students, both medical and graduate, and post-docs and brings different cultures into the mix. We have learned a lot about biodiversity in the world around us and we should apply these lessons to recruitment.

The next task for the committee is to make a short list for possible interviews. Once a few top candidates are identified, they need to be invited to visit with members of the section or RIG as well as with the search committee members. Often the senior leaders of the department will participate at this time or will be reserved for the next visit. Of course, the department should cover the expenses for the visit. Usually several members of the search committee will take the candidate out for dinner.

If viable candidates are well received on the first visit to the department, they are invited back for a second look. This second visit could be offered to just one individual if that person was the very strongest of the chosen group. Or several candidates could be invited back if no clear leader emerged after the first visit. On the second visit, the chair and others need to meet the candidate, especially if down to one individual at that time.

Even if these candidates invited back for the second visit are mostly clinical, the department could benefit from presentations at a noon conference or other forum. The presentations would be ideally related to their research interests but could be clinical in nature as well. Such presentations would provide the search committee and departmental leadership with some insight into their presentation skills. For PhD candidates, a "chalk talk" may be useful since it provides an opportunity to examine in more detail the research the individual is actually doing. Individuals with language difficulties often do fairly well in interviews but may not do so well in a formal presentation or a chalk talk.

Often the return candidates are asked to present to the committee, and perhaps the chair, their needs for a successful career. Sometimes it is useful at this juncture to learn a little about the expectations of the leading candidates. That knowledge may influence the decisions of the committee and may help determine the startup package that will be required.

The committee needs to pick the best candidates for the position and officially offer those names to the chair for consideration. Ideally the committee would be offering three individuals, all of which would be great choices. The committee should be asked to rank the three and should provide explanations for their choices to the chair. These communications are best in person and not written down, although the search process requires documentation of those considered and who was ultimately chosen. For most institutions, this documentation also includes information about minority status for each of the prospects.

Throughout the interview process, everyone involved needs to remember that each candidate needs to feel special and needs to be sold on the merits of the job. Everyone should be the best salesman possible and should always be thinking of every aspect of the institution, the department, and the location that might be appealing to the candidate in question.

What characteristics should be sought for such positions? For MDs, we have already stated that the primary driver is for clinical coverage in a particular subspecialty. For PhDs, expertise in a particular area of research is the first consideration. But a number of factors beyond clinical expertise or research interest need to be considered. The chosen individual must be a team player, must be a good communicator, and must consider resident, fellow, student, or postdoc education to be a priority and must enjoy teaching. They need to be more than just strong clinically or in research but should also have a strong work ethic. And as we stated earlier in this chapter, look for individuals who are self-disciplined and will not require handholding and be what we call "high maintenance" faculty. Interpersonal skills do matter; professionalism counts. Be sensitive to signals in references that might suggest interpersonal difficulty and believe that you will not be able to change someone's stripes. If you really want a great clinician or scientist with poor interpersonal skills think very carefully about the role, and about the impact on relationships within and outside of the department.

Academically, depending on the series, radiologists should have a strong record in a particular research area and should have a track record of manuscript production. Even if they are fresh out of fellowship, if they are to be considered for the more academic series, they need to have demonstrated academic accomplishments or at least great promise.

Be careful about considering someone who is several years out of fellowship or out of graduate school and expresses interest in pursuing research funding yet has a poor academic record to date. These individuals are likely to be disappointed in any position since their expectations are not in line with reality.

Start-up Packages for Radiologists

Once the best candidate is identified, then the full-court press is on. Obviously, the chosen candidate needs to be invited back to the department, often after informing him/her that they are the first choice. And they should be asked to come back with specific plans for their career and specific needs that they have. They need to be prepared to start the discussions about their start-up package expectations.

All candidates for recruitment seem to feel that the only chance for getting what they want is to ask for it when they are being recruited. Often the expectations for what they will need to be successful are far different from your own and the sooner you know this discrepancy, the better. So what is a reasonable package for a radiologist you have selected for a position in your department?

Let's start this discussion considering a mostly clinical radiologist fresh out of fellowship training. If this individual really wants to be a clinician-educator and does not expect extra academic time to pursue a strong research agenda, then the start-up is fairly straightforward. At UCSF, the salary and benefits are relatively standard based on the rank and step as described in Chapter 3. The X + Y has targets based on the AAMC surveys and are adjusted for the steps in each rank to keep us competitive with research-intensive academic institutions around the country. The package for retirement, health benefits, and life and disability insurance are fairly generous and competitive.

They will need access to a shared administrative assistant and will need an office, hopefully close to the primary site for their clinical work. Obviously, they will be a part of one of our clinical sections, each with a subspecialty focus. Each new faculty gets a computer, travel allowance, and help with a mortgage if they are entering an academic tract (not our clinical tract). The offer letter will state that they are expected to work 163 clinical days unless they have extramural funding to cover some of the salary and benefits. These workdays translate into about a day per week for academic pursuits when not away for vacation or meetings. And we have a small "faculty recruitment allowance" or sign-on bonus as well.

If the individual is planning on a more rigorous research program and is going to be appointed in the in-residence series, then a different set of expectations are established. First of all, we only expect about 50 percent clinical time or 102 clinical workdays. We guarantee this for a period of two or three years with the understanding that the arrangement may be extended if the individual has shown strong efforts to get funding but the actual support has not yet materialized.

For these recruits with promise for obtaining grants, additional resources are often committed such as research scan time, animal support, wet lab space, contrast material, etc. Sometimes we offer a fixed amount per year with the proviso that any funds left over are split between the individual's program, the associated RIG, and the department. Of course, the actual expenses require the approval of the Vice Chair for Research.

It should be noted that the salary (X+Y) is the same for these different series and the opportunity for clinical bonus is the same although if a faculty is given additional academic time, they will be working fewer clinical days, and, therefore, may earn less clinical bonus.

Start-up Packages for PhD Scientists

For PhDs the approach is similar to that for MDs with a few exceptions. The salary is determined, as before, by rank and step and is competitive with AAMC surveys. Most of these recruitments are in the in-residence series since we expect them to be successful researchers and teachers. Since we have no regular mechanism for bonuses for these faculty, we instead set a higher target for those with sustained success in grant funding. They need to be part of one of our RIGs, instead of the clinical sections, and the office should be close to their lab.

The actual start-up packages can vary tremendously. Typically they need salary support for two to three years as well as cover for rent (if at our off-campus China Basin facility). Salaries for post-docs or graduate students often are needed as well. Sometimes specialized equipment is needed. They need to have all of their expenses for that period of time covered, such as animals and their care, scan time (recharges), and supplies. They will depend on their assigned mentor for guidance and direction but hopefully were connected to the right individuals outside of our department during the interviews for their needed collaborations.

Competition and Fairness

Over the years, we have grown to appreciate the importance of structure in our compensation plan and adherence to that plan for new recruitments. If one falls into the trap of offering more salary or better start-up packages to the newest recruit, then the faculty already onboard, especially those recently employed, will become very disillusioned. Having faculty who are at similar levels along the academic ladder will be somewhat competitive naturally and that is probably a healthy thing. But if they perceive that they are not being treated fairly, you and the department will be in trouble.

We are convinced that the department is better off losing out on a great recruitment if hiring that individual would cause great dissention in the ranks. Harmony and faculty comfort as well as being treated fairly is extremely important and should never be forgotten. Of course, if a new faculty is recruited in the same research area as an existing faculty, the competition could be difficult. Our advice is to weigh carefully the potential benefits and problems that such competition might bring before adding that individual to your faculty. Sometimes, such competition encourages the prior recruit to be more productive and other times that individual will find greener pastures elsewhere.

Diversity

As we mentioned earlier in this chapter, diversity is very important not only when recruiting residents and graduate students but also for faculty and staff. The department is so much richer with a diverse group of individuals working together sharing their ideas based on different cultures and backgrounds. Having different perspectives enriches whatever we are doing, as long as everyone shares in mutual respect and admiration for those varied cultural backgrounds. And that diversity is not limited to under-represented minorities but also includes gender and sexual orientation.

Much debate has centered on the issue of preferential hiring and promotion for under-represented minorities. Our only comment on this debate is that this diversity has value just like other particularly rich experiences found in the CV and needs to be weighed in the selection process just as one would weigh these other factors. And an environment where different opinions are welcome and seriously considered in decision making, and honest constructive debate is encouraged, allows the most creative and exciting ideas to emerge and blossom.

STAFF RECRUITMENT

How do you feel about the staff in your department? We would like to suggest that the Chair's attitude about the quality of staff recruitment and retention is as critical as his or her feelings about faculty recruitment. A high quality administrative team is the only way to help a chair grow a department, because there are truly not enough hours in the day to accomplish everything most chairs establish as goals. If you have a small department, you still need a small group of people – an administrator, financial officer or revenue manager, and someone competent in academic personnel issues – to get day to day tasks accomplished and help you achieve your vision. At UCSF, we have a fairly large administrative team, and hiring faculty assistants, research administration staff, IT professionals, financial analysts, and so on, is delegated to the department administrator.

We can tell you from an administrative perspective that the chair sets the tone in the department. However, our department administrator feels comfortable recruiting star performers and doing whatever it takes to keep them happy because there is a very good balance of tasks between faculty leaders and administrative leaders. We have found at UCSF, that most of the strong departments have excellent chair administrator teams, while it is almost always true that those departments lacking this are among the weaker players. As chair, do you encourage and fund training and development for your staff? Do you allow them to travel to conferences and meetings, to bring back new ideas and best practices? Do you encourage recognition events for the staff, provide bonuses for key administrators, and encourage promotions from within? Do you back up your staff, if appropriate, when there are conflicts with faculty? Do you as chair make sure faculty understand the importance of professionalism and using their positions wisely and appropriately? We would argue that all of these things will contribute to a strong team of people who will make sure you are successful in generating professional fees, accomplishing research goals and generally raising the profile of your department in your organization. One final word, because we feel fortunate to have this at UCSF – hire people you trust and can count on. This is true whether recruiting faculty or staff. Make sure you have at least one administrator you know will be totally and brutally honest with you as chair and don't be afraid to lean on the individual. People matter and your own behavior as chair needs to demonstrate that you believe this.

We would like to say a word about recruitment strategies, particularly for non-faculty positions. At UCSF, we empower our administrators to network with their colleagues both inside and outside the organization. We expect our key managers to play roles formally as mentors, and to participate in leadership development and other development activities. This has allowed us to identify and recruit talent from across the organization. For key positions, we almost always end up hiring candidates who have been identified through our own networking and informational interviewing. We have also been willing to create positions when we interview great candidates, even if we do not have something final to offer them.

For example, one of our best administrators applied for a lower level accounting job, but it was obvious to our administrative team that we needed her in Radiology. We created a "special projects" position for two years until a more direct operational opening was created by another person's retirement. While this was unbudgeted at the time, the value she added to the department has been considerable and worth the expense. Your responsibility as Chair is to try to hire the top one or two administrators in the department who have the people skills to effectively market your department within and outside your organization when it comes to new talent. Create a department where staff are clamoring to work, and you won't worry when your own staff are promoted themselves and leave Radiology for other positions; rather, this will become a bragging point for you as Chair.

REFERENCES

Collins, J. (2001). *Good to great: Why some companies make the leap…and others don't.* New York: HarperCollins.

Chapter 15

FACULTY RELATIONS AND MORALE

As we have already stated several times, the quickest way to undermine faculty morale is to create an environment of uncertainty and a sense of unfairness in treatment of the faculty. We will delve into the subject of transparency soon but first we should discuss mentoring, especially of junior faculty.

MENTORING

At UCSF, we have developed what we believe is a model junior faculty mentoring program. This program evolved from a concept originally developed by Dr. Gene Washington, former Chair of OBGYN at UCSF and current Dean at the UCLA School of Medicine. Our program utilizes the concept of team mentoring where all aspects of mentoring are not necessarily handled by the same individual. For MDs, our team consists of the Chair, the Vice Chair for Academic Affairs, the section chief for that junior faculty member, the chosen individual mentor, and a trusted clinician who serves on all of the group mentoring sessions. In addition, we ask one of the administrative analysts to attend the meetings to record the action items and follow-up on any outstanding issues. For PhD junior faculty, we include a trusted senior researcher instead of the clinician in our group meetings and we invite the RIG leader instead of a section chief.

The Vice Chair for Academic Affairs, Dr. Susan Wall, oversees this program and is critical to its success. Not only does she help choose the individual mentors but also assures that the mentoring sessions happen on time and that the contact between the mentor and mentee occurs as planned. The follow-up from the group sessions is handled by a secure website and the junior faculty and mentors alike are expected to utilize these tools on a regular basis.

The faculty member receiving the mentoring chooses the individual mentors but they are guided, as mentioned, by Dr. Wall. We deliberately choose mentors who are not the section chiefs or RIG leaders. In fact, we encourage the junior faculty to select individuals who are not in their sections or RIGs and occasionally from other departments. These mentors are then "trained" by Dr. Wall and are instructed to touch base with their mentee as often as necessary and desired. They must interact before the annual group session with all involved. Although the Chair is part of the group, the Vice Chair often handles the sessions by herself (after the initial session with that junior faculty) especially if everything seems on track.

Before the annual group meeting, the individual updates their CV and prepares for the meeting by discussing any career issues they are facing with their designated mentor. They will have already, hopefully, addressed any issues that were identified the previous year.

At the group session, the mentee summarizes his or her progress to date. The group then provides open and honest feedback – always constructive – and rarely critical. All aspects of career development are discussed, in this confidential setting. Any issues that need to be addressed are identified along with the expected solutions. The administrative analyst then posts these on the secure website with access restricted to the mentor, mentee, and the Vice Chair. During the session, the junior faculty member has the opportunity to discuss any barriers that exist on the road to a successful career and in this fashion can garner support to ask for help from the department for any needed resources.

Although just a few years old, this program has been considered very successful and the junior faculty have expressed their appreciation for it. The true goal of the mentoring program is to advance junior faculty as quickly as possible. We often have unexpected revelations in this process and we are convinced that we are making a significant difference. Other departments at UCSF have copied our program.

Such a mentoring program can be viewed as a vehicle to assure that our investments in junior faculty are successful. Each recruitment is such a vital resource for the department that any process to help nurture his or her success is worth the effort.

TRANSPARENCY AND FACULTY
INVOLVEMENT IN DEPARTMENTAL AFFAIRS

The word transparency is probably overused and there is such a thing as too much information. However, the faculty need to feel they are informed about what the department is doing and they need to feel that they have the opportunity to at least influence the direction the department takes.

The majority of issues about transparency relate to finances. Certainly faculty have to believe that their salaries are based on a sound rational basis and are at least competitive in their market area. This subject was dealt with in Chapter 3. But the use of departmental funds needs to be justified and the faculty need to feel they have a say in how their hard-earned revenue is used. Once a year, we present the annual "State of the Department" address in which we spend some time discussing the 50,000-foot view of the department's finances. Some of the data discussed in Chapter 4 are presented at this time. The focus is always on the funds that are available to the Chair, excluding restricted funds such as from grants and contracts.

In this fashion, the investments in research, recruitment, information systems, residency program, medical student education, and administration are all shown in the aggregate. An attempt is made to compare ourselves with our peer departments across the country. Obviously, there are clinical faculty who believe the investments in research could be reduced so that more funds would be available for their salaries. Some PhD researchers believe that more should be spent on the research enterprise. Some of the faculty believe we are spending too much on administration, yet they complain when their administrative needs are not addressed immediately. What is important is that the faculty believe a representative group of the faculty have an opportunity to influence how these funds are allocated among the many competing activities we face every day. This process will be discussed more in Chapter 16 under Department Organization.

But the faculty involvement must go well beyond financial planning and decisions. Of course, they need to be involved in committee activities and at least some of these committees need to be within the department. Frequently, at least monthly, faculty meetings should be used to discuss important events and to keep the faculty informed. Of course, faculty who cannot or will not attend these meetings should not complain of not knowing what happened. Minutes need to be distributed promptly and should be sent out by email so that those who did not attend may be brought up to speed and those that did may have a reference document.

Periodically, the department should hold a retreat. Retreats will be discussed more in Chapter 18 but suffice it to say that retreats can help shape faculty thinking and can boost morale, but only if handled carefully.

We keep a file of the departmental and external committees on which our faculty participates. For the departmental committees, we constantly look for opportunities to remove faculty who are not contributing effectively and put new faculty on in their place. We have made regular committee rotations the norm and everyone knows that they do not serve on these committees forever. We have not set absolute terms but we have thought about it seriously. Junior faculty need to begin serving on these committees both to put on their CVs and to gain knowledge about the department. We try to limit the committee work for junior faculty so that they have ample time to work on their research projects and their presentations. As will be mentioned in Chapter 22, we have a very active CME program and we invite our junior faculty to participate, but only in a limited way for the same reasons.

ENCOURAGING PARTICIPATION IN CAMPUS AFFAIRS

Faculty from the department need to populate almost all of the important school and campus committees in order for you to assure that they will be recognized and promoted, but also to protect the interests of the department. As chair, you must constantly be thinking of individual faculty who would like to serve on specific committees or you feel would contribute effectively to them. You need to understand how committee members are chosen and when. If you need to lobby for representation with committee chairs, do so early and often. You certainly want to have departmental representation on the various medical staff committees such as credentials, executive medical boards, quality and safety, and malpractice allocation.

Medical group committees that need departmental input include contracting, the executive committee, and billing. The medical school has research and teaching committees including IRB, animal protection, research space, medical student curriculum, and resident allocation. Medical center committees include capital budgets and information systems. And the campus usually has its own IT, capital, space, compliance, and fundraising committees. Of course, there are many more committees and which ones need Radiology input varies dramatically from one institution to another.

ENCOURAGING PARTICIPATION IN NATIONAL AND INTERNATIONAL ORGANIZATIONS

The Chair's personal influence on memberships in national and international organizations tends to be less than his/her ability to influence committee composition at the home institution. However, if the Chair is involved in leadership positions in these organizations, then such influence is certainly possible. Although more difficult, the Chair should once again take every opportunity to have faculty from his/her department serve on the various committees. This type of committee service is a prerequisite to leadership roles in those organizations. The faculty will likely find their own way, perhaps with encouragement, in their own subspecialty societies.

National organizations such as the RSNA, AUR, American Roentgen Ray Society (ARRS), and the ACR are somewhat different and each has a unique approach to populating committees with membership. The RSNA has a formal structure and rotation schedule. The various committee chairs and the board members all have responsibility for these assignments and they should be approached to learn the right time and the positions that are coming available in the near future. No matter which organization we are talking about, knowing the key members of the leadership group helps tremendously and a little active lobbying can only help get faculty involved.

As for the international committees, a willingness to speak at international meetings and participate when asked to serve as moderator or serve as manuscript reviewer always helps. Certainly getting involved with international committees inside of the national organizations provides the opportunity to get to know the movers and shakers in the international landscape.

One might draw the conclusion that encouraging your faculty to become well-known outside of the department could be inviting their recruitment elsewhere. If they are chosen for career-advancing positions, you should be proud of that departure and take the opportunity to advance another more junior member of the faculty. Broadening the horizons of the faculty in your department should only be considered a good thing and a feather in your cap as well as a great reflection on the department. When the Chair was working for IBM as an undergraduate and as a medical student, he was struck by the departure of successful and fully trained individuals who went on to start their own companies or take high-level jobs for other companies. The leadership of IBM commented that not only was this defection to other companies good for IBM, it was good for other companies and the country at large. Certainly more IBM computers were then sold to these other companies.

Chapter 16

DEPARTMENTAL ORGANIZATION

One of the tasks for a new chair is to decide on the best organizational structure for the department. Of course, the best course of action is to observe for a while until you understand the culture and the individuals more fully before making major changes. On the other hand, the "honeymoon" period for a new leader is not very long, estimated at between six months and a year for new chairs. You would like to make significant changes during that period. When the chair was recruited at UCSF, the chair of the department of Medicine, at that time, Floyd Rector, MD, took him to lunch to help orient him to his new job. The Chair of Medicine told him that the honeymoon period would last six months or so, but unfortunately he would not know what to do for a year or more! That statement turned out to have more truth than one would like.

In the *Good to Great* book, Collins describes how you first want to identify those leaders who you will rely on before you make major organizational and directional decisions. One of the most important tasks for you is to identify those leaders you can trust and that will support the changes you envision for the department early on. You probably should not depend on the prior leadership especially if they believe they should have been chosen for your job in the first place. And remember that any changes you institute will be viewed as criticism of how they did things before. Even if they have the best intentions initially, soon they will not be very supportive of you.

This chair felt that he could win over the entrenched senior members of the faculty when he was recruited. He deliberately left them in positions of power within the department, in spite of advice from other chairs at the time. Over the next few years, he learned the hard way that he should have followed their advice and put into leadership positions those he recruited or really felt he could trust. Keep in mind that change is never welcome to those not seeking it and that it takes time to develop trust among even the most open-minded faculty and staff toward a new chair. And it is hard to speed up that process.

VICE CHAIRS

During the honeymoon period described, you want to pick at least some of the executive group that you will depend on, which is likely to consist of a number of vice chairs. These individuals should be well respected by the faculty, especially for the areas you will appoint them to be responsible for. Typical vice chairs in academic Radiology departments include the following:

- Research
- Clinical Affairs
- Academic Affairs
- Education
- Informatics
- Technology and Capital Projects

The Vice Chair for Academic Affairs has the responsibility of oversight for promotions and mentoring as well as faculty discipline and counseling. This position should be the chair of the promotions committee in the department and should serve on all search committees in an ex-officio role. In that fashion, you can make sure that all searches are conducted according to the university rules, diversity is adequately considered, and that the proper emphasis is considered for academic excellence.

The Vice Chair for Informatics is becoming more and more common in departments across the country and after reading Chapter 17 you will understand why. We are in the information business although many of us believe we are here to interpret scans. How we handle that information is becoming more complex as well as more important.

We have a physicist that is a Vice Chair for Technology and Capital Projects and many departments could probably use a similar leader. The major equipment and construction projects are such an important part of what we do that this position became obvious. And this Vice Chair position is another example of first identifying the right people for leadership roles and then deciding how best to organize around them. This individual not only is in charge of the described areas but is also the primary physicist for the department and a member of the executive team.

An Executive Vice Chair (EVC) is the individual who will act instead of the chair when that individual is not available for whatever reason. The EVC is also the individual who the chair can turn to for advice on salary information for the other vice chairs or other issues that need such isolated attention. Many tough issues are addressed by the kitchen cabinet, which will be explained later in this chapter.

The other key individual in the leadership team is the administrator for the department, which we call the Director of Administration. This person may have a variety of titles but is the individual who must be responsible for all of the staff in the department as well as in charge of finances, space, and equipment other than the large imaging devices discussed already. This person must be a strong member of the executive team and be able to hold his/her own with this obviously strong group. Although this person could have grown up the ranks of the technologists or nurses in the department, more and more often this position must include true administrative skills and often requires an MBA or similar high-level degree.

The relationship between the chair and this person is critical to the success of the department. This point cannot be over-emphasized. This team needs to be in sync in so many ways and they clearly must have a high-level of mutual trust and respect.

Often, especially in large departments, another high-level individual will be directly responsible for the hospital operations, such as a Director of Medical Center Operations.

The Director of Medical Center Operations is the individual who is responsible for all of the hospital clinical personnel as well as the technical side of the equation. This person often reports to one of the hospital administrators but should also report to the chair or the departmental administrator. Later in this chapter we will discuss alternative organizational structures (Please refer to the organizational chart for UCSF, Figure 16–1).

UCSF Radiology and Biomedical Imaging
Senior Leadership

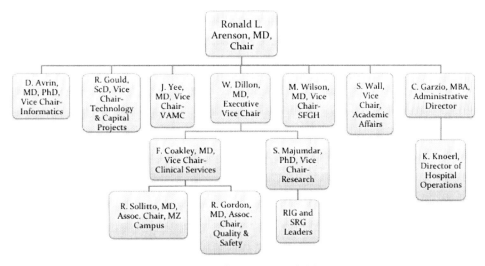

Figure 16–1. Organizational Chart.

KITCHEN CABINET

In *Good to Great,* the CEO has a select group of advisors to provide information and react to his/her ideas and plans. We have a similar group known as the "kitchen cabinet." This kitchen cabinet (KC) is made up of mostly vice chairs who are selected to represent different points of view yet have tremendous respect for each other. All of these individuals speak out and voice their opinions yet understand that the role is advisory and the chair has to ultimately make the decision. No notes are taken and no minutes are generated. Sensitive issues are discussed and most information that is exchanged is confidential.

The individuals who currently sit on the kitchen cabinet include the Executive Vice Chair, the Vice Chairs for Academic Affairs, Informatics, Technology and Capital Projects, and Clinical Affairs. The Director of Administration sits on the committee as well as the Vice Chair for the Veterans Administration Medical Center and the Vice Chair for San Francisco General Hospital. All of these individuals were selected because they are wise, experienced leaders and they represent strong and different perspectives. A number of others are well suited to be part of the KC but we really want to keep it to a small number for maximum effectiveness. And, frankly, we all fit into the chair's office!

This group is not at all afraid to tell the chair that he is off base and needs to change direction. But we do so with respect and with the knowledge that not only does the chair listen to us but usually follows our advice. We meet weekly for an hour and a half. This group of individuals who have strong opinions, also understand fully that our goals are aligned and we have a common vision of the needs of the department. But there is no room for "yes men" in this group!

EXECUTIVE COMMITTEE

This committee is much larger than the KC, made up of all clinical section heads as well as the vice chairs and administrative representatives. The administrative group includes the department's director of administration, the chief financial officer, and the Director of Medical Center Operations. The agenda is prepared in advance, minutes are taken and circulated, and standing reports are expected from several vice chairs. The Associate Chair for Quality and Safety attends and reports and the Program Director for the Residency Program (PD) also participates. In addition to the standing report on Quality and Safety, the Vice Chairs for Clinical Affairs, Technology and Capital Projects, and Research all give a report.

This committee is designed to discuss issues that need the input from the section chiefs and is also supposed to assure dissemination of information to the faculty, fellows, and residents through the section chiefs and the PD. The Executive Committee meets once a month for lunch and usually takes close to two hours each meeting.

FACULTY MEETINGS

All faculty are expected to attend meetings with the chair about once a month at one of the sites. The chair holds meetings at the VA Medical Center and San Francisco General Hospital (SFGH) with the faculty and has a separate meeting with the residents at those locations. In this fashion, the chair has the opportunity to meet with all faculty and residents at least once per month. At Parnassus – the main campus – these meetings alternate between early morning, 7:30 a.m., and lunch at noon, in order to give every section a chance to attend even with conflicting schedules. Of course, not everyone can attend at either time.

Standing reports are given at each of these meetings similar to the executive committee but also include the Revenue Director who is responsible for billing and compliance. These meetings provide the opportunity to cover topics that all faculty should understand fully and also to give them a chance to ask questions and comment. Generally speaking, not as much dialogue occurs at the faculty meetings as at the executive committee because of the size of the group. These meetings occur at the VA and SFGH as well as the main campus and our offsite research facility, China Basin. The latter will be discussed more in the next section. Attendance at these meetings is recorded and is used as part of the end-of-the-year review for all faculty. These meetings also provide the opportunity to discuss issues concerning quality and safety.

The faculty meetings that are held at China Basin consist of a general faculty meeting but also includes the Executive Research Council, discussed in Chapter 11. The Executive Research Council, made up of all RIG and SRG leaders, meets once per month at China Basin and includes the Chair, Executive Vice Chair, and Vice Chair for Research. In this fashion, research faculty are also given the opportunity to participate in the department's decisions and actions similar to the clinical faculty. Obviously, the topics for discussion tend to be more related to the research mission. Much of the agenda that is pertinent to the clinical faculty is of little interest to the research faculty and vice versa.

Some Radiology departments have a finance committee that is charged to periodically review the compensation plan or the overall financial planning for the department. Such a committee must be composed of senior members of the faculty who are judged to be fair and balance the competing needs of the various missions of the department. We have always felt that the KC is composed of such individuals and have used that group for financial discussions. The fact that we do not take minutes and the group is strictly advisory to the chair has limited the group's usefulness in this regard. We plan to officially appoint a finance committee, probably consisting of the same individuals – perhaps with a couple of additions – in order to address s few changes we need in our compensation plan.

SERVICE LINES

The medical center is likely to want to break down the departmental barriers – the silos – to make the clinical engine run more smoothly. Different institutions have tried various models for achieving this goal with the clear plan to increase admissions to the hospital and increase outpatient office visits to feed the inpatient census. If recruitment decisions are left solely to academic department chairs, then the need for additional clinicians may go unfilled. For example, the Chair of the Department of Medicine argues that they lose money on every primary care physician they hire, in spite of months of backlogged requests for appointments. He argues that pro fees are not enough to support these physicians, who generally collect only for E&M codes.

Although we have sections that, by their very nature, can't be easily profitable, other sections like Neuroradiology and Abdominal Radiology make up for them. In Medicine, and perhaps other departments, the Divisions are really like separate departments and do not cross the financial barriers to subsidize other Divisions that are not profitable. Although that difference is probably unfair for Radiology, the overall financial picture for Medicine is not as bright as for Radiology.

A different approach, used by the Mayo Clinic and other successful clinical enterprises, is for the enterprise or medical group to hire the clinical faculty needed. Decisions to hire another primary care physician, or radiologist, is based more on the clinical workload demands than on academic considerations.

The RVU payment model, described in Chapter 6, could make this process easier in that the financial implications of adding another physician are removed from the equation. No longer is the department on the hook for the start-up costs of adding another mouth to feed. Certainly problems of patient access to either primary care physicians or specialists can be solved with this approach.

If the enterprise is going to hire clinicians, then the academic departments have to be partners in order to issue faculty appointments, which should continue to be the key to hospital appointments.

Such academic appointments must drive criteria for hospital privileges or else the hospital will be headed to anyone getting privileges who seeks them.

Whatever approach is used must assure both the departments and the medical center that physicians interested in caring for patients can see patients in a timely fashion and that the departments would not be hurt financially for adding the needed additional faculty.

On the other hand, departments like Medicine must move away from the model of having strong academic faculty who see patients one day per week or are only on service for a month a year. The hospitalist model works well not only for quality inpatient care, but also to separate the academically focused faculty from the more efficient clinical service. But it is also necessary to have primary care physicians who are dedicated to seeing patients, one way or the other.

Another approach is the so-called service line which theoretically pulls together departments under the banner of the service such as Neurosciences. That service line includes Neurology, Neurosurgery, and Neuroradiology. The medical center is also a major party to the service line. For the service line to be effective, the director of the service line should be able to make decisions such as hiring another neurologist or even planning for the next MRI machine. For some service lines, it would make sense to co-locate the practitioners for more efficient and timely service. Such authority in the hands of the director can be threatening to the independent department chairs, especially the Radiology chair who really should be in practically every service line.

One of the possible goals for the service line is to cross-subsidize departments based on profitability. In that fashion, professional fees from Neuroradiology could be used to help support Neurology, for example. Such financial manipulation would destroy the ability to support losing sections in Radiology from the profits on Neuroradiology as well as undermine the authority and control currently exercised by the department chair.

The basic structure of academic departments is that the leadership of the department are basically responsible for all missions: education, clinical, and research. The department is the fundamental unit where these often-competing interests are kept in balance. Failure to balance these forces is a reason to change chairs. Fiddling with any portion of this balanced structure or the powers associated with it can bring unintended consequences.

So what is the best model to assure patient access while keeping the departmental focus? We would need to write another book to take on that issue but the simple answer is some combination of RVU-based medical center strategic support and financially independent departments. And the ability for the medical group or clinical enterprise to hire needed clinicians in partnership with departments is critical to this approach. Then service lines could be used simply for organizing and coordinating the patient centered care.

Chapter 17

INFORMATION SYSTEMS

In the world of Information Technology (IT) medicine is referred to as "the last paper industry." Historically, medicine has under-invested in IT at an annual rate of about three percent of total expenses compared to most other service industries that hover around 10 percent. The US economy has increasingly become an information economy relative to traditional manufacturing. The new emphasis placed on the role of the Electronic Medical Record (EMR) for quality, consistency, safety, and cost is already moving medicine toward the IT mainstream. "Information is the lifeblood of modern medicine," according to David Blumenthal, MD, MPP, President Obama's National Coordinator for Health Information Technology (HIT) (Blumenthal, 2010). Radiology has clearly been a pioneer and innovation leader in the "meaningful use" of IT in medicine for several decades. Many challenges remain. Productive use of IT, and planning for the future is the focus of this chapter.

At UCSF we have purchased, licensed, and built a large number of systems to empower and inform the various activities of the department, as listed in Table 17–1. The discussion will be divided into clinical, educational, research, business, and web systems, as well as support and personnel for these activities. Standards and integration are the glue that binds these systems together in a useful way.

The multiple missions of the department are vitally dependent on the information systems described in the following pages.

185

Table 17–1.

System	Clinical	Research	Education	Admin/ Business	Web/ Other
Radiology Info. Sys. (RIS)	X	X		X	
Radiology Dept. PACS	X	X			
Enterprise Web PACS	X	X	X		X
US PACS	X	X	X		
Mammo. PACS	X	X			
Nuc. Med Systems	X	X			
Voice Recog. Dictation (VR)	X			X	
Wet-Read Module	X		X		
Custom Work lists	X			X	
Custom Prefetching	X				
High Interest Case File (TF)		X	X		X
RIS/PACS = Film: Deprecated	X				
DICOM Enterprise Storage	X	X			
3D Processing	X	X	X		
Virtual Colonoscopy	X	X	X		
Data Analytics (AltoSoft ™)	X	X		X	X
UCSF Report Mining		X	X		X
Vendor Report Mining		X	X		
Faculty Scheduling	X			X	X
Interp. Decision Support	X		X		X
Rad Order Entry w/DS*	X	X	X	X	
Mammo. Registry	X	X			
Subcritical Findings DB	X	X		X	
Research PACS		X			
Research DB Server		X			
Department Website	X		X	X	X

*In planning phase

CLINICAL SYSTEMS

Radiology Information System (RIS)

RIS enables and monitors the life-cycle of a radiology study: ordering, scheduling, protocoling, performing, interpreting, signing, reporting, and billing (or communication to a billing system). The reference standard for Radiology Information Systems was developed by a multi-institutional team and consortium (Radiology Information Systems Consortium – RISC) led by the author while at the University of Pennsylvania (Arenson, 1984; Arenson et al., 1982). The prototype system was further developed and marketed by Digital Equipment Corporation as DECrad. Subsequently it was sold to IDX Corporation, and then General Electric, under the names of IDXrad and ImageCast. This system addressed successfully all of the issues surrounding scheduling, performing, reporting and, in the pre-PACS era, storing film-based exams. As such, it provided a reference implementation model that was inherited by all of the various commercial systems developed subsequently. It also provided for transmission of study and patient information to institutional billing systems. Since almost all academic Radiology departments now use PACS, storage of film-based exams is irrelevant, but most of the other functionality remains relevant and essential to efficient and safe operations. The transcription portion of the reporting process has also been subsumed by dedicated voice recognition reporting systems, discussed below. Tracking of technically completed but non-dictated exams is a continuous process of the RIS with feedback to PACS and the voice recognition dictation system.

Installation of RIS requires the building of dictionaries representing the institution's examination codes, as well as tabulations of the various locations or sites and specific equipment where the studies are performed. While the former should be similar from institution to institution, it is not, while obviously the latter, known as resources, will be very site specific. Categories of resources, such as CT, MR, etc., are similar across institutions.

Integration of the "front end" of RIS with the Master Patient Index (MPI) and the Electronic Medical Record (EMR) is essential for unambiguous patient identification, usually through the Health Level 7 (HL7) standard (Health Level Seven International, 2007). In the near future, integration with the institution's EMR will occur. Computerized Provider Order Entry (CPOE) is perhaps radiology's greatest opportunity for impacting the cost of healthcare through optimized referring physician ordering (Khorasani, 2010; Sistrom, 2009). Early developers of these systems segregate out the Radiology specific ordering from the overall CPOE as a Radiology Order Entry (ROE) system.

PACS

Picture Archiving and Communication Systems (PACS – not our favorite acronym for medical image management systems) were pioneered by academic Radiology departments. While initially they were demonstrated for the "low-hanging fruit" of digital modalities like CT and nuclear medicine, they have expanded to encompass all modalities, including high-resolution mammography. Probably the largest force in the widespread deployment of PACS has been the proliferation of multi-detector CT scanners that typically create many hundreds of images per study. It is simply impossible to view and interpret such studies on film, multiplied by the need for multiple window-level settings (soft tissue, liver, lung, and bone), further compounded by comparison with prior studies. This change on the modality side forced widespread conversion to PACS.

Early visionary developers of PACS (Dwyer, 1996) saw the convergence of predictably declinable cost/performance measures in computer hardware, specifically including storage and networking, and the development of inherently digital imaging modalities such as Nuclear Medicine cameras, CT, and Ultrasound, followed quickly by digital subtraction angiography (DSA) and MR imaging. Conventional projection radiography was actually the most challenging modality to integrate into PACS for reasons that are beyond the scope of this book. For further information please refer to Horii's article entitled "Image acquisitions. Sites, technologies, and approaches." Which can be found in the *Radiology of Clinical North America.* (1996).

Ten year ago the digital media storage cost became less than the cost of film and widespread adoption of PACS was delayed. However, academic medical centers and some visionary community hospital enterprises, as well as the VA hospital system, and the military, adopted the program. Although study size in terms of the number of images has been increasing, at approximately a linear rate, particularly for multi-detector CT, the cost of storage has been going down even faster, following the exponential Moore's law of the semiconductor industry. In Figure 17–1, the log-scale graph shows that over the past two decades the digital size of studies has been going up relatively linearly while the cost of storage has been going down exponentially with Moore's Law, resulting in a very low cost of storage per study, despite the increase in size. (Cost of disk storage is given as the available price at the time for raw storage component, e.g., a hard disk drive of given capacity, not the total cost of storage system component such as the Redundant Array of Inexpensive Disks controller).

The two principle reasons for the delayed adoption were the total cost of ownership and the challenges in change management. Radio-

Study Storage Cost (Log)

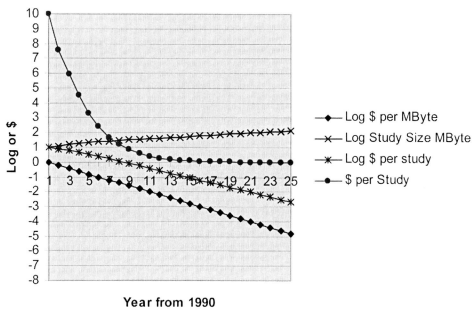

Figure 17–1.

logists were used to working in the film world and referring clinicians needed a simple but robust web solution for the enterprise outside of radiology. Certain care environments, such as the operating room, were particularly challenging.

There are still two competing technical architectures for PACS: the traditional client-server model, and a web or web-services model, as shown in Figure 17–2. A block diagram of traditional thick client PACS is on the left, versus web PACS on the right. These systems can exist alone, together but independently, or combined. For example, at UCSF the web PACS and thin web client is used for enterprise (clinician) access, but is populated as a destination from the thick client. At institutions where the web client is also the primary PACS (with dedicated radiologist workstations), such as SFVA and MD Anderson, the web PACS is populated directly from the modalities (dashed line). For redundancy, some, such as emergency department CT and digital radiography, or all imaging devices, could double send to both systems, depending on device and network speed. The client-server model works well for the Radiology department, but not for the large enterprise supporting thousands of secure and locked-down PC's. The web model works better for the enterprise, but still can be Windows/Apple asymmetric, require downloads and installations of small to large executables, and can be variable with regard to particular browsers. The web model also lends itself to easy EMR integration via Universal Resource Locater (URL) linkages to imaging studies and reports. Web clients tend to lack the sophisticated visualization tools and multi study, multi series viewing requirements of radiologists. The recent trend toward "zero" footprint web clients (no downloadable installed component) that are browser and platform agnostic is a huge step in the right direction.

For CT and MR intensive sections such as Neuroradiology and Abdominal Imaging, the conversion to PACS from film resulted in an estimated 50 percent improvement in radiologist efficiency. With improved workflow tools, particularly automated access to prior studies and reports, and navigation through large datasets, efficiency continues to improve, but at a slower rate. Some PACS are still challenged

Figure 17-2: Web versus Thick Client PACS

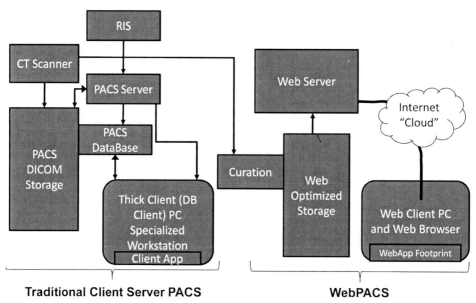

Figure 17–2.

by automated identification of relevant priors, particularly when the work list is driven by an integrated but separate voice recognition system, which is our typical workflow for resident readout by attending radiologist (Andriole et al., 2000).

From the beginning, we have been careful about proper demographic identification of patient studies by matching the incoming Digital Imaging and Communication in Medicine (DICOM) header demographics with pending orders. The four most common problems are misidentification because the technologist failed to properly close the immediate prior performed study on the device, picking the wrong patient from the DICOM Modality Work list, mistyping the medical record number on manual entry (manual entry is to be avoided whenever possible as a 15 percent error rate in ED environment at night has been documented), and wrong patient identification because the ID bracelet was not checked. For this last issue, we are in the process of installing automated barcode patient ID from the bracelet. A fifth problem area is portable CR in the ICU environment, with a stack of CR cassettes for a group of patients, brought to a CR device for input. This risk can be eliminated with portable DR units that complete the identity process at the bedside, but it is only cost-effective for high volume environments.

The vast majority of our workstations are of the 1-1.5K lateral resolution variety, i.e. conventional resolution monitors, and 2-2.5K monitors are reserved for high volume, plain chest and bone radiograph environments. When those studies occasionally need to be reviewed on the lower resolution workstations, magnify and roam tools work quite well, and we have had no resolution related complaints or incidents. We feel comfortable using carefully selected commercial (non-medical) grade mass market LCD monitors. We do look carefully at dynamic range and brightness. We have had no major issues using color monitors for gray scale display, and those can be advantageous for ultrasound and nuclear medicine display. For CT and MR, which are low spatial resolution images, commercial grade monitors are more than sufficient provided dynamic range is satisfactory. Bit depth of CT and MR is usually twelve, representing 4096 shades of gray, which requires good window level and width tools, and monitor dynamic range. Ultrasound can be as low as 8, representing 256 shades of gray, and is much less demanding.

Yet mammography presents even greater challenges with both image size and display monitor spatial resolution. Since we view at least two views of each breast compared to the same views on the previous examination, we need two monitors of at least five Megapixel resolution (2.5K to 2K in pixel resolution). Fortunately, dedicated PACS systems are available to address these requirements and these dedicated PACS systems can be properly interfaced with the general PACS. In a similar fashion, dedicated ultrasound PACS are also available to deal more effectively with the multiple video clips that are part of most modern ultrasound studies.

Interestingly, our biggest technical and change management challenges have been in the enterprise image distribution arena. It was surprisingly difficult to get rid of the last vestiges of film printing for our referring clinicians. Instead of listing all of the problems, I will describe our solutions. Most importantly, our solution had to be a web-based solution which was part of the department PACS, or well integrated to it. It needed to have sufficient time depth for access to relevant priors, and/or fast query capability back to PACS archive. It needed to contain or have instant access to reports on all studies. Ideally it should have a "zero footprint" for installation on the thousands of potential client machines. If not, the install package needed to be simple or automatic and coordinated with institutional IT. Ideally, it should run on any mainstream browser, and should not be limited to Microsoft Internet Explorer because of Active-X components. It needs to have "single sign-on" context management integration with EMR. It needs to be self-instructing – "rental car simple" to use – and must include patient and study navigation. We have deployed our enterprise solution in the operating room on large monitors, rather than our main PACS workstations, so it needs to have mission-critical reliability and uptime. More zero footprint applications are becoming available as this is written, which is promising. When configured as an extension of PACS from a different vendor, we have had issues with relay delay of studies for instant teleradiology coverage, transfer of conference work lists, and transfer of image markups (measurements, arrows, etc.). There are many different purchase/licensing cost models for enterprise web server access.

As an academic referral center, we receive a large number of studies from elsewhere daily (Lu et al., 2010). We bring foreign studies into our PACS even if they do not have a UCSF Medical Record Number, at least temporarily. If demographics are done carefully, we do not believe that there is any legal liability for importing these studies. On the contrary, we feel strongly that access to prior studies is good for patient care, and a positive role for Radiology to be the imaging advocate for the patient. We are asked to issue a second interpretation on about 10 percent of these studies. We are currently examining the professional economics of that practice, and it has been looked at elsewhere (Yousem, 2010). The cost of storage continues to decline faster than the increased size and volume of studies (Avrin, 2009). Figure 17–3 shows the trend of outside studies on PACS. The percentage of storage is steady at about 15 percent (lower line on graph), and the monthly burn or utilization rate has climbed to 200 GBytes per month at UCSF (solid square data points). Compared to the positive value to patient care, the cost is trivial.

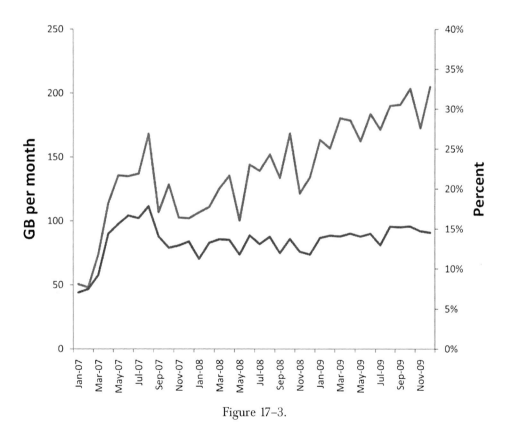

Figure 17–3.

Integration and Standards

The HIT world of the future will be one of multiple integrated systems rather than a single monolithic one. The principle two reasons are that a single system cannot capture the wide range of activities and data needs of a Radiology department; and that integrated systems allow the selection of "best of breed" component systems. Even the enthusiasm for combined RIS/PACS has waned, as is discussed below.

In order to integrate, standards are needed for data format or description, and message exchange or communication protocols. The two most common standards used in radiology today are DICOM (Digital Imaging and Communications in Medicine) and HL7 (Health Level Seven International, 2007). DICOM is used for movement of images and related data from imaging devices to PACS and from PACS to specialized visualization workstations and back. It is occasionally used for generic PACS workstations, but most vendors use more efficient (faster) transfer methods. DICOM does not require DICOM transfers within the boundaries of a single vendor system, which is why it is difficult to "mix and match" one vendor's workstations with another vendor's core servers. The DICOM standard is quite mature and unambiguous for data format and transfer between components of different vendors.

HL7 is used for patient demographics, registration, and ordering. It is also used for results reporting, conveying reports from VR/RIS to PACS and the Electronic Medical Record (EMR). It has a history and reputation of being unfortunately flexible and ambiguous in its implementation. The messages can be human interpreted as text, which aids in resolving problems. The newest version of HL7 implements XML data definitions and tags, which should improve its "standardization." HL7 is used to receive patient demographic information from the MPI and registration systems, receive orders, send reports, and send billing information back to the appropriate systems.

DICOM Modality Work list (MW) integrates the imaging modality computer with RIS through DICOM, enabling the display for technologist selection of scheduled patients and studies, avoiding the errors that frequently occur when typing demographics – names, medical records (MRN) and accession numbers.

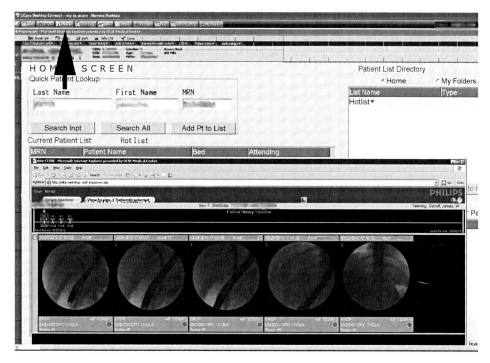

Figure 17–4.

Integration is crucial for successful deployment of PACS, CPOE/ ROE, linkage of Radiology reports and imaging studies to the EMR, and back end billing systems. Figure 17–4 demonstrates web PACS iSite on UCARE. At UCSF enterprise web PACS is integrated with the EMR remote desktop environment with single-sign-on user authentication, and patient context. Logging on to the EMR automatically provides access to web PACS, and when the web PACS tab (arrow) is clicked it automatically opens to the patient selected in the EMR. This is achieved through "context management," e.g., authenticated user (MD) and patient identity across systems.

Combined RIS/PACS

Because there was an overlap of data between RIS and PACS, specifically Patient ID and Exam History, several years ago there was a movement toward combined RIS/PACS. That movement seems to have abated, in favor of the "best-of-breed" approach combined with integration specifications that we have used at UCSF. Selection of IT systems always involves trade-offs, and weighing those becomes exceedingly complex with dual-purpose systems: for example an RIS/PACS may have an excellent enterprise-wide image distribution system but a poor scheduling module. Isolating the functionality makes it easier to evaluate trade-offs, outweighing the benefits of having a single common patient ID table.

Just as the RIS and PACS have been combined, so has the RIS and EMR. There are commercial EMRs that claim to have RIS modules and some of these systems offer a number of advantages. First of all, scheduling for patients can be across the enterprise, both on the inpatient side and for outpatients. Certainly such scheduling, if it includes Radiology along with other consultations and tests, can simplify the efforts of the referring physician as well as the patient.

The other portions of a modern RIS may be more difficult to find in an EMR, such as picking the proper protocol for patients' procedures or the management and interfaces with speech recognition systems, not to mention the close interface needed with the PACS in order to streamline the reading process.

CPOE/ROE

One of the most important new EMR IT developments is that of Computerized Physician/Provider Order Entry (CPOE), and more specifically Radiology Order Entry (ROE). These systems are being deployed in some institutions that have EMRs. One of the major benefits to Radiology is that they have the potential of providing more accurate clinically relevant reasons for ordering a study, and better tracking and communication back to the requestor. Some systems are integrated with online scheduling for providers or patients, once the order has been accepted.

ROE can exist within a CPOE, or be accessible by a link to an external system. This permits enhancement of the CPOE function specific to radiology. It also enables the addition of Decision Support Systems (DSS) (Health Level Seven International, 2007; Sistrom et al., 2009), which conduct an online instantaneous interaction with the ordering provider, regarding appropriateness for the given indication, based on a rules-set developed empirically or provided through the ACR Appropriateness Criteria, for example. Figure 17–5, demonstrates CPOE/ROE at the Brigham and Women's Hospital, where a

CPOE system is deployed. However when an order for an imaging study is initiated, the user is transferred seamlessly to an ROE system with built-in decision support (DSS) to insure that studies are only ordered for appropriate indications, based upon various guidelines. The recommendations can be over-ridden by the requesting physician, by clicking "Ignore" circled in the figure, and a dialog can occur with an on-call radiologist.

DSS implementation is controversial for several reasons. First, it has the potential to reduce high reimbursement imaging referrals. However, if it can substitute for the prior approval process or Radiology Benefit Management (RBM) companies, it could expedite appropriate referrals and decrease the use of resources to obtain approval. Furthermore, there is some rationale for the concerns of the federal government and Content Management System (CMS), the Medicare and Medicaid payer, that the large regional variation they see in their data at least suggests that some of these studies are unnecessary. It is better to be involved in the control process than have it inflicted upon us. It is consistent with cost-effective care and outcomes research.

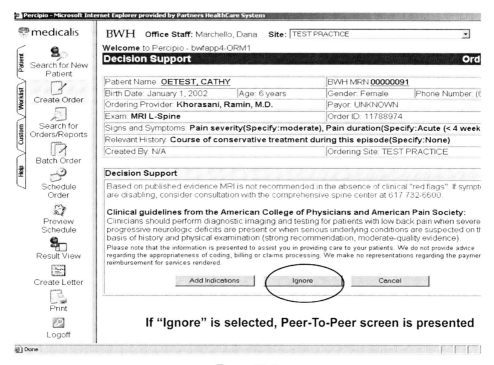

Figure 17–5.

Two independent, large development efforts at the two Harvard hospitals, Brigham and Women's (BW) and Massachusetts General (MGH), have demonstrated reduction in high-end imaging utilization (Sistrom et al., 2009). Both systems have been commercialized by Medicalis and Nuance respectively. They differ somewhat in style and philosophy. The MGH system appears to be quicker to navigate but gives less feedback or analysis, while the BW system acts as a more intelligent and informative partner in the process, providing details of the prior experience of the provider for the particular study in question. Acceptance by referring providers has been achieved over time with diplomacy.

DSS also exists for the interpretation process, ranging from Google to subscription vetted content systems such as STATdx (Amirsys, 2011).

Voice Recognition

Probably no other IT issue has captured as much attention and intensity as the debate about the appropriateness of voice or speech recognition (VR) software use. Historically voice recognition designated systems would identify the speaker, not transcribe speech. The advantages are clear: immediate transmission of reports to the care environment with the click of a mouse or a voice command such as "sign report." Several good systems are available in the marketplace, with varying degrees of integration to RIS and PACS.

The value of immediate availability of authorized reports is two-fold in the academic environment. First, the preliminary report issued by a trainee is instantly available to clinical decision makers. This involves Radiology intimately in the clinical process, without any transcription delay. Second, the quick availability of the final attending approved report at a median of less than seven hours is far better than our pre VR approximate twenty-four hour turnaround time. Simply put, our reports represent our intellectual added value as radiologists to the uninterpreted imaging study in the clinical care process. These shortened turnaround times at the time of diagnostic evaluation have been demonstrated to shorten hospital stay time, and thereby reduce the cost of care (Pezzullo et al., 2008).

The disadvantages are technical and philosophical. Technical problems include primarily accuracy and speed. Both have improved significantly, but still not as fast (for the radiologist user) or as accurately as an experienced radiology transcriptionist. Foreign accents have become less of a problem. The philosophical issues revolve around slightly decreased productivity, and performing a task (transcription substitution) for the medical center without any commensurate compensation. In our opinion, the immediate availability of reports with images trumps the opposition. The speed issue negatively affects efficiency, particularly of sections that perform a large number of plain radiograph interpretations, such as chest and bone. Accuracy issues require that the reports be read carefully before signing. Our median turnaround time from completion/interpretation to signing and release went from over twenty hours to less than seven hours after implementation (see Chapter 8).

Integration of VR and RIS

Even if the VR and RIS systems are from the same vendor, they are often separate components that require bidirectional integration to each other. Both systems also require integration to PACS, and in particular the VR integration needs to be bidirectional. This allows VR work lists and histories (e.g., reports "touched" or to be signed today) to drive the PACS to immediately display the images in the study of interest with a mouse click, and obviously to allow dictation of the new study on display, without entering a Medical Record Number or an accession number (unique procedure identifier in RIS).

Figure 17–6 demonstrates the VR system work list driving PACS. Similar to the EMR integration in Figure 17–4, it is useful to have bidirectional integration between PACS and VR. Forward direction efficiently insures that dictations belong to the patient and study on PACS, while the reverse direction allows the radiologist to open a study when reviewing reports. This is very helpful in an academic environment to review a list of pre-dictated reports by advanced residents, and see the associated image study. Unfortunately, in most vendor systems today, external work list selections do not trigger loading of relevant prior exams.

Templates and Structured Reports

The advent of speech recognition for reporting – using templates – has developed in parallel with increased interest in structured report-

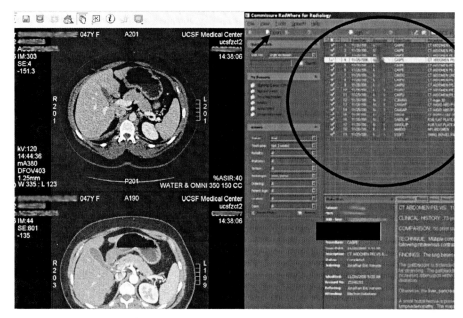

Figure 17–6.

ing. There is a natural symbiosis between these two trends. Some reported clinician surveys indicate that they prefer structured reports because of the standardization and predictability (Noumeir, 2006). They are also useful for backend data mining of the reports for findings, quality, etc. This is an area that will receive a lot of interest and scrutiny over the next few years.

In addition, use of newly available standardized structured report templates improves the efficiency of voice recognition, a partial example of which is shown in Figure 17–7. VR efficiency is improved with the use of templates when possible. RSNA has generated, through subspecialty experts, a set of templates freely downloadable by VR vendors or radiologists. They are available as standard text (shown) or xml encoded (Radiological Society of North America, 2011). The brackets indicate fields to be filled in by limited choice lists, dates, numbers, or free text.

Wet Read Module/Subacute Findings Notification

Years ago, one of our affiliated graduate students (Tellis & Andriole, 2005), developed a system to report preliminary interpretations by

FINDINGS:

Right kidney: [Unremarkable, no concerning cystic or solid mass lesions.*]

{Module for description and characterization of a renal mass. Replace default statement with the following description.}

Lesion: [none |solitary*] [ ]{add number for 2 or more}

- Location: Lesion centered in:[]
{Anterior/posterior/posteromedial/anteromedial/lateral}
{upper pole/mid/lower pole}

- Image location: series [#] image [#]

- Size: [# x # cm]

- Solid lesion enhancement: [Not applicable | homogeneous enhancement | heterogeneous enhancement] Hounsfield unit change from pre-contrast: [ ]

- Renal vein invasion: [present | not present]. Extent: [ ]

Figure 17–7.

radiology resident trainees to our Emergency Department, and record and track any discrepancy between the preliminary and final attending interpretation. This tool has been of tremendous benefit to our ED colleagues and now our ICU physicians, and to our internal assessment of our group and individual performance. The wet read module is fully and quite seamlessly integrated to our PACS by patient, exam, resident, and readout attending. This system is considered a quality assurance tool, and as such, in California, is protected from discovery by the California evidence code.

The module opens automatically with patient and exam context preloaded on the resident's workstation, as shown in Figure 17–8. The preliminary report is created via the VR system described above. This report text is copied into the wet-read module, and transmitted to the ED or ICU for after hour's cases. The preliminary report is also available in the EMR and on PACS. When the study is reviewed several hours later, the module opens automatically with the opening of the study on PACS, and the attending scores the wet-read as either no discrepancy, minor discrepancy, or major discrepancy in the module.

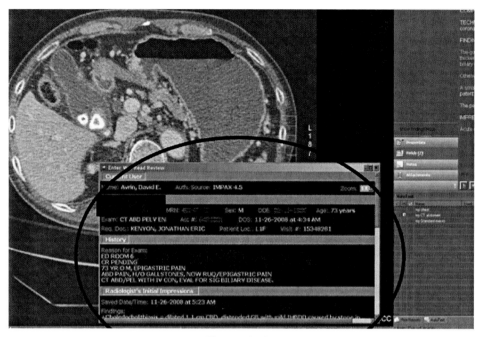

Figure 17–8.

Discrepancies are called to the appropriate unit and documented regarding time and name of contact. Data are reviewed annually. The wet-read module is the QA tool, and also provides a repository for the preliminary report upon which clinical decisions may have been based. In most EMRs, the preliminary report is overwritten by the final, so the wet-read module provides a way to persist the report version history. In an on-call environment, the preliminary wet read can be provided to the Emergency Department through PACS or other types of electronic communication, and is automatically displayed with the images, also facilitating attending review for accuracy and quality assurance.

A more recent area of increasing risk and therefore of great interest is the reporting, notification, and tracking of subcritical but significant findings, such as an eight millimeter lung nodule. We have found that the problem encompasses all of our three patient components: outpatient, ED, and inpatient. Oftentimes an imaging study will be ordered by a specialty physician who is not the patient's "primary" physician, and often the primary physician has no direct affiliation with our institution, and therefore no simple electronic communication pathway.

Identification of the correct physician most responsible for the patient's care remains a challenge, being addressed at UCSF by redesign
of the inpatient and outpatient admission questionnaire.

We have developed a system whereby the line of the report
IMPRESSION, which is the concluding section of the report, contain
the subcritical finding requiring follow-up which can be "tagged" by a
macro voice command in our voice dictation system. The entire report
stream is passed through a filter to detect these tags on a daily basis,
and those reports and related demographic information are inserted
into a database, ultimately merged with a better process for identifying primary or caring physicians. Appropriately trained personnel will
work through the entries in this database to provide direct notification
to the target clinician. Figure 17–9 demonstrates an actual log documenting the successful contact of someone at the primary care physician's office of an incidental finding that needs non-urgent follow-up,
such as a lung nodule. The database of course can be sorted or filtered
by date, patient name, physician name, etc.

An additional pathway may be to involve and inform the patient,
similar to Mammography Quality Standards Act regulations for mammography, that there is a finding that needs follow-up. Patient access
to images and reports is discussed below.

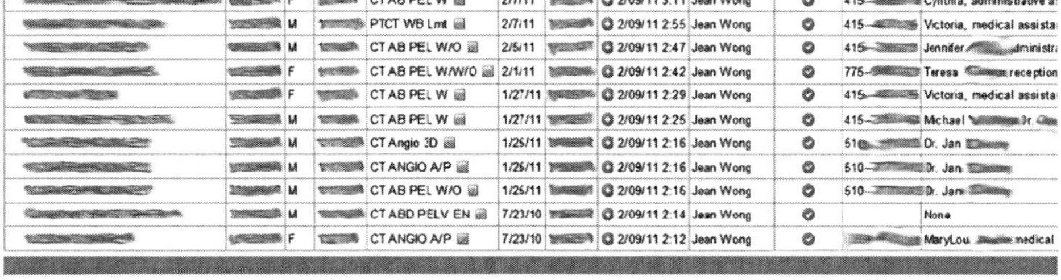

Figure 17–9.

Business Systems Integration

The RIS is the source of departmental billing information. At typical academic department rates of 1000 studies per day, it is essential that tight integration exists between the RIS and backend billing systems. As described in Chapter 5, billing systems may be departmental, institutional, medical practice, or contracted. Charges for imaging services contain two components: technical, for the equipment, overhead, personnel, and supplies; and professional, for interpretation, and procedure when appropriate. Except for department managed billing, procedures need to be in place to monitor the performance of the non-departmental billing service. Studies performed in an outpatient environment may be billed with a single combined technical and professional charge, of which a percentage is provided to the radiology practice.

One particular detail is worth mentioning as a problem to be avoided: Accession number linkage to the back end billing process. Most of our patients have multiple imaging studies. Unfortunately our billing system was patient and "visit" centric, but there was no direct linkage between the visit number and the RIS Accession number, which made it very difficult to audit for which studies we had been paid. It is essential that you have internal departmental tools to monitor the performance of an external billing service, whether it is on contract to the Radiology department, or provided by the academic group practice.

Unless an academic practice does its own billing, the business system integration needs to be monitored and managed. The most important parameter to verify is that the number of procedures billed equals the number performed. More detailed analysis must then be performed to verify that the exam types and various modifiers are correct. Next, traditional accounting measures such as aged accounts receivable (or number of days), need to be tracked. Thirty days is excellent performance, while sixty days is poor.

Non-recoverable billing (non-payment) is the next most important parameter. This segues into the difficult area of payer and contract analysis, which is beyond the scope of this chapter. However, it is the RIS data that provides the fuel for this essential business analytic activity. Analysis by a referring physician is also essential to detect changes in referral patterns that can be the first evidence of larger problems in your department.

Integration can also provide a tool to better manage the authorization referral problem.

Data Mining, Clinical and Business Intelligence

While our IT systems are designed primarily for "transactions" (e.g., schedule an exam on a patient, complete the exam, dictate/sign the report, etc.), these systems contain a wealth of data that can be used to manage our department better. Unfortunately, other than for some simple summaries on volume and time intervals, transactional systems are not very useful for analytics.

The past decade has witnessed the development of powerful data mining or "business intelligence" tools for the non-medical world. These tools from a variety of vendors can be put to use for business as well as quality data contained within our operational systems. We, and others, have found that the best way to maximize the information yield is to install a system where the various RIS, PACS, VR data is "rolled up" into a data "cube," which creates a mineable repository that can respond to many and varied queries. In order to accomplish this, the transactional data from the source systems has to be exported and transformed into a database format that lends itself to analysis. In a conceptual way, the dimensions on the edges of the multi-dimensional cube contain metrics that are key to understanding the functions of the department: obviously time, but also modality, specific imaging devices, inpatients vs. outpatients (patient type), locations, interpreting radiologists, technologists, referring clinicians, etc.

When properly configured, these systems can deliver standard as well as custom reports, or dashboards, and metrics known as key performance indicators (KPIs) of your choice and design. Some common KPIs include MR and CT volumes by patient category and location, referring physician metrics, and various payer analyses.

Figure 17–10 demonstrates, for example, pediatric CT extracted from our RIS. Other KPIs or dashboards monitor the volume of our outpatient CT and MR studies. This reporting and visualization tool extracts data from the RIS and optimizes it for analysis. The graph and data can be drilled down to expose the detail of individual studies, and accession number, which provides linkage to the patient, referring clinician, and even physician or patient zip code. Many commercial (we use AltoSoft™) and open-source tools are available for building a

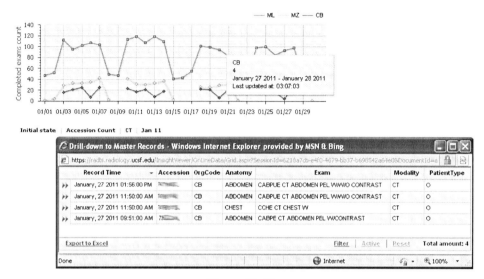

Figure 17–10.

data warehouse and optimizing analytics and the generation of KPIs.

Dr. Reuben Mezrich at Maryland, and his former informatics director Paul Nagy, Ph.D. make a convincing case that "you can't manage what you can't measure" (Deming, 2009; Nagy & Mezrich, 2007). The goal is to have data driven strategic and tactical discussions, decisions, and actions by the department leadership team.

EDUCATIONAL SYSTEMS

Teaching file

One of the early and enduring benefits of PACS for the academic department is that it truly enables computer-based education (Arenson, 1996). In order to capitalize on that benefit, it is essential to maintain a digital repository of cases of high interest, for education and research. To be successful, it is also essential that it be tightly integrated to PACS on the input side so that it can be populated at the time of readout. In our experience, the percentage of capture of interesting cases is related to the ease of entry. Writing down medical record numbers or study accession numbers on a scrap of paper and hoping to enter the case and capture the images is highly unlikely. It is also important that the collection of associated information be easily accessible. Security, HIPAA (Health Insurance Portability and Accountability Act of 1996) compliance and/or anonymization are required.

As shown in Figure 17–11, the front end user interface (on the left) is tightly integrated to PACS, preloading all demographic and study information automatically. The only requirement is creation of a summary series, and selection of at least one anatomic and pathologic code, as shown, which can be edited later. Multiple differential diagnoses are supported, as are key words – ultimately automatic inclusion of the actual report – and the name of the contributor, all of which can be queried remotely and securely. Images can be dragged and dropped into PowerPoint for presentations. A list of studies can also be generated and the images displayed as unknowns.

The DICOM header contains eighteen items of Protected Health Information (PHI), including the patient's name, date of birth, medical record number, etc. (www.research.ucsf.edu). These items are listed in Table 17–2.

One additional requirement is that a presumed or verified pathological diagnosis/code must be associated with every case (RadLex terms from the RSNA should be used for this), or the collection

UCSF TF

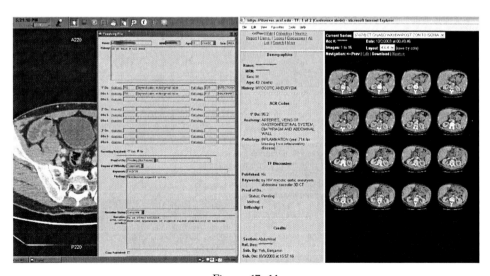

Figure 17–11.

Table 17–2.
HIPAA–PHI (Protected Health Information): LIST OF EIGHTEEN IDENTIFIERS

1. Names;
2. Address: All geographical subdivisions smaller than a State, unless the zip code has more than 20,000 people, then first three digits of zip code if aggregate of all such zip codes contains more than 20,000 people.
3. All elements of dates (except year) for dates directly related to an individual, including birth date, admission date, discharge date, date of death
4. Phone numbers;
5. Fax numbers;
6. Electronic mail addresses;
7. Social Security numbers;
8. Medical record numbers;
9. Health plan beneficiary numbers;
10. Account numbers;
11. Certificate/license numbers;
12. Vehicle identifiers and serial numbers, including license plate numbers;
13. Device identifiers and serial numbers;
14. Web Universal Resource Locators (URLs);
15. Internet Protocol (IP) address numbers;
16. Biometric identifiers, including finger and voice prints;
17. Full face photographic images and any comparable images; and
18. Any other unique identifying number, characteristic, or code (note this does not mean the unique code assigned by the investigator to code the data).

(From UCSF) Reference above

becomes unsearchable and useless. A system such as this is highly preferable to a hierarchical set of folders containing images.

We created such a system thirteen years ago, with the cooperation of our PACS vendor to accomplish the tight integration. It now contains approximately 60,000 cases with over two million images, and is the source of virtually all of the visual academic output of the department.

With the markedly reduced cost of storage enabling a trend toward "all-spinning" RAID current and historical clinical storage, it is now more feasible to consider "tagging" studies in the clinical PACS as having academic value, since one of the major challenges a decade ago was to have the academic collection rapidly accessible for visual browsing. However, we still believe that a separate but integrated solution is preferable because it can be made a richer resource than PACS tagging.

An excellent alternative to a "homegrown" system is the Medical Imaging Resource Center (MIRC) which offers free and open source software available through RSNA. However, integration with PACS, even with the creation of the IHE Teaching and Clinical Trial Export (TCE) profile has proven to be a difficult business, but not a technical challenge. The TCE profile provides PACS vendors with an integration tool to create and send a manifest or list of key image objects to a TCE compliant server. This server can then perform a DICOM request of the images in the manifest for automated and integrated input to the local MIRC server and database. It is hoped that more, and eventually all, PACS vendors will support these efforts for the future benefit of our profession and our trainees.

Report Mining

Closely related to the interesting case repository is the need for an ability to mine the text of reports for various purposes. The reports of the vast majority, if not all the academic departments, are held within database systems, either the RIS or a separate report database. In addition to fields associated with the report, which can be easily queried – such as MRN, accession number, date of exam, exam code, ICD–9 code etc. – one or more large text fields contains the narrative of the findings and impression. Technology known as Natural Language Processing (NLP) (www.amia.org) exists that enables the mining of those text fields for words, synonyms, or phrases. One of the largest challenges in NLP is the handling of negatives such as "no evidence of intracranial hemorrhage" in a search for cases with intracranial hemorrhage, for example.

Figure 17–12 is an example of the output of our UCSF built (using open source tools) NLP report searching application for "tension pneumothorax." Reports and images are available by selecting the case of interest.

Sistrom and Dreyer (Sistrom et al., 2009) et al. used NLP to report on the frequency of radiologist recommendations for follow-up imaging. Most of the work at our institution has focused on the retrieval of cases for teaching or research (e.g., a cohort of patients with similar findings or radiological diagnosis).

It is clear that NLP is useful for both the academic as well as the quality, safety, and management efforts of the department. Years ago we had a very popular internally crafted solution that could search through the text of hundreds of thousands of reports in less than one

Search Parameters

Keywords:	tension pneumothorax		Submit
Section:	Entire Report	▾	
Sex:	Any	▾	
Age:	Any ▾	0 Year(s) ▾	
Exam Date:		to	
Modality:	☐An ☐CR ☐CT ☐da ☐DR ☐DS ☐DX ☐FL ☐li ☐MG ☐mo ☐MR ☐f		

Displaying results **1 through 10** of 500 matches returned in 8.1 seconds **Download**

CT CHEST UNENH - (08-16-2006) [100] ☐
pneumothorax and bronchopleural fistula. FINDINGS: A large **tension pneumothorax** is identified on the right...
Demographics: 56 year old female
View Images (Requires V6)

ABSCESS DRAIN, - (03-28-2008) [67] ☐
tension pneumothorax. IMPRESSION: Moderate right-sided **pneumothorax** under **tension**. Evacuation by placement of a 12 French...
Demographics: 36 year old female
View Images (Requires V6)

CHEST, 1 VIEW - (12-05-2005) [58] ☐
tension pneumothorax. The cardiac silhouette is not enlarged. The comparison study demonstrated diffuse pulmonary...
Demographics: 3 day old female
View Images (Requires V6)

CHEST, 1 VIEW - (04-08-2005) [58] ☐
tension pneumothorax. IMPRESSION: The endotracheal tube tip is located between carina and thoracic

Figure 17–12.

minute (Ramaswamy et al., 1996). Unfortunately, that particular piece of software could not be maintained when the faculty developer left. We and many others are attempting to create similar search capabilities, and at least three commercial products exist that use NLP in radiology, and one even provides a direct mouse-click link to studies and images of the identified report (SofTek Illuminate™), when integrated with our web PACS (Philips iSite™).

As the practice of radiology becomes increasingly IT intensive, radiologists need a unified language for analysis and retrieval. Many terminologies have existed in the past, from various sources. RadLex, from the RSNA is a single unified source of radiology that is designed to fill this need (Radiological Society of North America, 2011).

Many of the benefits of clinical information technology cannot be realized unless information is stored using standard terms in a structured format. Unfortunately, almost all radiology reports are stored as text narratives rather than in a structured format, thereby hampering radiologists' ability to participate in the ongoing changes in our healthcare system, which are increasingly driven by information technology.

The RadLex project is sponsored by the RSNA, which has enlisted the collaboration of other radiology organizations, including the American College of Radiology (ACR), to develop a comprehensive radiology lexicon. It has been designed to satisfy the needs of software developers, system vendors, and radiology users by adopting the best features of existing terminology systems, while producing new terms to fill critical gaps. RadLex also provides a comprehensive and technology-friendly replacement for the ACR Index for Radiological Diagnoses. Rather than "reinventing the wheel," RadLex unifies and supplements other lexicons and standards, such as SNOMED-CT, and DICOM.

RESEARCH SYSTEMS

RRCS Recharge

In order to provide the IT infrastructure for our extensive academic and research missions, we maintain an internal two-team support service: academic and research computing systems. While it is possible that the academic PC support crew could be well served in some institutions by similar resources from the school of medicine, we prefer our independence and try to provide these services economically.

On the research side, particularly with the server and storage technical complexities, combined with increased vigilance regarding security and HIPAA protection of PHI, a dedicated department team is essential. One of the principle operating goals is to eliminate redundant and inefficient efforts by focusing the responsibilities on a highly capable crew, rather than having each individual research team duplicate that effort in ways that have variable quality. Furthermore, the network and system security requirements properly imposed upon us by the institution require this approach. Only our trusted team members have administrative access to research servers. We have also aggregated storage into central RAID devices.

We recently redesigned our recharge system for connection to our departmental networks and use of storage (and backup). We have a two-tiered system that more accurately reflects actual usage of resources, both equipment and personnel, and have revised that system in response to faculty comments.

Research PACS

Internal research as well as collaboration with colleagues from other departments on image-based projects is resulting in increasing demand for "Research PACS" capabilities. We have retained a small but skillful team to address these various needs using open-source software and "virtualized" server systems. The source of the imaging data may be from our clinical PACS or outside sources, even animal data, and may or may not need to be anonymized. We believe that this is an important service and resource for our institution, and as such have developed a recharge account to support it. We are attempting to transition it into a recognized research "core" service of the institution. One of our key goals is to support "quantitative" imaging (e.g., serial tumor size, comparison of agents, etc.).

OTHER IT SYSTEMS AND ISSUES

Departmental Website and Patient Access

We maintain and have recently redesigned our department website. In this era, this portal represents your vision to the outside world: potential patients, residents applicants, future faculty, etc. It is divided into sections on patient care, education, and research, and has external publicly accessible content as well as internal content restricted to UCSF staff onsite or through a virtual private network (VPN) login.

A new issue with the advent of patient portals and patient controlled record repositories is that of web access to patients for reports and images. Some institutions such as Memorial Sloan-Kettering have taken steps in that direction, provided the impression or summary report, as well as access to images. We plan to have a patient portal to our new EMR, and are analyzing the various options for patient access to medical imaging.

Two controversies surround patient access to their imaging studies and reports. First, some referring clinicians want to be in the initial communication loop with their patients regarding studies that may have significant implications. Clinicians have some concerns that they will lose control of their patients, which is probably an overreaction. Second, in spite of the trend toward and interest in patient-centered care, many patients will have difficulty understanding radiology reports, and perhaps more importantly, the implications. Who will be available to answer the many questions that arise, and relieve anxiety? Most departments are not prepared to do that.

Academic Personnel Systems and Physician Scheduling

As described above, we are able to track the clinical productivity of our faculty, but have been challenged to relate output to clinical time effort. Our faculty receives significant academic time to support the department missions, and therefore have variable clinical efforts. We are finishing the development of a scheduling and tracking system to support academically flexible scheduling but that assures clinical coverage with radiologists of the needed skillset, and tracks the amount of clinical time on service as well as research time.

Figure 17–13 demonstrates actual input dialog for our new faculty scheduling system. It automatically checks conflicts with requested time off or research days, prevents double scheduling of conflicting

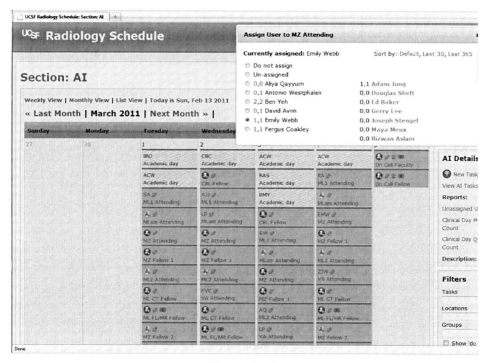

Figure 17–13.

tasks, and "red-flags" unassigned tasks. It provides summary statistics of clinical, research, meeting, and vacation time. Finally, it publishes individual assignments out to Exchange Calendar. The one and only true source of accurate, up-to-date information is on the web-accessible server, or Exchange calendar for individual faculty.

A few institutions have also developed computer-based faculty evaluation systems that combine clinical, academic, and service productivity by a scoring system (Mezrich & Nagy, 2007).

Safe Practices: Back-up and Redundancy

It is clear that an academic Radiology department maintains many mission-critical systems for itself and the parent institutions. The last decade has seen progressive emphasis on security and privacy, which are related but separate. Management and the Radiology IT team need to understand the unique demands of each.

Besides being safe stewards of patient and research data, departments and institutions have become increasingly concerned about clinical and business "continuity" and protection from interruptions, which goes far beyond offsite back-up, for example. Redundancy is expensive and complicated – beyond the scope of this book – but needs to be well planned, budgeted, implemented, and tested. RIS, PACS, reporting, research, education, and the entire portfolio with a measured effort that matches the time requirement for continuity, is necessary.

The most fundamental responsibility is to safeguard the digital imaging portion of the legal medical record. Historically, for comparison, usually only a single film copy of studies was kept, subject to fire, loss, and "missing in action." In the film era, at any point in time, 15–20 percent of requested prior studies could not be located immediately, and never for a significant number (Vega, 2011).

Digital back-up can be accomplished in three ways. If an enterprise business continuity solution exists, this can be expanded to duplicate RAID at a separate physical location. Each RAID has its own internal mechanism for fault tolerance or protection against single disk failures, so this represents double redundancy for everything except a catastrophic event such as a fire or flood. For adults, studies must be maintained for seven years, for children up to twenty-eight years, and essentially forever for mammography. Therefore this is a somewhat expensive solution, although the price of RAID storage continues to decrease faster than the increase in study size. If done in conjunction with business continuity, some of the cost can be shared with or assigned to that business objective.

Alternatively, newly acquired data can be copied continuously in chronological order to back-up tapes, which are then transported to an offsite storage facility. This is probably the most cost-effective solution, but obviously does not help with true business continuity. Finally, there are commercial services affiliated or unaffiliated with specific PACS vendors that provide offsite RAID or tape storage over a network connection on a fee schedule. This avoids the physical creation and transport of tapes. Each department and medical center needs to determine the best solution for their environment.

Management and Staffing: Department vs. Institution

One of the most difficult and important decisions, which may have been made years before the arrival of a new chairman, is the ownership of radiology systems: department versus institution. And those departments that manage their own RIS, PACS, and networks are under increasing pressure to turn over those systems to hospital IT or some similar entity.

We have been very successful at making the argument and have continued to manage our own systems, largely because of the quality of our performance. There is a lot of "domain knowledge" in radiology, and no one cares as much about quality of performance, workflow, and reliability as the chairman and his/her leadership team. Our RIS server hardware is in the hospital IT data center and maintained by them, but managed and configured by our departmental IT team.

Many hospitals, such as the University of Utah, want to consolidate all patient data and security, and medical imaging is the 900 pound gorilla. PACS servers can be housed in hospital IT data centers, but it is best that the configuration and management – apart from basic maintenance – be by Radiology personnel.

Because of the geographic dispersion of the UCSF imaging facilities, we have a mixed network configuration. The majority of modalities, PACS servers, and main department workstations are on a dedicated and isolated network that we maintain with no direct access to the internet. However, some modalities and workstations are in locations that are serviced by the hospital IT or academic institutional network, and quality of service has been a challenge at times, particularly related to security protocols.

Personnel

As you can see from the inventory above, the successful and cutting-edge academic department requires a significant IT investment and infrastructure. It is particularly important to have "the right people on the bus." This requires the correct mix of skillsets – network, security, server savvy personnel, database, and RIS personnel with medical and radiology domain expertise, interface experts, people knowledgeable about back-up, redundancy, business continuity, business intelligence types, creative web-masters, and innovative programmers for unique in-house projects.

Besides needing the skillset described above the team needs to be as compact, and cost-efficient as possible to stand up to external management scrutiny. And they need to be highly competent and motivated.

We are fortunate to have a wonderful crew, not by accident.

Meaningful Use

The Obama administration views HIT as one of the key tools in managing the cost of care, appropriateness, and outcomes (Blumenthal, 2009). Upon coming into office, the new administration first successfully promoted a bill to increase the individual penalty on each event of improper disclosure of PHI significantly to $50,000 per occurrence (maximum of $1.5 million per year) to convince the privacy lobby that they were serious about HIT and protecting patients' sensitive information (American Medical Association, 2009).

Next, coincident with a major funding effort in 2009 through CMS, the Obama administration promulgated a concept of "meaningful use." CMS would provide incentives for investment in HIT systems that satisfied an evolving set of rules for demonstration of meaningful use. Over the next few years, these incentives will turn into penalties for non-adopters (Khorasani, 2010).

Two groups can qualify for these incentives: institutions, and eligible providers. When first drafted, very little of the meaningful use guidelines impinged upon radiology, leaving Radiology "out in the cold." Through efforts of our major national radiology organizations, refinement of the meaningful use guidelines will impact radiology.

That being said, however, academic departments practice within large institutions, and radiology – even with PACS and RIS – will only have a minor impact on the ability of an institution to qualify for the meaningful use incentives. ROE/CPOE is perhaps the best opportunity, combined with outcomes research, to convincingly demonstrate true meaningful use. The initial set of rules has been modified to now make it easier and hopefully possible for a radiology practice, including academic practices, that have a significant outpatient practice to qualify for the substantial incentive payments (up to $44,000 per practitioner) and avoid potential penalties in future years. It is important for you to work with your RIS, PACS, VR, and CPOE/ROE vendors to ensure that they are each on the path to become "certified" systems, under the regulations. Then you can document your use of these systems according to the guidelines to qualify for the meaningful use incentive payments.

CONCLUSION

We acknowledge that UCSF is somewhat unique in having a chairman with an undergraduate degree in applied math, who developed software for IBM while attending medical school, and who was instrumental in creating the benchmark RIS, and believed in the connection between clinical PACS and the educational and research missions.

Table 17–1 is a list of all of the systems we have deployed at UCSF to meet the IT challenges of all four missions: Clinical Care, Education, Research, and Administration.

So what is a new chair to do to properly manage and ideally capitalize on informatics for his or her department? Even if one has the skillset, one may well not have the time to manage this part of the portfolio. Therefore it is essential to identify or recruit a suitable faculty member as the Vice Chair for Informatics. The Vice Chair level is important to identify the activities described in this chapter as the lifeblood and the pulse of the academic department.

In the absence of film, card files, darkrooms, wet processors, and film printers, these systems are mission-critical to the minute-by-minute activity of the department. Choice of systems, of vendor-partners, specification of integration requirements, maintenance of security, etc., requires a focused team and accountability. Success or failure in this arena will be reflected in the success or failure of your clinical, educational, and research missions.

REFERENCES

American Medical Association. (2011). Act of Congress: 42 USC § 1320d-5. Accessed February 5. http://www.ama-assn.org/ama/pub/physician-resources/solutions-managing -your-practice/coding-billing-insurance/hipaahealth-insurance-portability-accountability-act/hipaa-violations-enforcement.shtml.

American Medical Informatics Association. (2008). NLP. Accessed February 18. https:// www.amia.org/working-group/natural-language-processing.

Amirsys. (2011). Accessed February 5. http://www.amirsys.com.

Andriole, K. P., Avrin, D. E., Yin, L., Gould, R. G., & Arenson, R. L. (2000). PACS databases and enrichment of the folder manager concept. *Journal of Digital Imaging,* Vol. 13 (No. 1): 3–12.

Arenson, R. L. (1984). Automation of the radiology management function. *Radiology, 153*: 65–68.

Arenson, R. L. (1986). Teaching with computers. *RCNA,* (24) 1: 97–103.

Arenson, R. L., Gitlin, N. N., London, J. W., et al. (1982). The formation of a radiology computer consortium. Proceedings of the Seventh Conference on Computer Applications in Radiology, Chicago. *The American College of Radiology*: 153–164.

Avrin, D. (2009). Samuel Dwyer, III memorial lecture: Storage model. SIIM Annual Meeting. Charlotte, NC.

Blumenthal, D. (2010). Launching HITECH. The New England Journal of Medicine. Accessed February 18. http://www.nejm.org/doi/pdf/10.1056/NE-JMp0901592.

Deming, E. W. (2009). Curious Cat Management Improvement Connections. Manage what you can't measure. Accessed February 23. http://curiouscat.com/-deming/managewhatyoucantmeasure.cfm.

Digital Imaging and Communications in Medicine. Accessed February 18. http:// medical.nema.org/.

Dwyer, S. J. (1996). Imaging system architectures for picture archiving and communication systems. *Radiology of Clinical North America, 34*: 495–503.

Health Level Seven International. (2007). Accessed February 18. http://www.h-l7.org/about.

Horii, S. C. (1996). Image acquisitions. Sites, technologies, and approaches. *Radiology of Clinical North America, 34*: 469–494.

Khorasani, R. (2010). Can radiology professional society guidelines be converted to effective decision support? *Journal of American College Radiology, 7*: 561–562.

Khorasani, R. (2010). Health care reform through meaningful use of health care IT: Implications for radiologists. *Journal of American College Radiology, 7*: 152–153.

Lu M. T., Tellis, W. M., & Avrin, D. E. (2010). Three year experience importing outside hospital imaging to PACS: Utilization, storage, and formal reinterpretation. 96th Scientific Assembly and Annual Meeting of the RSNA, Chicago.

Mezrich, R., & Nagy, P. (2007). The academic RVU: A system for measuring academic productivity. *Journal of American College Radiology, 4*: 471–478.

Noumeir, R. (2006). Benefits of the DICOM structured report. *Journal of Digital Imaging, 19*: 295–306.

Pezzullo, J. A., Tung, G. A., et al. (2008). Voice recognition dictation: Radiologist as transcriptionist. *Journal of Digital Imaging, 21*: 384–389.

Radiological Society of North America. (2011). RadLex. Accessed February 18. http:// www.rsna.org/radlex/.

Radiological Society of North America. (2011). Reporting templates. Accessed February 18. http://www.rsna.org/informatics/radreports.cfm.

Ramaswamy, M. R., Patterson, D. S., et al. (1996). MoSearch: A radiologist-friendly tool for finding-based diagnostic report and image retrieval. *Radiographics, 16*: 923–933.

Sistrom, C. L., Dreyer, K. L., et al. (2009). Recommendations for additional imaging in radiology reports: Multifactorial analysis of 5.9 million examinations. *Radiology, 253*: 453–461.

Sistrom, C. L., Dang, P. A., et al. (2009). Effect of computerized order entry with integrated decision support on the growth of outpatient procedure volumes: Seven year time series analysis. *Radiology, 251*: 147–155.

Tellis, W. M., & Andriole, K. P. (2005). Integrating multiple clinical formation systems using the Java message service framework to enable the delivery of urgent exam results at the point of care. *Journal of Digital Imaging, 18*: 316–325.

UC Regents. (2003). PHI List. Accessed February 18. http://www.research.ucsf.edu/ chr/HIPAA/chrHIPAAphi.asp.

Vega, S., personal communication. 2011.

Yousem, D. (2010). Second opinion consultations. *The Outside Film Service*.

Chapter 18

LEADERSHIP DEVELOPMENT AND SUCCESSION PLANNING

One of our major concerns is the future of the department. We have all worked very hard at building a great department but we are concerned about sustaining that development and continuing to build upon it. Since the major strength of all departments is the people, both faculty and staff, we need to focus on them. What happens when we retire? What happens when some of our superstars get recruited to lead other departments or schools? How do we train the next generation of section chiefs, vice chairs, chairs, etc.? We need serious leadership development and succession planning.

Let's first define leadership. Wiktionary.org defines leadership as follows:

1. "The ability of an individual to influence, motivate, and enable others to contribute toward the effectiveness and success of the organizations of which they are members"
2. "One who, or that which, leads or conducts; a guide; a conductor. Especially:
   (a) One who goes first
   (b) One having authority to direct; a chief; a commander"

"True leadership only exists if people follow when they have the freedom not to" and "Holding a gun to someone's head will get results, but that is not leadership." These quotes are from Jim Collins who not only has written several books like *Good to Great* but also maintains a website, www.jimcollins.com. We encourage you to visit this website.

Putting these thoughts together, one can imagine a general leading his army on horseback toward the enemy line. The general is in front and his courage inspires his troops to follow. But we are talking about a less dramatic leader, the level five leader in *Good to Great*. The age-old debate continues about natural abilities of a leader versus what is learned. We believe a combination of personality traits, intelligence, interpersonal skills and management skills, both natural and learned, make real leaders as we know them.

We believe that the following characteristics which are borrowed from Jim Collins in *Good to Great* and from Daniel Goleman in *Emotional Intelligence* are critical to a leader's success:

- Level five characteristics: humility, putting the organization first, focusing on the right people, being rigorous, not ruthless, being disciplined, being passionate, and embracing the hedgehog concept
- Emotional Intelligence requires; gut sense, self-confidence, self-control, trustworthiness, flexibility, high standards, initiative, optimism, empathy, nurturing, maturity, motivation, and vision

As we are recruiting for leadership positions, we believe these make up the list of traits that we should look for. Now we will begin a discussion of some more concrete efforts at building leadership skills particularly in faculty, assuming we have chosen the right ones in the first place.

SECTION CHIEF LEADERSHIP

One way to develop leadership qualities in promising faculty is to have them take a shot at a section chief position. Of course, that is not possible if someone has that job for life. We started reviewing section chiefs recently and have written job descriptions detailing expectations for all of the more recent appointments. As part of our review, we hope to make it clear that five-year terms, which are renewable, are not expected to go on forever and we hope to give different faculty a chance to show their leadership qualities.

Some of our expectations of section chiefs, many of which we have put in job descriptions, include:

1. Hold regular section meetings and make sure faculty are informed of policy changes and critical decisions.
2. Conduct an annual section review and assess the entire section's academic and clinical productivity.
3. Regularly review RVU reports and other metrics and become knowledgeable regarding key clinical issues.
4. Maintain good relationships with clinical collaborators and referring clinicians.
5. Foster an attitude of customer service particularly as it relates to reading room behavior.
6. Be a model of outstanding radiologic skills and work ethic.
7. Oversee the education program in the section for residents, fellows, and medical students. If the fellowship is ACGME accredited, meet their standards.
8. Manage section finances: profits and losses, travel, and other expenses.
9. Support the academic development and advancement of junior faculty.
10. Encourage research projects in the section.
11. Manage section personnel (techs, RNs, administrative assistants, and clerks).
12. Participate in leadership in the department (Executive Committee and other committees as needed) as well as in the School of Medicine, the university and the medical center.
13. Be or become a recognized leader nationally in subspecialty area.
14. Maintain a high standard of professionalism throughout the section.
15. Lead recruitment of new faculty when open positions occur.

Leadership Courses

At the same time, we have started a series of workshops – described below – with our section chiefs to build their leadership skills, and we encourage them to take advantage of courses offered by SCARD, RSNA and the AUR on leadership. A list of RSNA/AUR/APDR/SCARD leadership courses can be found at http://www.raas1.org/. We firmly believe that although there are innate qualities of leadership, much can be learned, such as what you are currently doing by reading this book.

Seminars for Section Leaders

This series is a faculty development program for the more senior faculty. The goal of this program is to enhance the leadership skills of the faculty who have been appointed to leadership positions. This monthly meeting of Section Leaders is co-chaired by the Vice Chair for Academic Affairs and the Vice Chair for the VAMC. The group gathers for a one and a half hour free-form discussion of a variety of topics dealing with leadership. Some examples of the topics are listed below. Generally, the discussion is confidential in order to allow everyone to speak as freely as possible. This encourages the sharing of experiences so that new section leaders learn from those who are more experienced. The Co-Chairs prepare at least one "take home" lesson for each topic. Occasionally, the group invites a guest speaker who is an expert in a specific topic such as "conflict resolution" or "administration and finance." Attendance is voluntary but has been extremely high (averaging 90% with absences almost always related to out of town travel).

Topics discussed in 2010:

- Conflict: Tips for Dealing With It
- Professionalism: What Is It?
- How To Run a Service Oriented Section
- Administrative Pitfalls: How to Avoid Them
- How to Motivate the Unmotivated
- Understanding your Profit and Loss Statement
- Leadership in Dealing With Harassment (General and Sexual)
- New Clinical Fellows: Pitfalls and Tips
- Difficult Conversations
- Administrative Tips

The Medical School also offers some courses such as "Faculty Development Workshop for Division/Section Chiefs and Program Leaders" and we strongly encourage our Section Chiefs to participate.

Picking Likely Successors

Obviously, we need to select candidates for upcoming leadership positions carefully. We attempt to identify promising individuals and we attempt to groom them for the positions we have targeted. In this fashion, we are not caught off guard too much when someone decides to leave or when we decide to replace someone who has been serving as a section chief or as a vice chair for a while. And when we are recruiting new faculty or staff, we always look for leadership potential and we keep succession in mind.

For small sections with only two or three faculty in the section, such rotation of the chief can be difficult. It can be awkward to replace the section leader of a two to three person section with one of the other members. Because there are many other leadership roles in the department, the medical school and the university, we have been able to find strong and necessary positions for former section chiefs in smaller sections in order to promote or give an opportunity to a more junior person. Encouraging and recommending faculty to serve on committees is not only important for the academic advancement, it also allows these individuals to develop interpersonal skills and eventually leadership skills as they become committee chairs and fill other positions. By maintaining a list of our faculty and the committees they serve on, we can constantly look for opportunities for advancement and more experience.

FACULTY RETREATS

As mentioned in Chapter 15, faculty retreats can be very useful to reach general consensus among the faculty about contentious issues. These retreats are probably most constructive when selected topics are chosen (somehow the faculty should have the opportunity to suggest these topics). For the selected topics, in advance of the retreat, a committee or multiple committees of the faculty need to be established to draft white papers for discussion at the retreat. And some kind of follow-up is required to make sure the results of the retreat are not only well documented but needed change actually occurs. These retreats can be very constructive to steer the opinions of the faculty in new, difficult directions and can often be used to garner support for new concepts that would otherwise not be well received. Remember that change is always difficult, especially when everyone is complacent with the status quo.

Who should lead the retreat? The answer depends on the topic to be discussed. The chair should only lead the retreat if the key leaders in the department will support his/her opinion and when there is already strong support for the positions they will take. Otherwise, it is probably best that other leaders in the department take the lead and the chair can simply observe and comment periodically, if necessary. Obviously, this approach requires that other well respected leaders in the department are willing to stand up and lead the discussion in the direction desired.

As you can tell from the previous discussion, we do not think retreats should be a free-for-all and need to be structured carefully to achieve the desired results. The real debate and exploration of new ideas should occur in the smaller group meetings that may lead up to the final retreat.

The best retreats are probably off-campus and most likely held on a weekend to avoid the rush of clinical work during the week. The more relaxed the faculty can be, the better. Sometimes small group sessions can be used to tackle specific questions but these need to be structured as already described. The small groups could be formed in advance of the retreat and actually come prepared with draft reports. Such an approach assures progress and usually advances the discussion and conclusions. Sometimes different members of the faculty can be grouped together during the retreat in order to mix the faculty so that dominant individuals do not capitalize all of the discussion. Choosing who is in each group is obviously quite important.

The retreat should have specific goals and these should be rather focused so that the discussions can be fruitful. And if multiple small groups are used, one individual from each group should report for the group to the retreat participants as a whole.

It is essential to include the key staff members of the department. Not only can they bring valuable information and ideas to the table but their inclusion solidifies their roles in the department.

Chapter 19

STRATEGIC PLANNING AND
SCENARIO PLANNING

Faculty retreats might be used for strategic planning for the department. However, there are a variety of ways to conduct strategic planning. Why do it at all? Is it important? The department's missions are clear: excellence in patient care, education, and research. Although everyone probably knows the missions of the department, many faculty may not know how essential they are to the success in each of those areas. They may be more committed to their individual career goals and their own success, especially financial, that they lose sight of the department's interests. The department is really a team effort and everyone on the team must work in harmony with the others. Strategic planning can help galvanize the faculty to focus together on the important tasks for the department to advance in its missions.

Let's say that the department needs to make strategic investments in new PhD scientists and to purchase and install new research equipment. If the faculty does not understand the importance of the NIH rankings or the Dean's perspective of the value of the department to the school, their long-term interests may not be met. Through a strategic planning process, the clinical faculty should become convinced of the wisdom of such investments. Likewise, the importance of involvement of the faculty in recruiting resident applicants may not be high on some faculty's priority lists. Putting on the full-court press during the interviews could make the difference between a mediocre class and an outstanding one. Strategic planning could support such a message.

Or if investments in outpatient imaging centers seem like a way of assuring the future finances for the department, getting everyone onboard is important. Before you can divert large sums of hard-earned clinical revenue to such purposes, sharing the necessity for such an approach would be useful.

How does the department conduct strategic planning? One approach is to use a faculty retreat to bring the faculty together as discussed in the last chapter. Or a smaller group of faculty leaders along with a reasonable representation from junior faculty and research faculty could be used. And always include the key department staff, such as the Director of Administration.

A well designed strategic plan usually has several major components and often starts with the vision, mission, and core values. The vision is the future-looking description of what the department would look like if it were very successful at its mission. The mission describes the overall purpose of the department. We would argue that we have three missions, clinical work, teaching, and research. The core values are the principle qualities that we expect to be present in our environment and personnel. A discussion of core values frames future action plans by explicitly defining what is important and meaningful to a department faculty and staff. Refer back to your core values during planning meetings, and check future actions against your definitions.

The so-called SWOT analysis, looking at strengths, weaknesses, opportunities, and threats, is often carried out early in a strategic planning process and is very useful in determining the directions for the action plans that will emerge as well as being useful in getting everyone on the same page.

Strategic plans are usually designed to cover multiple years, from three years to ten years. We believe five years is about as far in the future as we dare to project. Strategic Goals are created next from the SWOT analysis by always keeping in mind the vision and mission. Under each Strategic Goal, four or five strategies should be articulated. These strategies may be at the level of actual actions to be taken or may be more conceptual. Either at this level or perhaps one more under each strategy, the action plans need to be planned.

The action plans are more detailed objectives, which should lead to yearly operating plans including resources needed and assignments for individual roles and responsibilities. These action plans need to be updated at least yearly and these updates should be based on key performance indicators.

SCENARIO PLANNING

One type of strategic planning is called scenario planning, in which various possible directions can be analyzed so that the department is not caught unprepared by surprise. These possible directions are usually forces outside of the department's direct control but are considered at least a strong possibility. In this fashion, as best as possible, the department can prepare for declines in reimbursement, turf issues, radiation scares, or outpatient DRGs. For each of these primary outside forces, three scenarios are presented, the best, worst, and more reasonable. Then the potential strategies to deal with each are explored.

In this process, the leadership must be careful not to paint a doomsday future where there are no good outcomes possible. In fact, the department should map out how best to thrive in the event different scenarios play out. Several good books have been written on this subject and a number of consultants would be glad to help with such planning. However, the department may use the faculty retreat and strategic planning approach to tackle the possible scenarios the department will face in the near future.

Chapter 20

MARKETING AND OUTREACH

Twenty-five years ago, a routine marketing course in a graduate school of business would have discussed the traditional "four Ps" of marketing – product, price, place, and promotion. In fact, as we began to think about integrating marketing concepts into our academic practice and activities at UCSF, we began with this approach. In more recent years, we have evolved our marketing program into a true cultural shift in attitude that impacts the rank and file faculty radiologists, and we hope everyone in the department. We have also begun new initiatives in social media marketing, whose success is yet to be determined. However, the social media initiatives go hand in hand with our efforts to create a service-oriented department, and to create web-based approaches that complement our traditional, research-based marketing plan. This chapter offers a case study in how we have used traditional and social media marketing techniques to reduce the leakage of outside referrals and to increase business from referring physicians outside of UCSF.

In other chapters of this book, we have discussed the unique healthcare environment in California, and the dominance of Kaiser Permanente in the San Francisco Bay Area market. UCSF Radiology is also a victim of its own educational success with many highly skilled and excellent resident and fellow alumni competing with us for business in a very tight radius of the main campus. Coupled with a medical center that invests a very small percentage of its operating budget in marketing and outreach, and without true service line integration, we found ourselves a few years ago struggling to attract business to a new outpatient imaging center which ultimately became a joint venture with our medical center. Once our capital (and significant amounts of it) was invested in the venture, our desire to market grew substantially.

Our Radiology department began its marketing efforts in a very straightforward way. In 2003, with the UCSF Medical Center, we opened an outpatient imaging center several miles away from the main campus, in an area of San Francisco that was still underdeveloped but had tremendous potential. The San Francisco Giants had built and moved to a new ballpark in the neighborhood in 2000, and UCSF itself opened and continued to develop a research campus and future hospital site in the same general area. However, at the time, our imaging center, was really the only patient care activity and outpost for the hospital in the area. While "China Basin" had name recognition from sports fans, as the home of the Giants, we knew it would be difficult to convince patients that it was easy and convenient to visit for imaging, despite its distance from their UCSF doctors' offices. We retained a marketing consultant to help us create some marketing communications materials ("promotion," one of the four Ps) and we approached it as a simple matter of "needing publicity." Needless to say, we discovered quite rapidly that our thinking was too narrow.

THE IMPORTANCE OF RESEARCH

As an academic leader and current or future Radiology Chair, we are sure you understand the importance of research to advancing your department's mission. But do you know what your key referring doctors think of you? Do you even know who they are? Do you know how much business is sent outside of your Radiology department and why? Does your faculty not just understand but also deeply believe that they have to earn every single referral? If you have answered no to any of these questions, then you are probably where we were several years ago and will learn very surprising things about your department and your faculty by undertaking serious marketing research.

Before we could jump into the communications pieces and promotion (what our faculty viewed as marketing), we needed to understand our customers so that we could tailor our message. From our RIS, we pulled the names and specialties of the key referrers to each modality we had expanded to the offsite location. We decided to use qualitative research rather than quantitative research, which means we used focus groups and one-on-one interviews with physicians instead of statistically significant surveys to solicit information, opinions, and feedback. We designed two survey approaches. The first included three structured focus groups with outside physicians (three different specialties) who might be willing to refer to our new imaging center because of geographic proximity. These groups were recruited, staffed, and facilitated by outside marketing experts with considerable experience in the technique. The second approach, also structured but a little more flexible, was a series of one-on-one interviews with our key referrers inside UCSF and the same outside marketing consultant conducted the interviews. In both cases, the information was summarized in formal reports, and we had the benefit of verbatim transcripts from the focus groups and quotations from the one-on-one interviews. We discovered that internal referring doctors were extremely happy to share their opinions about Radiology to a third party (our marketing consultant); it felt "safe" and they were honest and constructive in both their praise and their criticism. The information we gained from this research allowed us to craft a marketing communication message about the new site that was benefit-specific to referring doctors. This was one of our first marketing lessons – we needed to communicate what our referring doctors cared about, not what we cared about.

Within Radiology, we were very excited by a new facility, expansion of capacity, state-of-the-art equipment, proximity to our research facility, and a host of other things that only mattered to us! What did our referring doctors care about?

- How would their patients get to this new site and could they park when they got there?
- Who would read and interpret the images? Would the same faculty that the referring MDs were used to be reading these images?
- How fast could they get their reports?
- Would there be same-day availability and would we pay for a taxi if they needed to send a patient immediately?
- How would we staff it? Without a hospital nearby, what would we do in an emergency?

Our promotional materials then, were designed to talk about the outpatient-focused environment, the convenient and validated parking, the regular and immediate availability of the same faculty attendings, and a promise of fast turnaround on reports. We learned some other things, too. Simply by conducting interviews with our own UCSF referring doctors we heard about things we wanted to change. We heard about scheduling confusion and concerns with our call center. We heard about great difficulty getting authorizations for patients. We heard that our own doctors used outside imaging centers sometimes just to get reports hand-delivered to them. We heard about intimidating and unfriendly reading rooms. We heard about lack of input at tumor boards. We heard about long waits for appointments, and reports that were too long and did not get to the point or advise the doctor what to do next. Most importantly, we heard that our referring colleagues were so grateful to be asked their opinion of how Radiology could improve and serve them better! And we were surprised to hear these things, and took them seriously and to heart.

Between 2004 and 2007, our department began to work on marketing from the inside out. We focused our faculty away from an interest in brochures and handouts and promotional materials, and asked them to focus on relationships, service, communication, and old-fashioned friendliness. It sounds easy, but it is not. And this is an important marketing lesson – are you really ready to market? Can you handle the volume, the calls, the service expectations? Do your customers even know what service to expect? In this three year period, between qualitative research projects, we took a number of actions that were not easy, but set up the groundwork for successfully marketing our joint venture beginning in 2007:

1. We completely redesigned and reorganized our Radiology call center, moving the staff offsite, putting it under new management and instituting metrics and quality measures.
2. We began to regularly track key referring physicians to our higher-end imaging modalities, CT, MRI, and PET/CT and to ask our section chiefs to be comfortable communicating regularly with them.
3. We convinced our medical center that a centralized authorization unit was a necessity for its specialty clinics and we worked hard to help it get organized and functioning according to performance metrics.
4. We talked about reading room "friendliness" and we began to establish standards for what UCSF physicians could expect if

they walked in. As an aside, if you think your reading rooms are not a problem, send in a "mystery shopper" such as a resident from another specialty, or a new junior attending from medicine or surgery and have them report back to you, the chair. You might be surprised by what you learn.

5. We streamlined some of our requisition processes and made more information available on our website.

6. We refocused our efforts on wait times at all of our sites – not just our offsite imaging center – and then communicated across the institution as we expanded hours, days, and locations, and made other access changes.

7. We learned that no one is going to call Radiology and ask for news; we needed to do our own proactive communications and our own bragging. We also needed to acknowledge problems without defensiveness and then tell colleagues and medical center administration when the problem was fixed.

A BENEFITS FOCUSED MARKETING APPROACH

As our "marketing intelligence" grew, we began to establish clear plans with objectives and volume targets, and tried to define fit with our medical center's overall marketing strategy. In some institutions this might seem so obvious as to not need stating, but in the UCSF culture – with a focus on two major service lines, heart/vascular and neurosciences – Radiology did not often win a competition for marketing attention or dollars. Three years after our first experiment with qualitative research we did it again, this time as part of a launch of three specific service "bundles" within Radiology – cancer imaging, interventional spine imaging, and cardiac imaging. We felt UCSF Radiology services would benefit by efforts to:

• Organize Radiology's contributions in terms of the specific services being provided
• Differentiate on the basis of superior UCSF Radiology physician accomplishments and medical leadership
• Clarify the UCSF benefits by the combination of evidence-based protocols that utilize UCSF investments in cutting edge equipment

We were convinced that presenting services in "bundles" was closer to the way patients thought about diseases they were dealing with, and by creating methods for patients to "search" for these services would help them to ask their own doctors for UCSF services, and make it easier for physicians (whether UCSF or not) to find their way to UCSF Radiology and to our imaging centers.

As part of this effort, we asked our consultant to conduct a complete competitive assessment of the imaging center landscape. This step was critically important, first of all because of the data we gathered as a result, but also because it again helped to define service expectations from our internal and external customers. We also repeated one-on-one interviews with referring oncologists, surgeons and neurologists. We discovered that some of the referral "leakage" outside of our own institution was based on poor information and misperception. We want to emphasize the importance here of holding up a mirror to your operations and getting a clear view of what others see. As a result of doing interviews twice in three years, we could see where we had improved – but no one noticed because we didn't tell them – and where we really had to do better. Some opportunities we identified through this process that might be applicable to your institution include:

Create a "we'll see you right now" attitude inside your department.

1. Remember that not every computer in the institution can display images as well as Radiology, or as quickly. Help your referring colleagues solve problems with webPACS, hardware or other image-delivery issues even if not under your direct control.

2. Educate the referring community about the actual schedule, capacity, and hours – don't allow rumors about access – educate instead. Through our research, we found practices handing out photocopies of radiology phone numbers, locations, and hours that did not even exist anymore. It is amazing what is being handed to patients.

3. We undertook a complete web redesign as part of this process, to allow easy information look up for doctors, their office staff, as well as patients.

4. Use your expertise to educate referring MDs, particularly primary care, about radiation risk.

5. Offer alternatives to electronic delivery of reports if physicians require it.
6. Remember that referring MDs can't always see what a radiologist sees on an image – they need to be shown and told in a non-intimidating and non-patronizing way.
7. Keep your referring colleagues out of your turf battles with other specialties.
8. Share your knowledge and advice through contact with referring MDs – you can positively impact patient care.
9. Create virtual tours of your off-campus sites so referring MDs and practices can quickly see what is available for their patients so that patients can become comfortable with travel routes and amenities in advance.
10. Communicate all the ways you keep patients safe – particularly if you have offsite locations away from the hospital or hospitals.
11. Consider a true sales function within the Radiology department.

SETTING MARKETING GOALS

Each academic practice and market is different, but here we offer some generic marketing goals that you might consider as you enter a department as a new chair. At the very least, we suggest you develop a series of questions around these goals, and ask for data. If you are very lucky, your hospital marketing department is sophisticated and helps with market analysis, marketing communications, social media and other strategies. Or, perhaps, your department has some or all of these functions. If the department or hospital administration does not have dedicated marketing staff, perhaps this is a service you will need to buy from outside consultants. In any of these scenarios, though, it is good to have some overall goals in mind. This list is based on one overriding goal and that is to build volume in good-paying modalities and increase professional fee revenue to support the academic mission. Here are some of our thoughts to guide your goal-setting:

1. You should conduct qualitative marketing research as described above to help you prioritize the services you will mar-

ket. You won't have the funds or time to do everything, so it is best to highlight the services – whether new or existing – that your referring physician customers demand.

2. What do your marketing communications emphasize and what do you want them to emphasize? You should be describing benefits that emerge as important in your research, rather than what is important to you as academic radiologists. Be clear about why your department is superior to its competition, and question whether you are telling the right story about who you are and what you offer. A world-famous subspecialist on your faculty might be known to you – but have you told your referrers or your community?

3. Are your positioning concepts clearly developed from your market research? These can include things that matter to patients and referring MDs such as newest or one-of-a-kind equipment, convenient hours and locations, service focus, evidence-based protocols, and expertise.

4. Is there a true sales function in the institution that Radiology could share as a starting point? Often, clinical laboratories have been ahead of Radiology in developing sophisticated reference lab sales techniques. At UCSF, we have partnered with clinical labs and share an outreach coordinator who visits referring physician offices regularly with information about imaging services. We should note that sales people cannot just be turned loose without information or regular contact. They need to really understand your goals and business, and their activity should be tracked. How many visits have there been? Who did they visit? Did the doctors end up making referrals? In other words, track and measure effectiveness of the effort.

5. Have you trained your existing staff on excellent customer service and practice marketing? Do they see themselves as ambassadors for the practice and responsible for making it easy for patients and physicians to come to you for imaging? We have found this one of the hardest things to do at UCSF. It is hard for many staff to step back from day to day operations and see this as a critical aspect of the job. We have found it easier to send two or three individuals in key roles – our Operations Director, Scheduling/Revenue Director, and Practice Managers – out to develop key internal relationships with

their counterparts and to act as ombudsmen and facilitators for those referring practices. We also repeat the visits regularly because there is so much turnover in referring doctor offices.

6. Do you have good customer service feedback tools, including written and web-based, and do you track and publish the responses? Recently we have begun to use Yelp and we have also instituted a customer service survey using iPads that has been very effective.

7. UCSF Medical Center measures access in terms of how many days to the third available appointment – we have always measured this, and we routinely share this information with referring practices.

8. Is there an ongoing program in place to develop quality written materials for patients and physicians? We have put a writer on retainer to help us with our internal and external communications materials. This includes invitations for outreach dinners which we hold two to three times a year with referring physicians, clinical articles geared to the physician community about our service "bundles," and updatable patient information materials. He also helps keep our patient material on the web coordinated with what we publish in print.

9. What are the radiologists doing to market the practice? At the very least, is there a radiology representative at every tumor board? We have discussed elsewhere the importance of tracking report turnaround time and publishing the results. Do your section chiefs know their top ten referring MDs? Have they seen them lately or asked for feedback? You can set goals for each section chief in this area – give them the referring MD data and then ask them to set quarterly targets. Ask for a schedule of tumor board and conference attendance by section. Set expectations for communication, and then ask fellow chairs from other specialties for honest feedback.

One obvious question is what is an appropriate level of marketing budget for all of these activities? Our recommendation is to budget one percent of cash receipts from outpatient activities. We have set our budget based on receipts from the outpatient imaging center, and we supplement this from professional fees for other activities that support education and research as well as the clinical mission.

A WORD ABOUT SOCIAL MEDIA

At UCSF, our marketing research and plan caused us to rethink our entire website and approach for patients, physicians, research collaborators, and trainees. We are novices in social media, and there are many expert resources online and elsewhere that can better describe social media marketing. However, we have become converts to the idea that we should be telling our story, describing our benefits, and educating patients and physicians, and the internet and social media give us a perfect mechanism for doing so. At a recent conference at UCSF on global health, the COO of Facebook was a guest speaker. She described how when the internet started (and she actually remembered a time before the internet!) people used it to search and passively acquire information. As the internet has grown and applications and possibilities have grown, it has obviously become much more interactive. She described a social media, like Facebook, as less about finding information, and more like walking down a hall and telling someone what you're doing right that minute – only the "someone" is a global population of billions of people. So what is the implication?

We have discussed in this chapter the critical importance of knowing your customer through market research and then describing your services in terms of the benefit to the customer. Doesn't this sound like walking down a hospital hall and telling your patient or MD colleague what you're doing? Can we use Facebook, Twitter, and other media to explain to our audiences "what we're doing right now," in a way that describes why it should matter to them? That is our goal at UCSF as we take some small steps into using this technology. If you want to expand your thinking about this, and about the multiplier effect it can have, we suggest a book called *Tribes* by Seth Godin. It is a very easy read, not like a typical business book. It is more like a book of sound bites or tweets. However, it gives some insight into how crafted communication using these mechanisms can create followers on a scale that is faster, less expensive, and larger than anything we've seen before.

Chapter 21

FUNDRAISING AND ALUMNI RELATIONS

The chairs of most specialties have active fundraising efforts centered on grateful patients. They are able to create endowed chairs, research funds, and even research or clinical buildings from donated funds. Radiology traditionally has not been so fortunate in that we rely on referrals from other physicians and our interactions are more with them than the patients. Our referring physicians claim the wealthy patients as theirs and are reluctant to share any funds raised. However, they often ask us for images to show one disease or another in their fundraising efforts.

DEVELOPMENT OFFICER

What can we do? Well, the first step in raising money is getting a fundraiser who is dedicated to your department. Perhaps you may wish to share an individual with another department, preferably one that is not competitive with your own. Such an individual needs to be at least welcomed by the central campus fundraising organization if not reporting directly to them. Your fundraiser must focus, at least half of the time, on Radiology and should represent your department within the Development Office. Opportunities to collaborate with others to raise money are most likely under those circumstances.

Interestingly, at UCSF, the development function has undergone massive reorganization under the guidance of a new Chancellor. The new leadership reversed the organizational chart, hiring many more targeted fundraisers, and eliminating administrative positions. Despite the increase in fundraisers, targeted to new capital campaigns, areas of clinical excellence, major gifts, and so on, Radiology has still ended up with very little attention. Recently, this department's efforts have focused on corporate and foundation relationships, as it is probably a more successful avenue than grateful patients for Radiology. However, the argument for an embedded development officer still holds because even his more narrow focus results in competition for the Development office resources. It remains to be seen in UCSF Radiology, whether this approach will result in new gifts. One other avenue we have chosen to pursue holds more promise, and that is alumni relations.

ALUMNI SUPPORT

Alumni from the residency program and perhaps from the fellowship programs need the Chair's attention and the attention of organizational fundraisers. Almost twenty years ago, several alumni from the residency at UCSF approached the chair to consider creating an alumni organization. That humble beginning has led to a very successful fundraising organization called the Margulis Society. The Society raises over $50,000 each year to be applied in various ways, described below, as well as contributing to an endowment fund that has grown considerably over the years. In addition, because of the events and efforts of the Margulis Society, we have been able to establish two endowed chairs.

The Society has numerous functions each year including an annual job fair for residents and fellows and a panel of speakers representing both academics and private practice. This event, that lasts several hours, is hosted in the home of one of our alumni and another serves as the master of ceremonies. Another event is the annual presentations and awards for the best research projects and presentations. The cash awards are made by the Society.

At least once every other year, the Society hosts a gala event at one of the historic sites in San Francisco. A live auction is held and the event raises money for the society as well as getting alumni and faculty together for a great evening.

The Board of the Margulis Society is composed of alumni and current faculty and includes the chair of the department. The board members do not have fixed terms but tend to rotate on and off at a reasonable rate. They hold meetings about four times per year. There are representatives from each of the resident classes serving on the board.

The Society has almost always supported the residents to attend the AFIP in Washington. They tend to select one or two projects recommended by the residents to fund each year, such as new computers, books, projectors, as well as funding research projects. Every once in a while, they will tackle a big project such as renovating the department's library.

By any measure, this organization has been very successful, not only raising money but also establishing a wonderful interchange between the alumni and the faculty in the department. A number of the members of the Margulis Society also participate in teaching the residents as without-salary clinical faculty. One negative is that we continue to derive most of our support from older graduates and have not been able to capture uniformly support from the newer graduates in spite of their apparent enthusiasm for the program. This problem with the younger graduates is not unique to our department and may reflect the more global attitudes of this generation.

"IMAGES" MAGAZINE

We create an annual newsletter in the form of a magazine which we call "Images." We include a number of standard sections including residents, new faculty and fellows, grants, alumni news, CME calendars, and several articles highlighting our latest research activities. We distribute this publication to all of our alumni, chairs and academic leaders at UCSF, and chairs of some of our peer departments across the country. Leaders of some of our corporate partners also receive "Images." In addition, we give this magazine to our resident applicants when they interview with us as well as other guests coming to our department.

Some individuals have questioned the cost and time and effort to produce this publication. The university provides the layout and publishing at cost and our real out-of-pocket expenses are for postage. We view this magazine as a major part of our fundraising efforts as well as a showcase of the accomplishments of our department for the year. Having produced this magazine for many years now also provides an excellent historical record for the department. The most recent edition is available on our website (Radiology website, 2011).

INDUSTRIAL PARTNERSHIPS

The next category of support for the department is industrial partnerships. Although they have been a very important part of our research support in the past, we are very concerned about the future. As you know, the government and others are putting a lot of pressure on academia and industry to resolve the potential conflicts of interest between these groups.

Our industrial partnerships have been centered on research, usually attempting to bring new devices, equipment, or techniques to the market. Some of these have been our own creations, some with grant support, and some have been trying out new prototype devices created by the manufacturers. Often these companies approach us as a large prestigious department with knowledgeable faculty and staff. We have a reputation for thoroughly testing new equipment and rigorously adhering to IRB requirements, etc.

We have enjoyed long and fruitful relationships with many major equipment manufacturers. We have developed software packages such as MR spectroscopy and have worked with RIS and PACS vendors to produce important additional modules. A number of radiopharmaceutical advances have been developed at UCSF as well as contrast agents for CT and MR.

Typically we start with an introductory meeting at our site with scientists from a company and a number of our faculty. The company often presents some of their latest developments in equipment or software and, in turn, we present some of our related recent advances. If there is mutual interest, we agree to proceed with a contract for further development, usually under a broad research agreement that deals with intellectual property and confidentiality. Our university, like most others, takes a hard line on intellectual property to protect the faculty and the university. However, UCSF is fair and accepts the notion of intellectual property that is developed by individuals from both the university and the company as having dual or split ownership. Joint patents and copyrights are produced accordingly.

Publications are also protected although we may give the company the opportunity to review material before it is published to make sure that it is accurate from their standpoint and that any confidential material of theirs is protected. They do not have veto rights, however.

We do not know what the future holds, and certainly companies are no longer going to be able to consign FDA approved devices without documenting compensation for their expenses by the department. We believe that these new regulations, although well intended, will dampen progress and development in the future. However, we expect to continue industrial partnerships in the future. In fact, with a new chancellor recently appointed from a pharmaceutical company, overall campus interest in encouraging these relationships and streamlining the university rules around them is actually growing. Radiology might be better positioned than most departments to take advantage of a simplification of university procedures, given existing research relationships. It remains to be seen whether this strategy will be successful within the hierarchy of a ten campus university system.

One comment on royalties from patents is worthwhile. Most campuses have fairly similar rules about how patent royalties are distributed. Although the percentages might vary somewhat, typically the inventor, the lab/department, the school, and the university are all included. At UCSF, the lab/department is excluded unless a portion of the proceeds are shared from the inventor's percentage by a pre-arranged agreement. And there is no software copyright regulation that includes the department which typically supports the time and effort of this faculty. We believe having the department share clearly articulated encourages more investment in these areas.

REFERENCES

Radiology website. (2011). Accessed February 5. http://www.radiology.ucsf.edu/.

Chapter 22

POST-GRADUATE EDUCATION

Post-graduate education is almost entirely CME as defined by the Accreditation Council for Continuing Medical Education (ACC-ME). A faculty committee (to be described) oversees our post-graduate education efforts and we have an office for CME that has a small, dedicated staff to run the program. Although we fall under the School of Medicine's CME program and have to comply with their requirements, we actually staff our own courses and manage the finances accordingly.

POST-GRADUATE COMMITTEE

This committee provides the direction for the program and actually chooses the course director and faculty for each course. They decide on the best program content, location, and timing for each course and review the history of each course to decide on the changes needed for the coming year. They are also responsible to review the objectives for each course and to assess the needs for future courses.

COMPETITION

Radiology at UCSF has an active program, perhaps the largest in the country for Radiology departments consisting of about twenty CME courses each year as well as visiting fellowships in our department. Our competition is mainly subspecialty societies and some commercial entities. We specialize in relatively boutique smaller courses in nice places often away from San Francisco. And we conduct some off-shore courses periodically depending on our assessment of the marketplace.

VALUE TO THE DEPARTMENT

Why do we conduct CME courses? They take the faculty away from the department, the CME program is risky, and the financial return is relatively small compared to this risk. Each year some courses lose money and have to be reevaluated regularly. In fact, the revenue from the CME program is less than two percent of our total revenue. Although the department gets very little of the profits, they are important to the sections and are the primary source of discretionary funds for the sections. In addition, junior faculty have the opportunity to hone their skills at presentations and help develop their reputations. It allows faculty to interact with practicing radiologists from around the country, as well as with each other. These courses provide an opportunity for faculty to socialize with each other, often in a nice resort, away from the day to day routine.

UCSF Radiology CME has an active marketing program, via direct mail pieces and the web, and conducts robust evaluations after each course. It has also been our practice to engage a marketing consultant from time to time to review our activities and marketing materials. We are strong believers in the use of focus groups, and have engaged a consultant to conduct telephone interviews with practicing radiologists in targeted parts of the country to better target our courses to physician needs. The use of focus groups, as we discussed in the marketing chapter, has applicability to a wide range of department activities, and despite the subjectivity of the data, we have found them to be cost-effective and rich in useful information.

The evaluations by our attendees continue to be excellent and we feel that we continue to advance the quality of clinical radiology across the country. Most of our attendees are in private practice and many return for multiple courses. We have a frequent attendee discount that is popular and well used among our attendees and is another marketing strategy.

Would we recommend that you embark on a program this comprehensive? When our administrator has made presentations to other managers, mentioning that the program generates $200,000 plus for the department and sections each year, the response is nearly always – how can I get in? The reality is, for very little money, an enormous amount of time and attention to detail is required to run such a large program. We negotiate hotel and meal contracts, transportation, venue issues, and we must adhere strictly to OCME and ACCME guidelines. Our recommendation, if you are not currently offering CME, is to start small. Perhaps you have a clinical specialty or program that could be turned into a course offering. First go to the web and survey the competition. Remember the "Four Ps" of marketing – is the *product* unique? Can you afford it at the market *price* point? What location or *place* will you hold it and can you attract enough attendees to break even or turn a profit? What will be the unique selling points in your *promotion*? Finally, how will you staff it and pay attention to the details? We would strongly recommend against putting the reins for CME in the hands of an already busy faculty member; the business risk is just too great.

Chapter 23

QUALITY AND SAFETY

Perhaps one of the most important aspects of our department's activities centers on assuring the quality and safety of our procedures and interactions with our patients. We have a strong and active program in quality and safety that will be described in this chapter.

SAFETY

First, let's look at the big picture. Do we make a lot of mistakes now? According to the Commonwealth Fund and as shown in Figure 23–1, 34 percent of Americans claim to have suffered from a medical mistake, more than other industrialized nations (Commonwealth Fund, 2005). The Institute of Medicine's (IOM) report on medical errors claims that medical errors cause 44,000–98,000 deaths per year in the US (IOM, 1999). The IOM also stated that two percent of admissions experience medication errors costing $2 billion per year and that preventable medical mistakes cost $17–21 billion per year. Unfortunately, mistakes can happen in Radiology quite easily. We will begin this chapter by exploring the kinds of mistakes that can be made in Radiology.

Opportunities in Radiology for Safety Mistakes

In order to remember the areas of vulnerability in Radiology, we have come up with an acronym, "Perfect Aims to Avoid Safety Problems" with the letters in PERFECT AIMS matching the oppor-

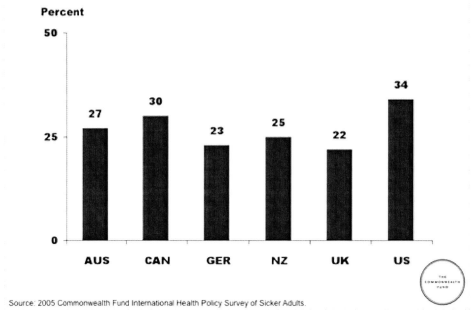

Source: 2005 Commonwealth Fund International Health Policy Survey of Sicker Adults.

Figure 23–1.

tunities to make a medical error:

- Patient misidentification
- Equipment – failure
- Reading – misinterpretation
- Fall – patient fall
- Environment – spill
- Communication – with referring physician
- Test – wrong exam/complication/excess radiation
- Allergy
- Injection – wrong material/dose/extravasations
- Metal – in magnet
- Side – wrong side

Patient Misidentification

We will explore many of these in more detail. First, patient misidentification can be due to performing a procedure on the wrong patient, giving the wrong patient injections or drugs, or the technologist placing the wrong patient's identifiers on the images. And the radiologist can dictate an interpretation for the wrong patient or the transcriptionist can mix up patients. As we will discuss later, the RIS/PACS/ voice recognition systems and interfaces have solved many of these problems to a very large extent.

However, if the patient is not properly identified up front, although consistent thereafter, we could still be in error. Unfortunately, it is very easy for the technologist to identify a patient properly on entering the examination room, but to use the identifiers of the previous patient for that exam. Luckily, the technologist often corrects this problem right away, but not always. One method of assuring the right patient is a combination of using armbands, even for outpatients, and a barcode or radio-frequency identification (RFID) associated with the armband. Once the patient is positively identified initially, then the armband assures accurate identification thereafter. When the patient is placed on the examination table, the barcode or RFID positively identifies the patient in the RIS or the scanner work list. Two different procedures for the same patient may still be on the work list but only that patient will be available for the technologist to choose. This technique can also help reduce confusion for portable examinations when using computed radiography plates, often trying to keep multiple plates identified prior to reading them into a scanner. Using the RFID or barcode can eliminate placing erroneous identification on a plate.

Miscommunication

Miscommunication can occur in a number of ways. First, so-called wet readings, which may be nothing more than a phone call or a curbside consult, leaves much to interpretation by the referring physician or nurse asking for the answers. Poorly constructed reports or perhaps resident interpretations off-hours (already discussed in Chapter 8) can lead to misunderstanding by the referring physician. Or if the referring physician is not paying close attention or if the report is too verbose, it is possible for the physician to miss an important finding. And mixing up right and left in our reports is also possible, even with voice recognition. And confusing abbreviations are also possible, although not usually much of a problem with VR.

Wet-readings are best communicated in a written form, although usually rather brief. We have instituted a wet-read module, described in Chapter 17, that provides the preliminary reports to the emergency department and the intensive care units. This system also provides feedback about changes from resident provided wet-readings and the final interpretation that is made later on. At least with such an approach, the referring physician, who relied on the previous wet reading for taking specific actions on a patient, is not left holding the bag when a change is made before the final report.

Of course, the referring physician can also make mistakes such as a poor clinical history on the requisition or not indicating why the examination was requested in the first place. And it is not uncommon for the requisition to state the wrong patient, the wrong procedure, or the wrong side! And if the patient is inadequately prepared for many procedures, the results are compromised to varying degrees. We have already discussed the possibility that a referring physician does not read the report properly or completely.

The possibility that the referring physician may not read the report carefully or understand the report is one of the reasons for the emphasis on structured reporting. Structured reporting, like in mammography, can reduce the verbiage and increase the likelihood of proper understanding. The RSNA has launched a large effort, with funding from the National Institute of Biomedical Imaging and Bioengineering (NIBIB) of the NIH, to create structured reports for most procedures but that effort has a long way to go. These structured reports will utilize the lexicon created by the RSNA called RadLex that is available in the public domain.

And the referring physician who uses decision-support order entry for Radiology procedures is more likely to choose the proper examination for a patient than is otherwise the case. These decision-support systems will hopefully be in widespread use in the next few years.

Radiation

Medical errors are a big problem for Radiology since we are not familiar with the patients – we see a large number of patients every day and there are many steps involved from registration to the final report – and we use contrast and other drugs on our patients. In Interventional Radiology, we use other devices such as catheters and guide wires, and in many parts of our department, we use radiation. Radiation has become a big issue for us, mainly because of mistakes made at a few prominent facilities. And recent publications have stated the wide variation in dose for the same procedures from one institution to another (Smith-Bindman et al., 2009).

As radiologists, we have been adequately trained in radiation physics, yet we have not taken radiation as seriously as perhaps we should have. Certainly the recent emphasis on children and the "Image Gently" campaign has raised our awareness. And the "as low as reasonably achievable" concepts (ALARA) should be followed all of the time. RIS and PACS have always warned us of prior similar examinations but we have not attempted in the past to record or analyze the possible cumulative radiation dose for our patients. And there is plenty of disagreement among experts about the cumulative effects of radiation from medical imaging. We have to assume the worst and act as if the radiation is strictly cumulative. For that reason, we need to start looking toward ultrasound, especially in children or MR in situations where CT has been utilized before.

Through the Medical Imaging and Technology Alliance (MITA), the manufacturers have started to produce the Dose-Length Product (DLP) which is an attempt to record particular CT examination settings in MAS, and the approximate radiation exposure that a patient should have received. This DLP can be read out of the DICOM header for a procedure and can be captured by the RIS or PACS. At UCSF, we recently started providing this data to our Emergency Room physicians after educating them about what the DLP means. We have started to notice a decline in CTs and an increase in ultrasound and MR which we believe is at least partly due to this notification. We intend to extend this process to more areas of the medical center and are beginning to store this data in our patient records in the RIS.

Yet the DLP is not enough. The physicists will tell you that in addition to the DLP, one needs the examination type, the size of the patient, the patient's age, and the exact critical organ distribution to begin to estimate actual radiation exposure for a particular patient. And that cumulative information is not complete without knowledge of other radiation exposures such as high altitude flying, sun exposure, radon gas, etc. The question is what is good enough?

We need to encourage our manufacturers to provide the DLP for all examinations producing radiation as well as record some of the other data described above so that the RIS or PACS might keep track of the cumulative dose for each patient in the future. And the RSNA and ACR are working on the communication of this information to a central registry so that this information can follow a patient from one institution to another. This central registry will also allow for comparisons between institutions so that we can indeed achieve ALARA everywhere. The RSNA is working on the transmission of information from institutions' PACS to a clearinghouse and a Personal Health Record (PHR) with funding from the NIBIB. This work is an extension of the existing effort called the "Integrating the Healthcare Enterprise" or IHE, which is a combined activity of the RSNA and the Healthcare Information and Management Systems Society (HIMSS). The ACR is establishing the radiation registry.

QUALITY

We have discussed the various kinds of safety issues in Radiology and now we will dive into other aspects of quality. Reed Dunnick, MD, the chair of Radiology at Michigan, simplified the process of clinical work in Radiology as follows:

- Appropriate examination
- Conveniently scheduled
- Safely performed
- Accurately interpreted
- Clearly and promptly communicated

We have addressed most of these steps except for accurately interpreted. Of course, an error in diagnosis can lead to the wrong therapy as well as chasing incidental findings can lead to more invasive tests and associated risks. We dealt with some aspects of incidental findings in Chapter 8 and incidental findings in human research studies in Chapter 11. We have come a long ways to assure that the best radiologist is interpreting studies by subspecialization. And Radiology has embraced Computer Aided Diagnosis for mammography and for high-resolution chest CT as well as skeletal bone age in children. These systems perform nearly as well as the best experts and improves on the average General Radiologist who is not an expert in these various areas.

We have also previously addressed the issue of poor clinical history, which can be partially solved by the radiologist referring to the electronic medical record before rendering the final interpretation. Of course, it requires additional time to find the appropriate information in the electronic record unless the needed data is summarized specifically for the radiologist. More and more systems are moving in this direction.

Department Commitment to Quality

Several years ago the department leadership became concerned with our vulnerability regarding patient safety and were convinced that quality should have a more prominent place in our collective thinking. We embarked on a path to elevate safety and quality throughout everything we did. The first step was the appointment of an Associate Chair for Quality and Safety. A senior member of our faculty took on this role with a passion that has pushed all of us to think more about the issues involved. We next selected a senior nurse in our department to be the primary staff person for this activity. We now hold monthly meetings (for a while they occurred twice per month) in which various sections are expected to report on their issues and solutions regarding safety and quality.

These meetings alternate with Operations Committee meetings and both sets of meetings have representation from each clinical section. The Operations Committee was initiated when the chair arrived at UCSF many years ago. This committee brings together the technical staff leaders with section faculty, and usually the section chiefs, in order to have a dialogue between these individuals as well as make sure they all are on the same page concerning significant clinical issues. Now these individuals are much more knowledgeable, have more understanding of the issues facing each other, and together they can forge the best solutions. That committee, as stated earlier, is now chaired by the Vice Chair, Clinical Affairs.

Importance of Quality Metrics

In Chapter 17, this topic was addressed. However, it is appropriate under the banner of safety and quality to point out that measuring important aspects of what we do is essential to understanding what issues we need to fix. We are clearly in the business of information and we need to have the data to monitor how well we are doing and to use the data for corrective action. The need for such information cannot be emphasized enough regarding safety and quality. We need to measure all of the possible safety errors such as patient misidentification, misinterpretations, patient falls, miscommunications, wrong procedures, etc. We need to collect radiation data, allergy information, and data related to giving incorrect dosages or drugs.

Patient identification errors occur all too frequently in spite of our best attempts at solving these problems and these errors must be discovered promptly and individuals who may have received erroneous information must be contacted. In the era of very fast image and report communication, this problem is magnified. We work on these daily and have a weekly meeting for PACS issues at which we focus on these mistakes during the first part of the meeting.

Almost always human mistakes are the cause for these errors but there are system problems that need to be addressed to overcome human limitations. One of the reasons that the wrong patient is associated with the images is the lack of system implementation by the equipment manufacturers of a notification to the RIS and PACS that the previous patient's examination is complete. Failure to indicate this completion step allows the technologist to record images for the subsequent patient under the name of the last patient. For this reason, as already described, we are moving to the barcode or RFID solutions for limiting mistakes in the technologist work lists.

At our Operations Committee meeting, we also look at any missing reports and the so-called complete, but not reported list. Most of these exams end up being research studies that do not require a report but often the technologist does not know that a report is really not needed. The default for these cases is to expect a report.

REFERENCES

Institute of Medicine. (1999). To err is human: Building a safer health system. Accessed May 9. http://www.iom.edu/~/media/Files/Report%20Files/1999/To-Err-is-Human/To%20 Err%20is%20Human%201999%20%20report%20brief.pdf.

Smith-Bindman R., Lipson, J., Marcus, R., Kim, K. P., Mahesh, M., Gould, R., Berrington de González, A., & Miglioretti, D. L. (2009). Radiation dose associated with common computed tomography examinations and the associated lifetime attributable risk of cancer. *Archives of Internal Medicine, 169* (22): 2078–2086.

The Commonwealth Fund. (2005). International survey: U.S. leads in medical errors. Accessed May 17. http://www.commonwealthfund.org/Content/News/-News-Releases/2005/Nov/International-Survey--U-S--Leads-in-Medical-Errors.aspx.

Chapter 24

CULTURE

One of the hardest lessons a new chair learns is that culture trumps nearly everything else! The institutional culture can keep a department from realizing its potential or can make a department seem better than it is. A new chair must consider the culture of the department and institution before embarking on new programs and initiatives.

How does one assess the existing culture? There is no easy answer to that question but careful observation and asking the right questions surely helps. Our administrator always says to "walk around and really listen." We favor an approach of getting out of the department and talking to as many stakeholders as possible in the early days of becoming a chair (or really assuming any leadership position in a department). If your calendar is loaded with standing meetings in your first few months on the job, change it! Yes, you need to immediately get involved, but you also need to set time aside to meet section chiefs, Dean's office staff, hospital administrators, key department staff, and many others. This due diligence will help you assess your department's and institution's culture and more importantly, will help you to begin to identify strong and weak players, and those you can count on to move your initiatives forward.

Let's look at a couple of examples that will help explain this issue, both of which have existed here and probably many other institutions. First, think about a department that has been living on its reputation and actually not creating significant new science in many years. There are few radiologists with NIH funding and only a few older PhDs who conduct most of the funded research in the department. The Dean recruits a new and ambitious chair who has come from a department rich in a tradition of NIH funding for radiologist faculty and sets the expectation for this new chair that he should significantly increase NIH funding in the department. The Dean has given the new chair space and money to achieve this goal.

The new chair recruits a couple of young promising radiologists and gives them a high salary, space, and new research equipment. The existing faculty perceive this move as playing favorites and are very disgruntled. Soon they are angry that the new chair has ignored the clinical side of the department which, after all, generates all of the revenue needed for the academic department. While the chair continues to focus on research, referring physicians are upset that reports are delayed, equipment is breaking down, and patients are waiting longer and longer for their studies. He has also ignored the residents and fellows, and the existing PhD faculty see the new equipment and space going to new faculty. How long do you think this new chair will last? No more than one term for sure before the faculty that he inherited ask that he be removed.

Another example would be the same new chair expected by the Dean to clean up the clinical department where faculty have grown used to academic days, short hours each day, poor access for patients, and long delays in report turnaround. The new chair ignores the scientists, including the PhDs who have the NIH funding, and puts most of his attention on the clinical enterprise. Soon, the top NIH funded investigators leave, the department's ranking falls, and the chair is looking for a new job.

What lessons can be learned from these examples? In both examples, if the chair had spent some time asking questions and listening in his own department, he would have discovered which faculty had strengths in the areas the Dean felt needed improvement. He would have begun to hear recurring themes about priorities around the Dean's goals and could have used those discussions to solidify support for what actions he wanted to take first, second, and so on. We agree it is important for the new chair to understand the Dean's priorities, but we also believe success has to be built from the ground up. A department resting on its laurels isn't suddenly going to start winning new NIH grants without an infusion of new scientists, but those new scientists will be more successful if they enter a culture where all the scientists are valued and all successes are celebrated.

At UCSF, we have undergone some leadership training that asks us to look for what is working, and then try to do more of that. This first chair might have asked the older PhDs how they have been successful – what in the department helped them in the past, and how could he do more of that? The second chair might have tried to pick a section with the greatest productivity and referring physician satisfaction – how did they achieve this? What's working? How can the department replicate this in one more section, then one more, and so on until the culture changes?

We highly recommend a book on change that really provides simple suggestions about changing an organizational culture called *Switch: How to Change Things when Change is Hard* by Chip Heath and Dan Heath. It is a relatively fast read and well worth your time.

We must say another word about institutional culture. Institutional culture must also be considered as explained to some extent in Chapter 11. One should not expect a department to be substantially better than the rest of the institution, in most areas, but particularly in research funding. The reputation of the institution and the collaborators in other departments have a very large impact on a department trying to be much better than the rest.

Likewise, if the institution does not value residency programs, there is little hope that a department can quickly become a top contender for the best resident applicants. These comments on culture should not be used as excuses for not working on problem areas but a tempering influence on a new chair attempting to make changes too quickly. The status quo is a strong force and should always be reckoned with. If you are trying to move your department ahead in an area that is not a strength for your institution, you might want to break the change into smaller steps.

To use the residency program example, if you want better residents, you need your current residents to help "sell" your program. Start by asking them what they would brag about and then do more of that thing. Find out what it would take for them to recommend the program to their best friend (if their best friend wanted to be a radiologist). Maybe engage the chief resident or other resident leader in the process; maybe he or she could survey programs with better reputations and find out the top two or three things that make it better. We're sure you can think of many other small changes yourself, but the point is, it's probably best not to start by tossing out the Program Director and cleaning house. Changing a department in the midst of a less positive institutional culture is never easy, but it's important to keep looking for small successes and publicize and celebrate them. Over time, these small victories will amount to substantial change.

Chapter 25

CONCLUSIONS AND SUMMARY

We have now finished highlighting the leadership and management issues in academic Radiology that we believe are important. We have used the Department of Radiology and Biomedical Imaging at UCSF as our example of what we think works and doesn't work so well, mainly because that is what we know best. We have tried to bring in examples of other departments that have good solutions to many of the problems we all face. We have always been amazed at the similarity of issues across different institutions and we hope you have found our thoughts useful to you.

Although this text was focused on individual academic faculty who aspire to leadership roles, especially chair positions, our hope is that every practicing radiologist and even some physicians in other specialties will find our advice and experience of some use. We also hope that administrators in Radiology as well as technologist leaders will be able to apply what we have presented in their daily lives.

We want to thank the many individuals who have helped us with this book, in particular David Avrin, MD, PhD, who not only wrote the chapter on informatics but also helped edit the entire text and added a number of important points. He has been a terrific addition to our team. We also want to thank Lynne Payne, assistant to the chair, who has not only edited the text but also sought references and helped shape our book. We also need to thank the following important people in our department who gave invaluable help:

- Robert Gould, ScD, Vice Chair Technology and Capital Projects
- Susan O'Hara, Chief Financial Officer
- Susan Wall, MD, Vice Chair Academic Affairs

• Many individuals in SCARD and AAARAD who have helped us over the years with our approach and helped refine what we have tried to implement.

We also need to thank our Dean, Dr. Sam Hawgood, who allowed the chair to take a sabbatical – the only one at UCSF – in order to get this book written. And lastly, I want to express my deep appreciation to Cathy Garzio for agreeing to share the authorship in spite of the fact she did not get a sabbatical!

INDEX

A

Academic Radiology, 11, 117, 162
Academy of Radiology Research (ARR), 9,
    121–122, 137
Accountability, 53–54, 218
Accreditation Council for Continuing
    Medical Education (ACCME), 244,
    246
Accreditation Council for Graduate Medical
    Education (ACGME), 83, 154
Alumni, 145, 229, 239–243
American College of Radiology (ACR), 11,
    39, 66, 111, 117, 211, 218
American Hospital Association (AHA), 86
American Journal of Neuroradiology, 96, 106,
    119
American Journal of Roentgenology, 119
American Medical Association (AMA), 112,
    218
American Recovery and Reinvestment Act
    (ARRA), 122
Animal imaging, 16, 47, 127, 129, 165–166
As low as reasonably achievable (ALARA),
    251–252
Association of Administrators in Academic
    Radiology Departments (AAARAD),
    32, 45, 47, 115
Association of American Medical Colleges
    (AAMC), 15, 28, 31–32, 39, 45, 47,
    81, 165–166
Association of University Radiologists
    (AUR), 7, 140, 154, 174, 222
Authorization, 63–64, 69, 71, 99–100, 232

B

Barcode, 191, 249, 254
Basic science, 12, 16, 125, 127, 129
Benchmark, 15, 31–32, 47–48, 52, 61, 80–81,
    83, 105, 112, 121, 217
Benefits, 29–30, 44–45, 48, 66, 76, 79, 83,
    116, 165, 219, 233, 238
Billing, 15, 29, 35, 43, 53, 55–56, 58–60, 72,
    79, 81, 111–112, 116, 187–188,
    194–195
Bonus, 15, 26–31, 24–39, 46, 52, 64–66, 147,
    165–166, 168
Budget, 18–19, 39–46, 48, 52, 56, 71, 77, 79,
    84–92, 174, 229, 237
Business Intelligence, 56, 205
Business system, 204

C

California Pacific Medical Center (CPMC),
    70–71
Campus core, 16 129
Capital budget, 18–19, 71, 77–78, 85–92, 174
Capitation, 64, 72
Certificate of Need (CON), 88
Chief executive officer (CEO), 5, 8, 10, 24,
    75, 91, 104, 108–109, 157, 179
Chief financial officer (CFO), 43, 55–56, 62
Chief operating officer (COO), 22, 104–105,
    238
China Basin, 127–128, 153, 166, 181, 230
Circular, A–21, 126
Citizenship, 29, 37

Clinical service, 22, 79, 101, 183
    access to, 98
    organization, 93
Clinical coverage, 95, 164
Co-pay, 65–66, 71
Commercial, 60, 62–64, 127, 187, 191, 196,
    205, 215
Commitment, 12, 14, 19, 41, 46–47, 53–54,
    56, 253
Communication, communicating, 52, 79,
    102–105, 142, 149, 186–187, 191, 194,
    196, 202–203, 230–237, 248
Community, 36, 63, 76, 234, 236–237
Compensation plan (comp plan), compensa-
    tion, 15, 26–29, 31–39, 44, 54–55, 68,
    75, 105, 166, 181–182, 243
Competition, 68, 70, 76, 100, 112, 132, 144,
    149, 166–167, 233, 240, 244, 246
Compliance, 30, 50–51, 53, 55–57, 63–64,
    66–67, 100, 174, 181, 207
Computerized Provider Order Entry
    (CPOE), 187, 195–197, 217
Computerized tomography (CT), 17, 19, 21,
    31–32, 61, 68–69, 71, 86, 90–91, 94,
    98, 101–103, 106, 110, 127, 133–135,
    187–191, 205, 232, 242, 251–252
Computerized tomography angiography
    (CTA), 63, 68, 110, 153
Conflict of interest, 54, 108, 140, 242
Content Management System (CMS), 197,
    216
Contingency, 46
Continuing medical education (CME),
    31–32, 43, 173, 241, 144–246
Contracting, 22, 42, 48, 59–68, 72
Controls, 53–54
Cost management, 47–66
Critical values, 102
Cube, 205
Culture, 49, 51, 54, 109, 121, 123, 125, 176,
    256–259
Current Procedural Terminology (CPT), 69,
    100, 112

D

Data mining, 186, 200, 205, 209
Depreciation, 19, 58, 86–87, 126, 130–132

Development officer, 239–240
Diagnosis Related Group (DRG), 91, 228
Diagnostic Radiology, 45, 60, 121–122, 124,
    146
Digital Imaging and Communication in
    Medicine (DICOM), 186, 191, 194,
    207, 209, 211, 219, 251
Digital Subtraction Angiography (DSA), 188
Discretionary expenditures, 49
Diversity, 167
Dose-Length Product (DLP), 251

E

Educational systems, 206
Electronic medical record (EMR), 56, 67,
    104, 185, 187, 190, 192, 194–196, 199,
    201, 202, 212
Emergency department (ED), 96, 106, 110,
    189, 201–202, 250
Endovascular, 87, 107–108, 110, 150
Executive Committee, 180
Executive Research Council (ERC), 134,
    161, 181
Expansion, 15, 19, 24, 78
Expenditure, 41, 43, 45, 49
Expense budget, 44–45
Extramural funds, 41, 44, 53, 56, 165

F

Faculty retreat, 173, 224–228
Faculty meetings, 180–182
Fee-for-service, 62, 64–65, 135
Fellowship, 31, 152–155, 159, 162, 164–165,
    222, 244
Flexible operating budget, 42–43
Finance team, 55–57
Forecasting, 40–41, 46
Foundation, 65–66, 70, 121, 128, 240
Full-time equivalent (FTE), 9, 29–30, 34–35,
    38, 81, 113–116
Fundraising, 239–243
Furlough, 48

G

Global bill, 71

Good to Great, 156
Graduate medical education, 78, 83
Grant bonuses, 38
Gross revenue, 29

H

HCFA 1500, 59
Health Information Technology (HIT), 185,
    194, 216, 218
Health Insurance Portability and
    Accountability Act (HIPAA),
    207–208, 211
Health Level Seven (HL7), 187, 194
Healthcare Information and Management
    Systems Society (HIMSS), 252

I

Illuminate, 210
Incentive, 26–39, 60, 75, 82, 101–102, 106,
    216–217
Incidental findings, 135–137, 203, 252
Industrial partnerships, 242–243, 247
Information technology, information system
    (IT), 66–67, 79, 99, 185–219
Institute of Medicine (IOM), 247
Insurance, 62–65, 67–71, 76, 113, 136, 165,
    207
Integrating the Health Care Enterprise
    (IHE), 252
Integrity, 53–54
Internal rate of return (IRR), 87–88
Interventional Radiology (IR), 45, 58, 72,
    94, 97, 150, 153, 250
Interview process, 142–144
Investment, 7, 17, 20, 30, 37–38, 41, 46,
    76–77, 86–87, 91, 99, 108, 130, 132,
    171–172, 216, 226–227, 233, 243

J

Joint Commission on Accreditation of
    Hospital Organizations (JCAHO),
    Joint Commission, 102, 150
Joint venture (JV), 19–21, 41, 43, 46, 53,
    74–83, 100, 112, 117, 232
Journal of Nuclear Medicine, 119

Journal of the American College of Radiology,
    119
Journal of the American Medical Association, 119

K

Kaiser, 65–66, 70–71, 229
Key performance indicators (KPI),
    205–206
Kitchen Cabinet (KC), 179–180

L

Length of stay (LOS), 87
Library, 13, 30, 241

M

Magnetic resonance angiography (MRA),
    63, 68
Malpractice, 30, 58, 113, 173
Mammography Quality Standards Act
    (MQSA), 203
Managed care, 58, 60, 64–65
Margulis Society, 145, 240–241
Marketing, 3, 47, 60, 66, 75, 87–88, 109,
    132, 137, 229–238, 245–246
Master Patient Index (MPI), 187
Mayo, 82, 182
Meaningful use, 67, 185, 216–218
Medicaid, 61, 70, 197
Medical Group Management Association
    (MGMA), 15, 32, 81
Medical Imaging and Technology Alliance
    (MITA), 251
Medical Imaging Resource Center (MIRC),
    208–209
Medical Record Number (MRN), 194, 199,
    209
Medical student, 9, 13, 29, 49, 144, 150,
    172–175, 222
Medicare, 16, 42, 53, 58–59, 61, 63, 66–69,
    83–84, 90–91, 112–113, 115–116, 197
Mentoring, 140–141, 170–171
Mezrich, 36, 39, 206, 214, 218
Microsoft, 87, 192
Miscommunication, 249, 254
Mission Bay Campus, 127, 129, 133

Molecular imaging, 47
Moore's Law, 188, 219
Morbidity and Mortality (M&M), 111
Motivation, 38, 221
Mt. Zion, 80, 114, 153

N

National Institute of Biomedical Imaging
      and Bioengineering (NIBIB), 250,
      252
National Institutes of Health (NIH), 9, 12,
      16, 18, 38, 47, 50, 55–56, 120–124,
      127, 133, 137–138, 159, 226, 250,
      256–257
Natural Language Processing (NLP),
      209–210, 218
Nature, 119
Negotiations, negotiating, 5, 8, 10, 12, 14–15,
      18–20, 22–24, 59, 61–63, 67–71, 77,
      108, 131
Neuroradiology, 32, 70, 94, 96, 113, 115,
      119, 141, 152–153, 182–183, 190
New England Journal of Medicine, 119
Nighthawk, 97–98
Nuclear medicine, 30–32, 45, 71, 94, 113,
      119, 152, 188, 191

O

Oakland Children's Hospital, 70
Office of CME (OCME), 246
Office of Management and Budget (OMB),
      126
Office of Statewide Health Planning and
      Development (OSHPD), 88
Offices, 10, 23–24, 100, 127, 230, 236–237
Operating Room (OR), 80, 96, 150, 189,
      192
Operation(s), 45, 55, 58, 75, 91, 98, 106,
      123, 130, 149, 169, 187, 234, 236,
      253–254
   clinical, 15, 23, 24, 60, 104
   hospital, 22, 43, 78, 178
   medical center, 104–105, 178, 180
Outreach, 134, 229, 236–237
Overhead, 11–12, 16, 29, 47–48, 77, 79, 87,
      116, 125

P

Package pricing, 72
Patient mix, 61
Pay for performance (P4P), 66
Payer, 42, 52, 59–64, 67, 72, 87, 197,
      204–205
Pediatric, 21, 30–31, 70, 80, 94, 97, 113, 134,
      152, 205
Pediatric radiology, 21, 30–31, 80, 94, 97,
      113, 152
Per person per month (PPM), 64
Personnel systems, 213
Preferred provider network (PPN), 63, 65
PET/CT, 31, 71, 101, 133, 232
Picture Archiving and Communication
      System (PACS), 79, 95, 97, 99,
      101–102, 111, 115, 130, 187–199,
      201–202, 205–212, 215, 217–218, 234,
      242, 249, 251–252, 254
Pneumothorax, 102, 209
Post-award, 45, 50–51, 56
Post-graduate education, 244–245
Pre-award, 50–51
Principle investigator (PI), 123, 125
Productivity, 27–29, 32, 36–37, 45, 48, 75,
      112, 115–118, 199, 213, 222, 258
Professional fee – pro fee, 15, 19–20, 40–44,
      46–47, 49, 52–53, 56, 59–60, 71, 74,
      112, 182–183, 235, 237
Professionalism, 37, 154, 168, 222–223
Profit and loss (P&L), 29, 52, 56, 222–223
Program support, 78, 80, 84
Protected Health Information (PHI),
      207–208, 211, 216, 219
Publication(s), 30, 36, 119–121, 146, 162,
      241, 243, 251
Purchased services, 78–79

Q

Quality metrics, 254

R

Radiation, 66, 90–91, 105, 228, 234, 248,
      250–252, 254–255
Radiation oncology, 79, 121

Radio-frequency identification (RFID), 249, 254

Radiographics, 119, 219

Radiological Society of North America (RSNA), 7, 49, 92, 154, 174, 200, 207, 209–210, 218–219, 222, 250, 252

Radiology, 119, 162

Radiology Benefit Management (RBM), 197

Radiology Information System (RIS), 79, 99–100, 104, 186–187, 194–196, 189–199, 204–205, 209, 214–217, 230, 242, 249, 251–252, 254

Radiology Information Systems Consortium (RISC), 186

Radiology Order Entry (ROE), 187, 195–197, 217

Radlex, 207, 210–211, 219, 250

Recharge, 45, 47, 56, 127, 129–132, 134, 137, 166, 211–212

Recruitment
  faculty, 156–167
  staff, 168–169
  start-up packages, 13, 164

Redundancy, 214, 216

Redundant Array of Inexpensive Disks (RAID), 208, 211, 214–215

Regulation(s), 203, 217, 243
  pending changes in, 90–91

Reimbursement, 21, 59, 61, 66–67, 71–72, 74, 76, 79–80, 83, 90–91, 115–117, 130–131, 136, 197, 228

Relative Value Unit (RVU), 9, 11, 21–23, 28, 31, 34–36, 48–49, 52, 60, 81–82, 112–117, 182, 184, 222

Renovation(s), 15, 23–24, 75, 85, 87, 92, 130

Report mining, 186, 209–211

Report turnaround, 27–29, 101–103, 237, 257

Research, 119–137
  facilities, competition for, 132–133
  interest group (RIG), 39, 44
  NIH funding, 120–124
  program, starting a, 124–125
  space, 11–12
  studies, reporting on, 135–136
  systems, 211–212

Reserves, 28, 37, 40–41, 44, 49, 52–53, 56, 75, 77–78, 126

and commitments, 46–47

Residency Review Committee (RRC), 83, 110, 139, 147, 153

Resident (s), 138–159
  call, 146–147
  chief, 148–149
  evaluation, 147–148
  financial perks for, 144
  rotations, 145–146

Retirement, 28, 30, 43, 44, 48, 165, 169

Retreat, 173, 224–228

Return on investment (ROI), 86–87

Robotics, 149–150

S

Safety, 87, 105, 149, 173, 180, 185, 209
  quality and, 247–255

Salary, 21, 26, 28, 31, 35, 38, 44–46, 48, 54–55, 66, 75, 79, 80, 97, 116, 121, 135, 165–166, 178, 241, 257

San Francisco General Hospital (SFGH) 70, 145, 151, 153, 180–181

Scenario planning, 226–228

Scheduling, 55, 99, 130, 186–187, 196, 213, 232, 236

School of Medicine (SOM), 7, 9–10, 24, 41, 52, 56, 78, 170, 211, 222, 244

Search committee, 161–164

Search process, 5–25

Section,
  accounts, 31–32
  leadership, 221–223
  profit and loss statement, 29–30

Self-pay, 62, 64

Service line, 18, 109, 182–184, 229

Social media, 229, 235, 238

Society of Chairman of Academic Radiology Departments (SCARD), 32, 115, 154, 222, 261

Space, 4, 9–17, 58, 85, 98, 178, 257
  allocation needs, 10, 128–129
  education, 13
  for clinical operations and offices, 23–25
  research, 9, 11–12, 17, 46, 127–130, 133–134, 165, 174

Specialized Resource Group (SRG), 44, 56, 133–134, 181

Square footage, square foot, 10–11, 13, 126–129
Stanford, 70, 143, 149
Start-up, 13–14, 18–19, 21, 27, 80, 159, 163–166, 182
STATdx, 198
Strategic, 41, 46, 66, 85, 134, 206
    planning, 226–228
    support, 19–23, 43, 74–82, 84, 137, 184

Strengths, Weaknesses, Opportunities and Threats (SWOT), 227
Structured report, 199–200, 219, 250
Subacute findings, 200
Subsidy, 21, 47, 49, 59, 80–81, 132
Subspecialty, 26–27, 31, 37, 45, 93, 95–98, 111, 113–115, 144–146, 152, 161–162, 164–165, 174, 200, 222, 244
Succession planning, 220–225

T

Tax, taxes, 15, 29, 32, 37, 43, 47–48, 92, 116
Teaching, 3, 6, 9, 14, 36, 54, 94–95, 100, 120, 139, 148–150, 159–160, 164, 174, 209, 227, 241
    file, 206
Teaching and Clinical Trial Export (TCE), 209
Technical revenue, 21–22, 41
Templates, 51, 199–200
Transparency, 84, 170, 172
Trauma center, 70, 97
Travel, 29, 31, 45, 49, 138, 145, 168, 222–223, 235
Turf, 17, 60, 82, 94, 107–111, 154, 228, 235

U

UB92, 59
Ultrasound, 80, 94, 97–98, 101, 108, 110–111, 113, 115, 153, 188, 191–192, 251
Universal Resource Locater (URL), 190, 208–209
University Health Consortium (UHC), 81
Utilization, 13, 65, 90, 193, 198

V

Vendor, 54, 90, 186, 192, 194, 199–200, 205, 208–209, 211, 215, 217–218, 242
Vice chair, 7, 40, 43–44, 46, 51, 55–56, 61, 79, 101, 105, 133–134, 161, 166, 170–171, 177–181, 217, 220, 223–224, 253, 260
Virtual private network (VPN), 212
Voice-recognition (VR), 100–102, 186, 191, 194, 198–201, 205, 217, 249

W

Website, 8, 38, 121, 132, 142, 154–155, 171, 212, 220, 233, 238, 242
Wet read, 95, 97–98, 100, 103, 200–202, 249–250
Workload, 9, 15, 20, 34–35, 81, 112–116, 144, 160, 182

X

X + Y, 28, 35, 39

SB3.